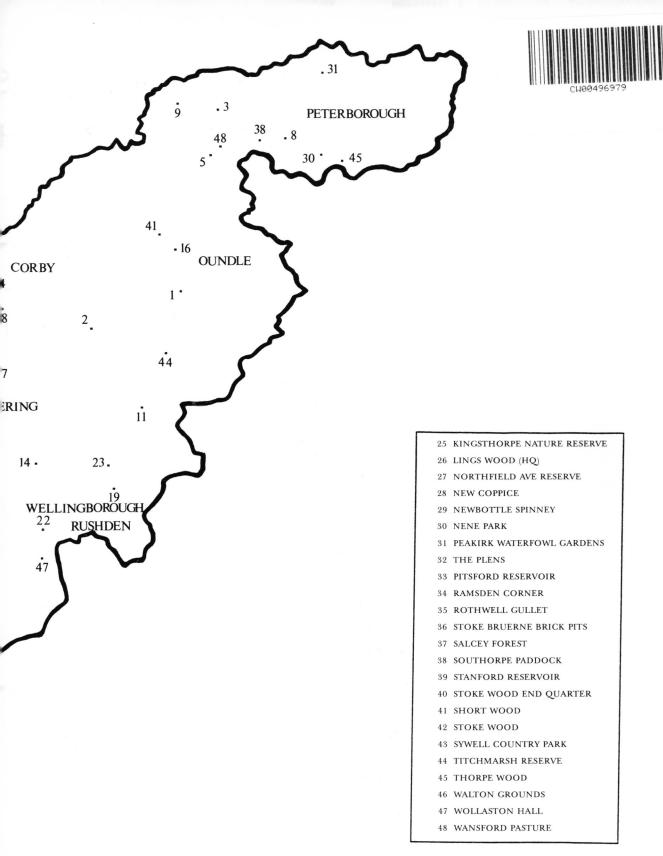

. 31

9   . 3   PETERBOROUGH

     48   38
          . 8
     5   30 .   . 45

CORBY

41 .

. 16

OUNDLE

1 .

2 .

44

ERING

11

14 .   23 .

WELLINGBOROUGH
22   19
RUSHDEN

47

25	KINGSTHORPE NATURE RESERVE
26	LINGS WOOD (HQ)
27	NORTHFIELD AVE RESERVE
28	NEW COPPICE
29	NEWBOTTLE SPINNEY
30	NENE PARK
31	PEAKIRK WATERFOWL GARDENS
32	THE PLENS
33	PITSFORD RESERVOIR
34	RAMSDEN CORNER
35	ROTHWELL GULLET
36	STOKE BRUERNE BRICK PITS
37	SALCEY FOREST
38	SOUTHORPE PADDOCK
39	STANFORD RESERVOIR
40	STOKE WOOD END QUARTER
41	SHORT WOOD
42	STOKE WOOD
43	SYWELL COUNTRY PARK
44	TITCHMARSH RESERVE
45	THORPE WOOD
46	WALTON GROUNDS
47	WOLLASTON HALL
48	WANSFORD PASTURE

The Nature of Northamptonshire 1989
has been published
as a Limited Edition
of which this is

Number 597

A list of subscribers
is printed at
the back of the book

THE NATURE OF NORTHAMPTONSHIRE

OVER: Woodland ride with goldfinches.(DJW-P)

D Watkins-Pitchford

THE NATURE OF NORTHAMPTONSHIRE

WILDLIFE, GEOLOGY AND CONSERVATION
OF THE COUNTY
INCLUDING THE SOKE OF PETERBOROUGH

Edited by
ADRIAN COLSTON AND FRANKLYN PERRING

Art Editor
ROSEMARY PARSLOW

Published in collaboration with, and in aid of,
THE NORTHAMPTONSHIRE WILDLIFE TRUST

BARRACUDA BOOKS LIMITED
BUCKINGHAM, ENGLAND
MCMLXXXIX

THE NATURE OF BRITAIN SERIES

PUBLISHED BY BARRACUDA BOOKS LIMITED
BUCKINGHAM, ENGLAND
AND PRINTED BY
MACDERMOTT & CHANT LIMITED
ENGLAND & WALES

BOUND BY
WBC BOOKBINDERS LIMITED
MAESTEG, WALES

JACKET PRINTED BY
CHENEY & SONS LIMITED
BANBURY, OXON

LITHOGRAPHY BY
CAMERA GRAPHIC LIMITED
AMERSHAM, ENGLAND

COLOUR LITHOGRAPHY BY
WESTFIELD STUDIO LIMITED
ABINGDON, ENGLAND

TEXT SET IN BASKERVILLE BY
GRAHAM BURN PRODUCTIONS
LEIGHTON BUZZARD, BEDFORDSHIRE

ISBN 0 86023 451 7

Contents

ratum – The Nature of Northamptonshire
ge 73 line 2 for (NO) read (BG) for
G) read (NO)
ge 89 line 3 after plant. read (FHP)
ge 104 line 2 for (FWW) read (PMW)
ge 114 line 1 after bellflower. read
); line 3 for (TB) read (RP)
e 124 line 4 for (FWW) read (PMW)
e 175 for 306 read D. Rone-Clarke

Pasqueflower.

Hedgehog

What do you dream of curled up there,
sleeping away the winter?

That you're a squirrel
springing through the trees?

Or a handsome buck,
nose tilted to the breeze?

Or a sleek, velvet mole,
keeper of a hundred galleries?

What a shock, then, to awake
and find you're still a flea-ridden brush.

Trevor Hold

Introduction

Written during 1988 and 1989, this volume has been published to mark the Silver Jubilee of the Northamptonshire Wildlife Trust, founded in 1963, and to draw attention to the richness and variety of a county which is still largely unknown to outside naturalists.

Having no hills above 800 feet, no coastline and a very efficient, increasingly arable, farming industry, and with several new or expanding towns within it or on its edges – Northampton, Milton Keynes, Daventry, Peterborough – cut by the M1, with the M40 and A1/M1 link to come, it is a county all too easy to pass through, unless the motorway is blocked! But those who do not stop are missing a middle England county, by tradition including the Soke of Peterborough, which has some of the finest and richest ancient woodlands in the Kingdom, remnants of the great Forests of Rockingham, Salcey and Whittlebury and, in the north-east, limestone grassland to match anything in the Cotswolds, 70 miles to the south-west. Through its centre winds the River Nene – a wet land, changing in character, but still providing a more or less continuous habitat for wildlife, especially birds, of national importance.

However unsung its treasures, Northamptonshire has not failed to produce naturalists in the past. Few other counties can boast a longer or more prestigious list: John Clare, the poet, George Claridge Druce, who wrote our *Flora* and towered over British botany for a generation, and H. N. Dixon, whose handbook on British mosses became the standard work and was still in use 90 years later. Then there were zoologists like Lord Lilford, whose two volumes on the birds of the county remain a monument to scholarship: he was followed by James Fisher, son of an Oundle headmaster, who settled here, helped found the Trust but was, for over a decade, the national voice of ornithology.

Above all else, perhaps Northamptonshire can claim to be the spiritual home of the Trust movement: it was Charles Rothschild who, living at Ashton, near Oundle, created the Society for the Promotion of Nature Reserves in 1912, which was to become in time, the Royal Society for Nature Conservation, the umbrella body of the 48 Conservation and Wildlife Trusts and many Urban Wildlife Groups which now cover the whole of the United Kingdom. It is particularly pleasing that his daughter, Dr Miriam Rothschild, President of the Northamptonshire Trust, who still lives at Ashton Wold, has made a major contribution to this volume. She is a vivid example of the way in which this county still attracts eminent naturalists to live within its boundaries and study its wildlife – and it is they who have made this book possible. With their many interests and enthusiasms they have contributed a kaleidoscopic account based on their research and first-hand experience. They deserve our gratitude.

Some of our naturalists have other talents. The county of Clare has now inspired Trevor Hold, whose poems periodically illuminate the text: our thanks go to *The Countryman* for permission to include several of these. Finally thanks to 'BB' (D.J. Watkins-Pitchford) for generously allowing us to reproduce many of his woodcuts, which catch the character of our landscape and its many hidden wonders. I hope that this blend of prose, poetry and pictures will make you rise from your chair, determined to discover the county for yourself and that you will then appreciate to the full the Nature of Northamptonshire.

Franklyn Perring
Oundle, February 1989

Acknowledgements

The authors would like to thank the following artists and photographers: Linda Aucott, (LA), Tim Barfield, (TB), Jeff Best, (JB), Bob Bullock, (RWB), Tom Chester, (TC), Adrian Colston, (AC), Alan Dawn, (AD), Brohna Dart, (BD) Richard Eden, (RE), Martin Elliott, (ME), F.W. Frohawk, (FWF), Basil Greenwood, (BG), John Mason, NCC, (JLM), Ruth Moffatt, (RM), Rodney Ingram, (RI), Craig Neate, (CN), Pippa Nuttall, (PN), Nick Owen, (NO), Rosemary Parslow, (RP), Frank Perring, (FHP), George Peterken, (GP), Phil Richardson, (PWR), Miriam Rothschild, (MR), Jonathon Spencer, (JS), Peter Wakely, NCC, (PW), D.J. Watkins-Pitchford, (DJW-P), Andy Wilson, (AW) and Peter Woollard, (PMW).

In addition the editors would like to thank the following organisations who have contributed photographs and illustrations: The Biological Records Centre, (BRC), Cambridge University Library, (CUL), the Nature Conservancy Council, (NCC) and the Northants Wildlife Trust.

The following people also helped the editors get the book ready in time: Steve Stringer of 3D Studios, Northampton printed a number of photos at short notice, Helen Parlsow helped with several of the maps and Lynn Farrell assisted with the labelling of the Short Wood map. Thank you to Jean Mullord who helped throughout the production of the book with typing, photocopying and other tasks. Finally thanks go to Mr Bob Gent for the loan of the painting for the cover.

Spotted flycatcher using nestbox. (RP)

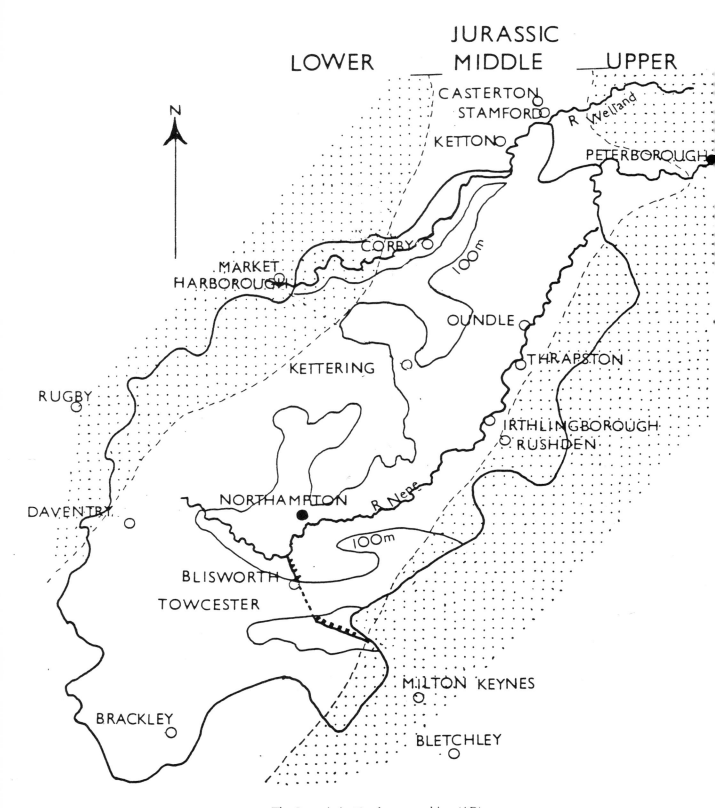

The Jurassic in Northamptonshire. (AD)

The Geology

by Alan Dawn, President, Stamford and District Geological Society

There are few places where the county's underlying geology naturally comes to the surface. Large areas are hidden beneath a covering of glacial boulder clays or river gravels, deposited by successive ice sheets during the last 1.8 million years. Elsewhere the low hills, rounded by the ice sheets, are under cultivation and only the soil types revealed by the plough give any indication of the rocks beneath. Thus we have to rely on industrial extraction sites or road works to study the deeper rocks. Any temporary hole in the ground is worth an inquisitive look.

All the geology of Northamptonshire, with the exception of the glacial cover, is of Jurassic age. The oldest rocks in the west of the county are some 150 million and the youngest in the east some 120 million years old. They are chiefly marine sediments laid down in fairly shallow sub-tropical seas, at a time when the area which is now northern Europe lay in latitudes between 30° and 40° north. There are some unconformities and freshwater beds when no marine sediments were formed. These indicate periods when the seas receded and there was some erosion of the land surface.

The Jurassic system can be divided broadly into three parts. The lower Jurassic consists largely of clays and shales with a few muddy limestones and ironstone beds. The middle Jurassic contains mostly shelly and oolitic limestones with a few clay bands. The upper Jurassic sees a return to clays and shales formed in muddy water conditions which inhibited the formation of limestones. Most of the Jurassic rocks are richly fossiliferous and the evolution patterns of creatures like ammonites, bivalves, fish and marine reptiles can be traced through their fossil remains.

The Jurassic rock beds of Northamptonshire are no longer horizontal, but dip gently downwards towards the east. Consequently, as one travels east the rocks exposed at the surface become progressively younger.

Moreover the county is rather long and narrow and its long axis lies along the strike of the beds. As one travels north east to south west the rocks change little, except where river valleys have cut their way downwards to expose the older beds in the valley bottoms.

These are the major formations, beginning with the oldest, with locations where they may be examined.

The Lower Lias   The word 'lias' may be a dialectical pronunciation of 'layers', referring to the alternate beds of clay and muddy limestone found in the cliffs at Lyme Regis in Dorset. The clays weather away more rapidly than the harder limestones, giving a step-like appearance when a cliff is revealed. The best exposure to be seen locally is just over the county

Diagrammatic section of strata from west to east. (AD)

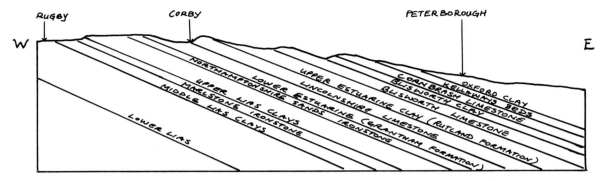

boundary in Warwickshire. The Rugby Cement Co extract the rock at Southam (SP420640). Some beds contain beautifully preserved ammonites, brachiopods and bivalves. Fish and marine reptile remains are also found. Complete skeletons are rare, but isolated bones, teeth and fish scales are not uncommon. The Southam quarry exposes more than 100 feet of the clays and limestones, but the total thickness of the Lower Lias is about 750 feet. Permission to visit the quarry should be sought in writing from the manager.

The Middle Lias   This can broadly be divided into a lower clay facies and an upper ironstone bed. The marlstone ironstone is a calcitic, sideritic, chamosite oolite. It has been extensively mined in the past for the making of iron and steel, as well as for building stone. Mining stopped some years ago when richer ores from abroad were found to be more economic. Now of course iron ore is no longer smelted at Corby. Many old quarries can still be found around Banbury and Daventry. The ironstone contains abundant 'nests' of the brachiopods *Lobothyris punctata* and *Tetrarhynchia tetraedra* near its base.

Brachiopods are almost extinct today. They appear on rare occasions in trawlermen's nets in Shetland, around New Zealand and Japan. They were becoming rarer throughout the Mesozoic, and bivalves were becoming more abundant. The rich golden brown of the marlstone can be seen in the buildings of older villages which lie near the outcrop.

The Upper Lias   Above the marlstone ironstone there are about 750 feet of clays and shales. In the past these have been worked for brickmaking in the south and west of the county. Exposures at the surface are rare. The old brick pits were abandoned long ago, but occasionally the Upper Lias appears in the Nene valley where gravel extraction uncovers them. Around Northampton, at Great Billing and Earl's Barton the clay beds are revealed by a combination of erosion by the River Nene, and a process known as 'valley bulging'.

Brachiopods from the Middle Lias: LEFT: *Tetrarynchia tetraedra;* RIGHT: *Lobothyris punctata.*
(AD)

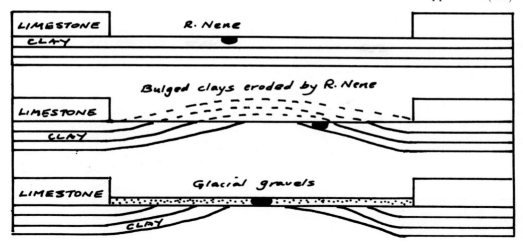

The river has carved its way down through the over-lying limestones and made itself quite a wide valley floor on the clays beneath. The pressure from the limestones above has squeezed the clays out into the valley, causing a bulge upwards. This bulge has then been smoothed off by the meandering river to expose some of the deeper clay beds. During the ice age these were again buried by the gravels from glacial outwash.

Modern gravel extraction enables us to see the Lias clays from time to time, and at some levels large numbers of ammonites occur. These belong to the genera *Harpoceras, Hildoceras* and *Dactylioceras,* together with a number of rarer forms.

The Northamptonshire Sands Ironstone   An ironstone bed averaging ten feet in thickness overlies the Upper Lias clays. It was an important economic resource and has been extensively quarried in the past, especially in the northern part of the county, and in south west Lincolnshire. The ironstone was smelted in the blast furnaces of Corby after being extracted from the ground in opencast workings. These were huge strip mines with a working face a mile or more long. Now abandoned, many have been infilled and levelled since the death of the Corby iron and steel industry. Some of the old quarries can still be seen. Where they are accessible the ironstone beds are visible at the foot of a considerable overburden of clays and limestones. This had to be removed by giant draglines which were, until quite recently, a spectacular feature of the landscape.

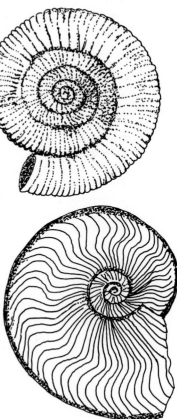

As the upper surface of the ironstone was exposed, a railway line was laid and smaller 'navvies' loaded the iron-bearing rock into the waggons, to be hauled away to the furnaces. Some of the limestone was calcined by heating to be used as a flux to draw away the impurities as slag in the smelting process. As the draglines worked across the countryside the railway had repeatedly to be re-laid.

Ammonites from the Upper Lias. (AD)

15

Any fossils in the ironstone have been much altered during the weathering process and are barely recognisable. A spectacular feature of the ironstone is the peculiar 'box' formation, which arises during the weathering of the iron content. Successive layers of geothite and limonite produce a cube-in-cube structure.

The Lower Estuarine series or Grantham Formation This is a bed which varies considerably both in thickness and in lithology. It has a maximum thickness of 25 feet and a minimum of three feet. It varies laterally from a sticky clay to a fine white pure silica sand. This sand was until recently quarried at Sibson (TL088961) for making refractory products.

Sadly this quarry is now a landfill site and will soon be completely lost. The clay beds sometimes show fossil root-beds. These appear as vertical tubes where reeds grew in the brackish marshy conditions when the beds were formed. Occasional thin coal bands are found and it is thought that the clays formed on a low-lying coastal plain or delta-flat.

The Collyweston Slates To the south of Stamford the village of Collyweston (SK995028) is famed for Collyweston slates. These are not true slates, but a thinly bedded sandy limestone lying at the base of the Lincolnshire limestone beds. There are a number of old drift mines near Collyweston from which the stone has been quarried. The slabs are left in the open and kept wet until the winter frosts cause them to cleave along the bedding planes. Once dry the slates will not cleave any further and will withstand all the elements when laid on roofs. Recent years have produced relatively mild winters so the supply of new slate has been limited. A rare and interesting fossil gastropod is found in the Collyweston slates – *Phyllocheilus bentleyi.*

Phyllocheilus bentleyi – a rare gastropod found in the Collyweston slates.
(AD)

The Lincolnshire Limestone The Lincolnshire limestone of the Inferior Oolite beds succeeds the Lower Estuarine and Collyweston beds. It is found in the north of the county, where it has a thickness of some 60 feet. It thins out southwards and disappears in the Oundle-Kettering area. There are many old quarries in the Lincolnshire limestone around King's Cliffe and Stamford, and it is exposed in most of the ironstone quarries around Corby.

Castle Cement quarries the limestone for cement making at Ketton in Rutland (SK980060). The face is about a mile long, making this the largest working in the area. The quarry was originally worked for building stone, and abandoned workings are now a nature reserve.

Much of the limestone is oolitic in structure, (oolite derived from the Greek *oon*, an egg). The rock consists of many small rounded grains said to resemble fish spawn. Each oolith is a small ovate spheroid of concentric layers of calcium carbonate, built around a small shell fragment. As the ocean currents moved the fragments around on the floor of a shallow tropical sea they each slowly accreted carbonate layers. It is estimated that each oolith took about 100 years to achieve a size too heavy to move further. The accreted ooliths build up quite thick beds of rock which show no bedding and no cleavage. This is known as freestone because it can be cut in any direction. It is a good building stone and can be seen in many fine buildings and churches in the area. Some 150 acres round the village of Barnack (TF075045) are covered by the remains of old quarry workings. Stone from Barnack was transported through the village of Pilsgate to wharves on the River Welland, whence it was carried by barges to build some of the great cathedrals of East Anglia. Much of the area south of Barnack is now the nature reserve known as the 'Hills and Holes'. A number of quarries around Stamford, Duddington and Corby are still worked for roadstone and a visit will often reward the collector with many species of marine fossils. Another fossiliferous site is the abandoned ironstone workings at Irchester Country Park, near Wellingborough (SP915660).

The Upper Estuarine Clays or Rutland Formation After the Lincolnshire limestone was formed there were some seven million years when the land rose slightly above sea level. Some of the limestone was eroded before the sea came back again and the Upper Estuarine clays were formed. These clays vary in thickness – about 45 feet around Stamford, only eight feet at Kettering but some 30 feet again around Towcester. They are still used in the manufacture of high quality bricks at the firm of Williamson Cliff in Stamford (TF014084). The clays are also used in the manufacture of cement at the Ketton Cement works. There are a number of disused quarries in the King's Cliffe area which expose the Upper Estuarine clays.

The lower nine feet of the clay is of freshwater origin – perhaps formed in a river delta or coastal lake. In 1968 a nearly complete skeleton of a land dwelling dinosaur named *Cetiosaurus oxoniensis* was found in the Williamson Cliff quarry. It must have met its death in the freshwater swamp, and been buried in the mud at the bottom of the lake. Much of the skeleton was embedded in an ironstone layer which probably formed in the early stages of diagenesis. The skeleton has now been reconstructed and is on display in Leicester City Museum.

The clay beds above the freshwater beds are of a cyclic nature, formed in shallow waters as the sea invaded the land. Each cycle of deposition starts with a brown clay at the base, followed by a shell bed of shallow water marine bivalves, gastropods and rare inarticulate brachiopods.

The shell bed is covered by green and purple clays, whose upper layers are penetrated by the roots of reeds which grew when the water became very shallow. A further rise in the sea level flooded the mud flats and the whole cycle began again. The fossilized root beds can be found in all the quarries which expose the clays. Often the holes have been infilled by pyrite, and casts of the reed roots can be picked up.

South of Kettering, the Upper Estuarine series lies directly on top of the lower, since the Inferior Oolite limestone is absent.

The Blisworth or Great Oolite Limestone Following the shallow water deposits of the Rutland Formation the sea deepened and the waters became clear of mud. Clear water limestone was laid down to a thickness of 15 to 25 feet in the Northamptonshire area. It is exposed in a number of old workings around Blisworth and has recently been widely excavated in road works on the A43 around Towcester, and in a road cutting on the Oundle by-pass. The latter can still be examined at the roadside on the A605 (TL045865). The brachiopod, *Kallirhynchia sharpii,* marks the top of the limestone. When exposed it is superabundant. Many other fossils are found, including echinoids, bivalves, brachiopods and occasional ammonites.

The LMS railway station quarry at Thrapston (TL000776) is a Site of Special Scientific Interest (SSSI) and displays the Blisworth limestone and the succeeding three formations.

The Blisworth Clay This lies on top of the limestone. It is from ten to 25 feet in thickness, and consists of greenish or purple clay, with a few thin oyster beds. At the base of the clay is a thin, intermittent ironstone band.

The Cornbrash Limestone Up to ten feet in thickness, this is yet another band of marine limestone formed in clear water. Richly fossiliferous, it is divided into upper and lower formations which have distinct faunal and lithological differences. The Lower Cornbrash is characterised by the ammonite *Clydoniceras discus.* The horizon between the Lower and Upper Cornbrash is marked by a prominent bed of worn, bored and encrusted pebbles which show

The plesiosaur *Cryptoclidus eurymerus*. (AD)

a purple centre when broken or cut. The Upper Cornbrash contains the ammonite *Macrocephalites macrocephalus* as well as many species of bivalves, brachiopods, gastropods and echinoids. A section can be seen at Thrapston and has recently been exposed in roadworks in the Peterborough area.

The Cornbrash is the uppermost of the clear water limestones to form before the return to the clays and shales of the Upper Jurassic.

The Kellaways Sands and Oxford Clay   These form a thickness of some 300 feet. The lower Kellaways sands were probably derived from the London landmass to the south, and are formed of a silica sand with some mudstones. They are poorly fossiliferous, unlike the overlying Oxford clays, which yield innumerable ammonites in many species. Also found are belemnites, bivalves, marine reptiles and large amounts of fossil wood. Extensive quarries at Peterborough, Stewartby, Calvert and Bletchley extract the clay for making bricks by the Fletton process. The clay is blue/black when dug. It is fairly soft, has the right water content and contains much bituminous material, which makes the bricks self-firing once they have been heated to the combustion temperature. This ensures a relatively cheap brick.

Marine reptiles are especially abundant in the Peterborough area and specimens from these pits can be found in museums all over the world. The most recent discovery, in September 1987, was a complete skeleton of the plesiosaur *Cryptoclidus eurymerus*. This is now on display in Peterborough Museum.

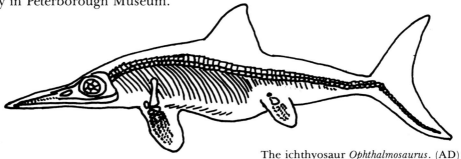

The ichthyosaur *Ophthalmosaurus*. (AD)

Other reptile remains frequently found belong to the ichthyosaur *Ophthalmosaurus,* the marine crocodiles *Steneosaurus* and *Metriorhynchus,* the giant pliosaur *Peloneustes* and others. Many fish are found, including the whale-sized *Leedsichthys problematicus.*

Fossil wood is found from trees such as ginkgo and cycad: flowering plants had not evolved at this time in the earth's history. Plant remains are fairly scarce in the marine deposits elsewhere in the Jurassic of this area. Rare fern leaves can be found in some of the limestones. *Phlebopteris woodwardii* fronds are found in the Lincolnshire limestone in an old ironstone mine at Pilton, near Morcott (SK926016).

Some 25 million years ago, during the late Tertiary period, the folding of the Alps caused some flexuring of the rocks of southern and central Britain. This resulted in the gentle eastward dip of the rocks of Northamptonshire and also induced some small faults. These have continued to move at intervals up to the present day, causing occasional minor earth tremors.

One fault runs for some 18 miles in an east-west direction from the fens east of Peterborough to a point between Stamford and Oakham. It then runs for a further six miles southwards towards Oundle. A series of three faults arising east of Corby extends as far as Oundle. Several smaller faults lie to the west and south west of Northampton.

During the last 1.8 million years of the Pleistocene period the landscape has undergone many successive advances and retreats of ice sheets. These have planed and rounded the hills when the ice has crept forward, and left huge deposits of clay and stone when the ice melted. During the melting of ice large quantities of water have carried gravels and pebbles to leave extensive deposits in the valleys of the Nene, Welland and other smaller valleys. These gravel beds can be dated to several different periods. Between the advances of the ice there have been warm periods, some with mediterranean climate. Each ice advance and ensuing warm period has lasted for a long time – some up to 100,000 years or more.

From Great Billing (SP80-62-) and Little Houghton (SP80-59-) comes evidence of a treeless, tundra-like landscape at the end of a period of climatic amelioration just before the last ice age. This supported marsh-marigold, spearwort, cuckooflower, mouse-ear, sandwort, tormentil, sheep's sorrel, pondweeds, rushes, sedges, grasses and moss, arctic birch and dwarf willow. The fauna included ostracods, molluscs, flies and predatory beetles, with no less than woolly mammoth, woolly rhinoceros, reindeer, wild horse and bison grazing upon the steppe-like vegetation, some 28,000 years ago. At Apethorpe (TL02-95-), there is a sequence of deposits, the plant and animal remains of which divulge dramatic changes between Late-Devensian (c15,000-10,500B.P.) and modern times. Musk ox, red deer, roe deer and voles have been recovered from a number of Middle and Late-Devensian deposits along the Nene valley. The presence of extensive clearings of open grassland harbouring sheep/goat (the bones of the two are difficult to tell apart) and cattle, with roe deer in oak-hazel woodland beyond, is attested by a Neolithic site at Ecton (SP82-63-), although evidence of later clearance of original woodland comes from further along the valley, where the Beaker people occupied a similar situation in Bronze age times. Sheep, pigs, cattle and cereal farming are seemingly characteristic of the plentiful Bronze Age and Iron Age settlement sites within the valley of our principal river, with deer and wild boar roaming the not too distant woodland. Meanwhile, deposits adjacent to its tributaries, the Harper's Brook and River Ise, currently under investigation, include abundant seeds, hazel nuts, logs, branches and fragments of beetles – possibly of Boreal age, when Mesolithic hunter-gatherers foraged in the district. Detailed assay and interpretation of a bedded sequence of tufa deposits rich in well-preserved molluscs, probably of later Atlantic 'climatic climax' date, from a quarry near Wellingborough is also under way.

We are today living in a warm inter-glacial period. The ice is still retreating towards the poles and back into the mountain valley glaciers. But it is quite possible that some time in the future ice will re-advance and once again make the British Isles and much of the northern hemisphere uninhabitable for thousands of years.

The dinosaur *Cetiosaurus oxoniensis*. (AD)

20

Our Naturalists

by Ioan Thomas, formerly Head of Biology, Oundle School

In 1712 John Morton, Rector of Oxendon, published *The Natural History of Northamptonshire*. It gives a detailed description of the county and is of great value in providing a foundation for later accounts. Even then he was deploring the reduction in Rockingham Forest – the great area of woodland in the north of the county which was important for hunting and for charcoal for iron smelting.

'In all probability it was anciently one entire or continuous tract of wood, and a forest of far larger extent than it now is.'

The book can be seen at the County Records Office at Delapré, and in the Northampton Public Library. Much of it is concerned with geology, perhaps because of the importance of the Jurassic oolite as building stone. The county was already noted for its 'spires and squires' and Morton records that: 'there are more parks in Northamptonshire than in all the rest of England; and more in England than in all the rest of Europe.'

Morton records particular plants in places where they are still found, like shining crane's-bill on the stone walls at Barnack, wall-rue under Lilford Bridge and lily-of-the-valley – 'the woods north of Kingscliffe are full of it'. And he is probably the first person to quote Dr Bowles' description, in 1650, of Barnack Hills and Holes as 'as fine a place for variety of rare plants as ever I beheld'. Botanists before him had recorded plants in the county, but his was the first systematic record of the flora and the places where the plants were to be found. Druce wrote that 'John Morton is the one to whom Natural Science in Northamptonshire owes most', but Druce's own *Flora* would now challenge the truth of that opinion.

Botanists George Claridge Druce (1850–1932) wrote his first paper on the plants in the county in 1880, when he was thirty, and brought all his studies together fifty years later in *The Flora of Northamptonshire* which was published in 1930. He was a man of immense charm and energy and a skilful scientist who became a Fellow of the Royal Society. In an obituary H.N. Dixon wrote: 'There was a great attractiveness about him. Few gathered friends so easily; did anyone ever gather around him so many botanical friends?'

OPPOSITE ABOVE: Quarrying at Cowthick (NCC) and BELOW: Cranford Quarry. (PW)

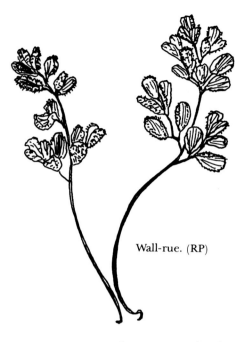

Wall-rue. (RP)

Druce was born at Potter's Pury in Northamptonshire and his interests in plants started early – he says that at the age of six he knew the four violets. Ten years later he became an apprentice to a firm of chemists in Northampton. His love of plants deepened and was strengthened by the botanical walks of the Pharmaceutical Association, an organisation he helped to found when he was 21. Two years later he began his herbarium and he continued to add to it for the rest of his life. Even though he left Northamptonshire in 1879, when he bought a chemist's shop in the High in Oxford, he continued to make frequent botanical excursions in the county, and he maintained strong links with the Northamptonshire Natural History Society; he became one of its founder members in 1876.

More than 60 pages of the *Flora* are concerned with the history of botanical research in the county, and the account of each species includes the details of early records. Druce found several first records for the county in the poems of John Clare and, when he was a boy, once saw Clare in Northampton. Several pages of the *Flora* are devoted to the plants in Clare's poems.

H.N. Dixon, (1861–1944) was also a distinguished botanist. He came to Northampton to teach in the Deaf and Dumb School, and soon became involved in the Natural History Society, becoming President of the Botanical Section in 1890, a position he held for 53 years. His special interest was mosses and his *Student's Handbook of British Mosses* (1896) became the standard work on that group.

Both Druce and Dixon knew Miles Joseph Berkeley (1803–1889). He was born at Biggin Hall near Oundle and, when he was Curate of Apethorpe and Woodnewton, he became an international authority on fungi. He was sent the fungi collected by Darwin on the voyage of the *Beagle,* and he also helped to establish the cause of potato blight – which was causing such a great disaster in Ireland – and of the rust disease of wheat. He presented his collection of 10,000 specimens of fungi to Kew, and Druce estimates that he was responsible for naming 6,000 species. Berkeley made several contributions to *The Flora of Northamptonshire,* making the first record in the county for man orchid, knapweed broomrape and alder buckthorn among others, and he also describes the woods near King's Cliffe as being full of lily-of-the-valley. He eventually became rural dean of Rothwell. For many years he contributed to the *Gardeners' Chronicle,* and in 1857 published his *Introduction to Cryptogamic Botany* which became the standard work.

Entomologists   There are several references to Northamptonshire in South's *Butterflies of the British Isles* (1906). Many of them originate in the records of Rev William Bree (1823–1917), curate of Polebrook near Oundle, 1847–62. The enthusiasm of Victorian lepidopterists is shown by this quotation from Rev F.O. Morris's *History of British Butterflies* (seventh edition 1893) in his account of the purple emperor: 'Thanks to the obliging hospitality of the Rev. William Bree, the curate of Polebrook, to whom I had no introduction but that which the freemasonry of Entomology supplies to its worthy brotherhood, I had the happiness of beholding His Majesty, or to speak more correctly, Their Majesties, though, as is only proper, at a most respectful distance; they at the top of a tree, and I on the humble ground. The next day, in the same wood, at Barnwell Wold, near Oundle, Northamptonshire, during my absence in successful search of the large blue, of which more anon, Mr Bree most cleverly captured one . . . That specimen, a male, now graces my cabinet, together with the first female that its captor had ever taken, both obligingly presented by him to me. Since then, I have just heard from him that he took another the day after I left him, in one of the ridings of the wood, in his hat. I hope that Her Most Gracious Majesty has no more profoundly loyal subject than myself, and I may therefore relate that, while plotting and planning an 'infernal machine' against his Imperial Majesties liberty and life the following summer, in the shape of a fifty foot net, and without any reference therefore to what is now going on in France, or any allusion to the career of Louis Napoleon, my toast that evening after dinner was (with as much sincerity as in the minds of the French), *Vive L'Empereur.* Since then, in 1854, Mr Bree captured nine in one day in three hours, three of which he has given to me.'

Such was their enthusiasm that toasting the long life of the Emperor did not conflict with capturing them for their cabinets! In 1857 W. Sturgess took 80 specimens of the purple emperor between 11 July and 24 July, 'in a 1300 acres wood near Kettering'. That note was published in *The Entomologists Weekly Intelligencer,* an unusual journal which could be bought for one penny every Saturday from 1856 to 1861. It was edited and published by Edward Newman, whose classic work *The Illustrated Natural History of British Butterflies* was published about 1870. In April 1856 in an editorial in *The Intelligencer* he wrote: 'Each discoverer has but to write one full notice of his discovery and forward it to us, and in ten days, at the very outside, it is in print and in the hands of nearly every Entomologist in the kingdom. Each Entomologist will find that he can live quicker and do more in a season . . .'

So the Victorians were almost as good at circulating news of rarities as the bird 'twitchers' are a hundred years later.

The main purpose of this news was collecting, and in the issue of Saturday 10 July 1858 W. Sturgess writes about the black hairstreak: 'When, last week, I announced the capture of Pruni in this locality, I made no offer of exchange, very few of my insects being in fine condition; notwithstanding, I have received so many pressing applications, that after parting with my own set, I am compelled to ask your permission to say, through the medium of the "Intelligencer" that my supply is exhausted; it being utterly impossible, at this busy season of the year, to answer individually every applicant.'

The black hairstreak was first known in Britain, from Monk's Wood in Huntingdonshire, in 1828. Specimens from there were sold as *Thecla W-album,* now called the white letter hairstreak, but Edward Newman noticed that the specimens he had been given differed from that species. When it became known that this was a new species for Britain the collector said that the locality was in fact not Monk's Wood but in Yorkshire – a county in which this species does not occur. But during the next thirty years the fact that its distribution is limited to Buckinghamshire, Cambridgeshire, Huntingdonshire, Northamptonshire and Oxfordshire became known.

The plate of the chequered skipper in Morris's book is from a specimen in William Bree's cabinet (named the spotted skipper). It was probably collected in Ashton Wold, but it was also recorded from Monk's Wood, Castor Hanglands and Barnwell Wold. Morris writes almost defiantly: 'I have heard that in one of these places the Lord of the Manor has forbid the "free warren" and "free entry" of the Entomologist, but I am unwilling to believe that any such interference with the "liberty of the subject" has been perpetrated.'

William Bree reported his find of the large blue butterfly in the *Zoologist* for 1852: 'The great prize of all the butterflies of the neighbourhood of Polebrook, I hold to be *Lycaena Arion,* which if I mistake not, was discovered here by myself thirteen or fourteen years since. It is confined entirely, as far as my experience goes, to Barnwell Wold and the adjoining rough fields, with the exception of a single specimen which I once met with in a rough field near Polebrook . . . Many Entomologists have of late years visited Barnwell

23

Purple Emperor. (DJW-P)

Wold in search of Arion; in short, a summer never passes without meeting in my rambles brother entomologists from different parts of the country; I rejoice, however, to be able to state that its annual occurrence does not appear to be diminished in consequence. Unless my memory fails me, I think Mr Wooley, of Trinity College, Cambridge, informed me that one year he captured, in a few days, between fifty and sixty specimens in and about Barnwell Wold, though, in point of weather, the days were anything but favourable.'

Alas Bree was wrong. Herbert Goss, in the *Victoria County History* (1902), writes that the large blue disappeared from Barnwell Wold in 1860 after an exceptionally wet summer, but he considered that over-collecting contributed to its extinction.

The 'brother Entomologists' who were collecting and recording at the same time as Bree included, in addition to W. Sturgess of Kettering, Rev Hamlet Clark who was curate of All Saints in Northampton and who collected near Towcester; he later became Curate of Quebec Chapel in Marylebone, London. Frederick Bond made several records concerning 'The Lynches' at Wodenham near Aldwinkle', presumably the wood of that name near Lilford. Rev T.C. Wilkinson and Rev W. Whall, both of Thurning Rectory, included records and requests for specimens in *The Intelligencer*. Rev F. Tearle of Kettering Grammar School was another collector.

William Bree was curate at Polebrook from 1847–62. If his memory of dates is correct then he must have been making his first observations of the large blue when he was only 16, long before he became curate. He became Rector on the death of Charles Eusery Isham in 1862, but ceded in 1863 to move to Warwickshire, where he became Rector and Patron of Allesley, where his father had been Rector. He later became Archdeacon of Coventry. We can guess that he was sorry to leave Polebrook and its fascinating butterflies.

Ornithologists Until the 1930s almost the only published records of ornithology in Northamptonshire were made by Thomas Littleton Powys, 4th Lord Lilford (1833–96). Rev H.H. Slater, Vicar of Irchester (1883–93) and rector of Thornaugh (1893–1906), in his account on birds in the *Victoria County History* states that little else has been written, and he makes a plea for more records: 'we want definite facts recorded every year (authenticated in the case of birds with which the observer is not personally well acquainted, by specimens).'

Though he was a keen shot I do not think that Lilford would have approved the requirement for specimens, because he often refers sadly to needless shooting of birds, but he was aware of the need for more records: 'but, as I have said before, ornithological records are lamentably wanting amongst us, and I feel convinced that our list of Northamptonshire's birds might be increased, on excellent authority, by at least fifty species, if only a few of those persons who possess some knowlege of ornithology would take the trouble to keep careful notes, and publish their observations, with the exact dates and localities, of any unusual occurrence.'

That was written in the *Journal of the Northamptonshire Natural History Society* in 1882, when Lilford contributed a long series of articles on the birds of the county which were eventually published, with some additions, in his book, *The Birds of Northamptonshire* (1895).

The book is full of his own observations. He took a special delight in owls and describes how he would climb up to various holes in old trees to see if his 'friends' were at home. He often bought birds for his aviary in the market in London and over several years released little owls at Lilford, setting free as many as forty in July 1888. At one time he had as many as twenty species of owls in the aviaries.

Other birds for the aviary were ordered specially from abroad, but he was surprised when his request for 'a good many' glossy ibis from a dealer in Seville resulted in 60 of these birds arriving for him in London!

Rare birds were in much danger from being shot, and collectors were particularly keen to get local specimens. Lilford's attitude is shown in his account of the night heron which, much to his grief later, he shot at Titchmarsh in 1868. He wrote to his nephew Mervyn in Cambridge on 15 July 1886: 'The chief news here is the appearance of a night heron on Tuesday evening, seen by Irby pretty nearly exactly in the same spot near Aldwinkle where I saw one in 1868. I am very anxious to preserve this bird alive; there is no reason why he should not live happily through the summer months on our river, as George Hunt is away.'

Encouraged by the long stay of this bird, and to atone for his own offence he attempted to introduce night herons from the aviary into the wild.

Lord Lilford built the duck decoy at Titchmarsh in 1885 and on 1 December of that year Lady Lilford wrote: 'Lilford thinks you will be glad to hear that twenty ducks have been caught in the newly made decoy.' But the heronry there now was not established in Lord Lilford's lifetime.

During the 1930s, records of birds in the *Journal of the Northamptonshire Natural History Society* became more frequent and more detailed. They were usually written by Ray Felton. In 1946 James Fisher got a group together to discuss the possibility of producing a *County Bird Report* and in 1969 this became an annual publication. Lilford would have been greatly delighted by the interest now shown in birds and conservation.

The influence of two other Northamptonshire naturalists, Charles Rothschild (1877–1923) and James Fisher (1912–1970), goes far beyond the county. Both were deeply concerned with the promotion of conservation and both were good at inspiring others. Miriam Rothschild has written in a *Memoir* on her father 'it has been said with an element of truth that he *invented* conservation, since, years ahead of his day, he realised the importance of protecting and preserving the habitat and special biotopes rather than the individual rare species threatened with extinction, and the necessity of obtaining government support and massive publicity.' In 1912 he called a meeting to inaugurate the Society for the Promotion of Nature Reserves, which has become the Royal Society for Nature Conservation the organisation which co-ordinates the work of all the County Wildlife Trusts. And he led the way for other landowners, by setting aside part of the estate at Ashton as a nature reserve, the first in the county. Rothschild was particularly interested in insects and became, like many other distinguished amateurs, more expert than the professionals. Throughout the world the study of fleas (which include the vector of plague which he described) will always be associated with his name.

James Fisher's professional interest was ornithology and much of his research was on birds of Britain's coasts. But his special skill was, through writing, radio and television, to make natural history accessible to everyone. His obituarist in *The Times* wrote: 'With his enthusiasm and engaging manner, and his well stored mind, he was a born evangelist for ornithology.' In 1968 he became Vice-Chairman of the Countryside Commission and the close co-operation which now takes place between that body and the County Wildlife Trusts would have given him much satisfaction. The Northamptonshire Trust was fortunate to have him as its founder Chairman in 1963.

The twenty-five years which have passed since the Northamptonshire Trust was founded have been a time when interest in the environment has become widespread. We owe a great deal to naturalists who have made careful records of the plants and animals in the county, and who promoted the conservation movement. Much still needs to be done, both in publishing detailed records of the plants and animals now present, and in maintaining the habitats in which they can flourish.

(We acknowledge with thanks the permission granted by Cambridge University Library to reproduce the portraits of Rev M.J. Berkeley and Lord Lilford.)

Reverend Morton's
Saturday Night

Jogging wearily back to Oxendon
From another foray afield, the Reverend John,
His satchel full of curious stones and flowers
And curiouser stories running through his head.

Late for supper. Late with his lifelong work
(Promised to subscribers years ago).
The more he finds, the more there is to know.
(The theories still refuse to face the facts).

He'll not be happy till he sees the title page:
'The Natural History of Northamptonshire . . .'
But tonight, weary, weary . . . These things must wait.
Time now for a quiet pipe, a leg-stretch by the fire . . .

* * *

Snoozing in his chair, he wakes with a start –
Saturday night, and the sermon still not done!
Pass me the Bible! What else shall I want? –
Pen and paper – where's that Commentary?

And tadpoles still swimming in the font!

Trevor Hold

OPPOSITE ABOVE: Rev M.J. Berkeley (from *Gardeners' Chronicle* 1871, 271), and BELOW: Lord Lilford in his study (from *Lord Lilford on Birds*, 1903). (Both CUL)

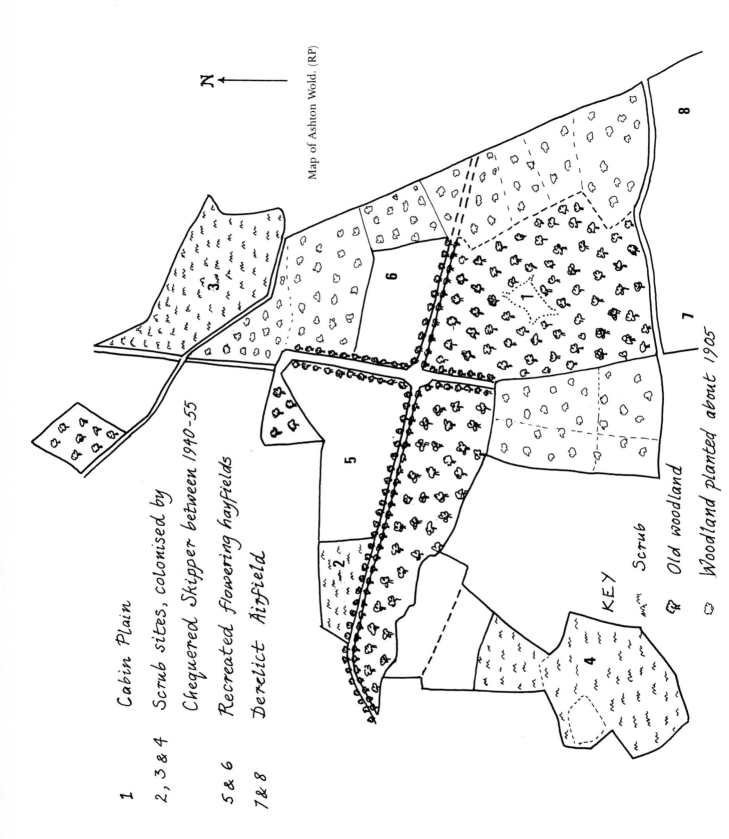

Map of Ashton Wold. (RP)

N

KEY

~~ Scrub

Ɋ Old woodland

Ø Woodland planted about 1905

1   Cabin Plain

2, 3 & 4   Scrub sites, colonised by Chequered Skipper between 1940-55

5 & 6   Recreated flowering hayfields

7 & 8   Derelict Airfield

Ashton Wold

(RP)

Some changes in the Fauna and Flora between 1900 and 1989
by Miriam Rothschild, President, Northamptonshire Wildlife Trust

Charles Rothschild, in his early twenties, visited Ashton Wold (TL09-87-) while exploring Rev William Bree's collecting areas around Polebrook. He was so enchanted by the fauna and flora of the wood, and the magnificence of the elm avenue, that he decided to try to buy it and preserve the ancient trees. Imagine his astonishment when he discovered the property belonged to his own father. Apparently 'Nattie' had accepted Ashton Wold as a token payment for a bad debt; he was quite delighted to pass it over to his son, and promptly built a house for him on the perimeter of the future reserve. Charles Rothschild realised that the ancient remnant of the open forest was dangerously small for the conservation of the interesting species found there, and he immediately planted up a belt of mixed woodland round three sides of the Wold as a protective buffer zone. It is striking how the rare insects, with the exception of the chequered skipper (see below), failed to invade these new plantations or scrub areas. Even when a species like the white admiral reappeared, after an absence of 50 years or more, it was in Cabin Plain in the centre of the ancient woodland that it was first seen, and where it bred for the next decade.

Ashton Wold is of considerable interest for three reasons:

Firstly, the old portion of the woodland and the elm avenue have been undisturbed for over 100 years. No silviculture has been carried out apart from clearing the ditches, maintaining the ridings and the removal of fallen timber. The oaks in the ancient part of the wood are, according to Dr George Peterken's estimate, the oldest in the county, approximately 250 years old. No other local woodland has been undisturbed for such a lengthy period.

Secondly, Ashton Wold has had two consecutive owners interested in entomology and general natural history, so that observations of the flora and fauna extend continuously over a period of virtually 90 years. Thus it has been possible to note the fluctuation in the abundance of certain species for a longer time than is usually possible.

Cowslip.(BD)

Thirdly, although the old portion of the wood is relatively small (with approximately 40ha (100 acres) originating before 1835 and 104ha (256 acres) before 1884) and parts of it were undoubtedly ploughed and cultivated, sometime before 1300 (more recently a piece at the west end must have been used as an orchard for growing raspberries, dewberries, apples and pears), the entomological fauna is rich and characteristic of ancient open woodland.

Dr Eric Duffey on two occasions collected spiders in the best entomological 'spot' in the Wold, Cabin Plain, and the species he obtained from sifting leaf litter (*Porhomma oblitum* and *Saloca diceros*) were, in his view, characteristic of areas of 'long established vegetation, where interference or exploitation has not destroyed the natural ancient habitat.' Up to 1930 Cabin Plain was a small grassy enclosure surrounded by rabbit netting, but it has now been largely grown over by bushes of privet, goat willow and blackthorn. Old maps give two spellings: Cabin Plane or Cabin Plain . The avifauna is especially rich numerically. Neil MacMahon, an ornithologist who made 20 visits to the area in 1987-88, noted: 'During the breeding season Ashton Wold must rank as one of the most densely populated woodland areas in the county'.

In order to provide some idea of the sort of long term fluctuations observed in the wood, the relative abundance of certain plants and butterflies are described below.

Vegetation The wood, as a whole, is considerably drier than it was in 1914, although the neglect of drainage and ditching, during and after World War II, has left some small areas subject to temporary flooding in the winter. The canopy is thicker and there are less clearings and open grassy enclosures, since the ash has regenerated naturally in these open spaces, and sycamore has invaded certain portions of the wood. This has resulted in the suppression of many low-growing plants: the bushes of blackthorn, hawthorn, goat willow, privet etc, tend to grow taller, with less foliage near the base. There is a considerable increase in honeysuckle throughout the old part of the wood.

Up to 1940 primroses were lacking. These first appeared along the banks of certain ditches near Cabin Plain and gradually spread to the more open areas of the wood; a decline in cowslips coincided with their advent. Along the banks of the primrose ditches two species of ferns appeared which had not previously been noted in the wood. Bracken, up till then represented by one or two plants only, spread in the so-called 20 acres of roughs known as the 'Gorse', while the gorse (*Ulex*) gradually died out. During the period 1940-1980 there was a steady increase in bugle throughout the wood, along ridings and in areas where the canopy was not dense.

Two major changes took place during these 40 years.

The first, chronologically, was the sudden dramatic increase in dog's mercury which occurred in the early fifties. A dense growth of this plant was first noted along the top of the banks of ditches in Cabin Plain. From there it spread rapidly, like a green tide, through the wood. One of the worst aspects of its general encroachment was the stifling of the sweet violet which is one of the food plants of various fritillaries, and this may well have contributed to their disappearance from Ashton Wold. Another, aesthetic, disadvantage of the rampaging dog's mercury was the destruction of the bluebell stands in the more open portions of the wood. Instead of the 'sea' of blue which had been such a beautiful feature of certain areas, the flowering spikes were drastically reduced and appeared singly or in small clumps.

I invited the botany department of Cambridge University to visit us and advise on the dog's mercury situation. The general opinion seemed to be that it was a phenomenon of 'natural succession' characteristic of our locality and there was nothing one could do about it. An ash tree had recently blown down in one of the invaded bluebell stands and we cut a 'dart board' from the trunk which was examined by one of the postgraduate students. He counted the rings and declared gloomily: 'One hundred and twenty-two wet summers'.

The second dramatic and more important change was due to the death of the elm trees throughout the wood. One of the obvious results of this disaster was the opening up of the canopy, and the associated penetration of more sunlight. However, this effect was less important where clearing could not be undertaken in certain areas of the old portion of the Wold.

All the giant elms in the Avenue died – a great tragedy. A number of dead stumps of these huge trees were left standing, in the hope that their exceedingly rich fauna of Hymenoptera might be preserved.

The Orchids Between 1900 and 1940 there had been only one record of bee orchid at Ashton (in 1920, mentioned in Druce, 1930). In 1940 several flowering spikes appeared in an uncut lawn round the house; today it is one of the most abundant orchids throughout the SSSI at Ashton. An equally clear-cut change in the opposite direction has occurred with common twayblade. This species was exceedingly abundant right through the wood between 1910 and 1935. Thereafter, it waned, and now, although still present, it is rare. Another abundant species was early-purple orchid which had much the same distribution as the twayblade, and which declined simultaneously. Unlike the twayblade it has once again become more numerous in those portions of the old wood where the dead elms have been removed.

Common spotted-orchid continues to be the most numerous species in the wood but there are perhaps fewer specimens where the boggy areas have become reduced. Greater butterfly-orchid, white helleborine and broad-leaved helleborine have been represented in the past by one or two occasional specimens but have not been recorded recently. The first Ashton Wold example of southern marsh-orchid was found in 1988.

Introductions or escapes Between 1900 and 1920 there were several garden escapes present in the west end of the Wold, such as raspberry bushes with red and yellow fruit, dewberries and daffodils, the latter planted in two rings round old ash trees. Except for the daffodils these plants all disappeared rather suddenly about 1920 – 23 and simultaneously there was a rapid increase of snowberry in the same area. In 1922 a flowering plant of monk's-hood appeared on the edge of a riding and this has spread gradually, so that about 50 plants are now present in close proximity to the first. In 1905 Charles Rothschild introduced the marsh sow-thistle along the banks of the swamp near the lake, where it flourished. About 45 years later it suddenly appeared in the water-garden near the house, about half a mile distant. Thirty-five years after that (1985) four plants, eight feet tall, flowered in an area in the wood from which dead elms had been removed; it had now jumped the 800 yards of woodland between the water-garden and this new site. In 1988 several new plants of the thistle – somewhat shorter – were growing round the original group of the four giants.

The other species which in all probability is a garden escape (it first flowered in the west end of the reserve where the monk's-hood and dewberry were found) is the giant bellflower which is spreading steadily if slowly in the west end of the reserve, but there are now dense stands where it first appeared.

Bluebells were present at Ashton Wold in 1900, but extra plants from a local source were added in the west end of the reserve and multiplied vigorously. I myself collected seed from Tring and scattered a few ounces under the beech tree in that section. About the same time that the dog's mercury invaded the western end the bluebell began to extend its range. Up till then it had not crossed the elm avenue, but now a few flowering plants appeared on the north side of the road and in the gorse. It also spread sparsely in the eastern perimeter alongside the ride known as Strawberry Riding.

The Butterflies Of the British species 44 have been taken by us at Ashton between 1900 and 1989. A single specimen of the swallowtail was captured near the lake a mile outside the wood in 1974. In addition F.O. Morris (1908) recorded large blue, black-veined white and large heath at Ashton, three species which we have never seen here. The butterflies recorded between 1900 and 1989 can be divided into five broad categories:

1) species which have increased in abundance,
2) species which have decreased in abundance,
3) species in which there is little or no change,
4) species of which one or two specimens only were taken,
5) species which have disappeared completely.

The comma, although present at Ashton about 1850 (according to Morris) was unquestionably absent between 1900 and 1922. A specimen was seen on the wing in 1922 and one was caught in 1923, and thereafter this butterfly increased in abundance, reaching a peak in the forties. It then declined, but is still well represented at Ashton and is present even in 'bad' years.

The white admiral was not recorded at Ashton by Morris although stated to be present in the surrounding district. It was certainly absent between 1900 and 1940, in which summer I saw several specimens on the wing in Cabin Plain. It thereafter increased in numbers and became abundant – also present in the garden and in the village. In the fifties and sixties it began to decline and by the seventies was once again absent and has not been seen here since. It is present at Lyveden about seven miles west of Ashton (SP98-86-).

The holly blue was not recorded by Morris at Ashton and his text suggests it was not then a common butterfly in the country as a whole. It was here, though scarce, from 1900, but began to increase steadily in the fifties and sixties and is now always present, albeit in moderate numbers; curiously enough its increase coincides with a decrease at Ashton of one of its principal food plants, the holly.

The speckled wood was present at Ashton from 1900, but during the last 20 years has undoubtedly increased in numbers, and it has extended its range in the wood.

The gatekeeper or hedge brown was present at Ashton from 1900 and Morris describes it as common everywhere. However, compared with all the other browns it was, relatively, rather scarce here. In 1980 it suddenly increased dramatically, and reached huge numbers in all the more or less open spaces in or around the wood, and was more plentiful than all the other browns present. Since then it has declined somewhat but still remains far more abundant than in Charles Rothschild's day (1900–1923).

Morris mentions Ashton Wold as a locality for the silver-spotted, dingy, grizzled and chequered skipper but does not record the presence of the small or Essex skipper. This is peculiar, but his text suggests it was absent here, although he does not state so specifically. That assiduous collector, the Vicar of Polebrook, who was always pottering about at Ashton, must surely have captured and recorded it, had it been present. From 1900 to 1923 both the small and Essex skipper were not uncommon, but at the same time that we experienced the gatekeeper 'explosion' the small skipper increased dramatically in numbers, and is still abundant.

The general impression is that the purple hairstreak has increased at Ashton. It appeared in the courtyard here and on the terrace, which is unusual. The same applied to the white-letter hairstreak up to three years ago. Now I am not sure about its status here. The following species are still present but numbers have been greatly reduced between 1920 and 1940: ringlet, meadow brown, small heath, common blue, small copper, large white, wall (slightly), black hairstreak.

T: The Avenue at Ashton Wold in winter. (MR) CENTRE: Great
ey Meadow showing ridge and furrow. (JB) RIGHT: Wet
nproved meadow along the River Nene near Northampton with
marsh-marigolds. (JB)

The numbers of the small white, green-veined white, orange tip, silver-spotted skipper, small tortoiseshell, red admiral, painted lady and peacock seem to be unaltered. This is strange where the orange-tip is concerned, since its most favoured food plant, the cuckooflower, has been drastically reduced by modern farming methods.

The species which have disappeared are the green and brown hairstreaks, marbled white (common until 1940 approx), silver-washed, high brown, dark green and Duke of Burgundy fritillaries, (this last species vanished in the mid-thirties – it was never abundant but always present up to 1935), white admiral, dingy, grizzled and chequered skipper. The latter was still abundant in 1952 and its extinction here is a mystery. It is one of the few species which more or less vacated the old woodland when the clearings became overgrown, and migrated into various roughs round the outside of the wood. It increased its numbers markedly in the Gorse, an area where its larval food plant, false brome and bugle – a favourite nectar source – were in close proximity.

Simultaneously it formed a colony in the rough area behind the lake, about a mile south of the wood, where it was also numerous. Another population was installed in Miriam's Cover, a rough scrub on the eastern border of one of Charles Rothschild's buffer zones. I can only repeat that its sudden disappearance from Ashton remains a complete enigma. In 1952 it seemed to be increasing and extending its range. The rough areas where it was flourishing were never disturbed and did not become overgrown. Yet suddenly in the sixties it went out like a light.

Between 1900 and 1988 single specimens were captured of marsh fritillary (1938), wood white (1940), large tortoiseshell (1940), and swallowtail (1974). All these species, except the latter, were recorded at Ashton by Morris.

In addition there have been isolated, especially 'good' years for certain species, like clouded yellow in 1980, white-letter hairstreak in 1974 and peacock in 1958.

Two insects other than Lepidoptera collected here (although the flea concerned was located on the fringe of the reserve) are worth mentioning, since their rise and fall in numbers suggest some long term cycling.

When Ashton Wold house has built in 1900 a colony of house martins installed themselves under the eaves and returned yearly to occupy the nests until the house was rebuilt in 1972. One pair always rested in the front hall! About 1904 Charles Rothschild collected fleas from a number of these nests and found that *Ceratophyllus rusticus* was extremely rare in the colony. In fact it was rare everywhere in England at that time. In 1940 I repeated my father's investigation of the house martin's nests under our eaves. Much to my surprise I found *C. rusticus* was one of the commonest fleas present. I then decided to examine nests of house martins from Tring, and found that there too, *C. rusticus* outnumbered all other species. Thus in the space of 40 years this flea had changed from one of the rarest British Hirundinid fleas to one of the commonest. Sixteen years later I examined a number of nests from the same situation and found that *C. rusticus* was once again completely absent in the colony.

		C.hirundinis		*C.rusticus*		*C.farreni*	
1946	In:	15 out of 16 nests		16 out of 16 nests		11 out of 16 nests	
1962	In:	1 out of 16 nests		nil out of 16 nests		16 out of 16 nests	
	Numbers:	M	F	M	F	M	F
1946		298	424	128	225	29	45
1962		1	nil	nil	nil	56	89

Another conspicuous insect which was absent from Ashton between 1900 and the forties was the hornet. I captured the first queen in 1940. Since then there has been an increase in the number of nests found in the wood and in the roofs of thatched cottages on the perimeter of the wood. Like many Hymenoptera, numbers fluctuate from year to year but since 1940 this handsome insect has been a permanent breeding resident at Ashton Wold.

The birds The birds at Ashton have not been allocated the same amount of watching-time as the insects, yet it would be an error to ignore one or two conspicuous changes which have occurred in the bird population of the Wold.

I have a strong impression that numbers (not species) have increased in Ashton Wold over the last 50 years. This applies especially to the occupants of the roughs round the perimeter of the wood as well as the wood itself. We have lost the nightjar and the little owl; up to the forties the latter was exceedingly common here and is now definitely absent. Until World War II and the wholesale ploughing up of the grass meadows round the wood, we had a large population of green woodpeckers and no spotted woodpeckers. At this period the green woodpecker disappeared and the two spotted species moved in. It is difficult not to associate the two events. During the last few years the green woodpecker, albeit in small numbers, has returned to Ashton Wold and all three species are now present.

F.W. Frohawk, the great entomologist, spent a considerable period at Ashton working for my father – in fact he enjoyed his second honeymoon here in 1911 – living in the Manor House and gave us an excellent sketch of the green woodpecker, watched through a telescope which my father had installed in his sitting room.

The sparrowhawk and kestrel, which disappeared temporarily in the 1960s (after wheat-seed in neighbouring farms was treated with dieldrin), have also returned. Both species are now breeding in the woodland. We have added five species to our list of breeding birds: hen harrier, wood warbler, collared dove, woodcock and mandarin duck.

During the past 50 years an occasional rare visitor has been recorded. The most unexpected of these was a pair of choughs (they stayed three days).

Conclusions It is possible to find many different and plausible explanations for the changes in the flora and fauna of Ashton Wold, apart from 'natural succession' and the use of noxious chemicals in adjoining farms. Heath (1974), for instance, attributes the reduction in the number of marbled whites to a change in agricultural practices, i.e the cultivation and ploughing up of medieval meadows, and with this I am in complete agreement. On the other hand, his suggestion that the chequered skipper disappeared because of 'changes in forestry practice' does not apply at Ashton. As we have said, the roughs on the perimeter of the wood occupied by this butterfly in relatively large numbers in the fifties, are completely unchanged as far as one can judge. Its sudden disappearance is a mystery and one can only speculate about such possibilities as a great sensitivity at different stages of its life-cycle to drifting insecticides from local farms, or the smoke from burning stubble.

It is difficult to attempt to assess the effect of climatic change on the fauna and flora, or the combination of factors such as climatic change and a lowering of the water table, brought about by dredging of the Nene, and so-called improved drainage. Nor can one guess why the comma, which extended its range to include Ashton in 1922, has remained in the Wold, while the white admiral has once again vanished, despite an increase in its larval food plant.

Even more puzzling is the dramatic increase of a parasite like *C. rusticus* which, presumably, is independent of man-made changes, and its equally sudden disappearance again 16 years later. In this case, one may assume the environment of the bird-host's body is relatively stable; the nesting sites were unchanged both there and at Tring. However, the larval stages are presumably exposed to temperature and climatic changes while in the empty nest.

It is tempting to speculate on the presence of some genetic long-term 'cycling factor', largely independent of environmental effects, which could be the underlying cause of these fluctuations. Is the rise and fall of numbers of benefit to long term survival? Is it a built-in protection against too much success? Does such a 'prudent' strategy prove disastrous within the novel framework of modern man, with hurricane machinery and the use of lethal chemicals? Instead of providing a moderate brake or useful check on uncontrolled expansion, does it now lead to sudden extinction? We do not know.

Future possibilities   Charles Rothschild was once described as 'the man of vision' and he certainly looked ahead some fifty years when he planted protective zones of trees round the old portion of Ashton Wold. I do not think much of interest would otherwise have remained in such a small relic of open forest, especially in view of the elm disaster. It is of great importance that the screen of trees provided by Water Gap and Lutton Common take the first impact of the prevailing westerly winds, laden with residual sprays and clouds of smoke and soot from the burnt stubble from the adjoining farmland. Unfortunately, the vital importance of such areas is not appreciated by those who laid down the guidelines for the delineation and classification of our Nature Reserves. For instance, the derelict Polebrook airfield, one of the most important of the buffer zones at Ashton (and incidentally of considerable interest in its own right), which was once proposed as an addition to the SSSI, has now been withdrawn, since it does not quite fit the new 'rules'. A glance at the map will show how exposed this leaves the best area of the reserve. It could bring a corn crop with all its attendant chemicals within five yards of the perimeter with only a road in between.

If the entomological interest of Ashton Wold is to be maintained in addition to the wooded and scrub protective zones, an effort should be made to recreate the grass meadows which once surrounded the wood, but which were ploughed up at the request of the Ministry of Supply during World War II. This has been achieved on the north side of the Avenue. After a period of four years of apparent entomological 'stagnation' a large number of meadow browns, ringlets, blues and skippers have appeared in the 60 acres of flowering hayfields.

This plan should be extended to include the 56 acres of grassland known as Stanborough Hill. It should then be possible to reintroduce several of the recently lost species, for instance the marbled white, and the grizzled and dingy skippers. An ideal site for the reintroduction of the two skippers and the Duke of Burgundy fritillary is the derelict airfield, which abounds in cowslips and perhaps a bit too much tor-grass.

In the past it was possible to envisage the natural reintroduction into a small reserve of 'lost' species from other local sites. But today 'deserts' of agricultural land separate reserves and it will be necessary to bridge these gaps by man-made efforts. It is also important to leave the core of the Wold undisturbed, apart from maintaining the clearings and protecting bushes like the old blackthorn (which supports the black hairstreaks) and the sallow bushes (where the purple emperor bred), from destruction by the generating ash. The National Trust holds protective covenants over Ashton Wold and it is hoped that, as well as the Nature Conservancy, this organisation will take an active interest in its natural history.

The Elm Avenue   When Charles Rothschild first saw the magnificent elms in the Avenue at Ashton they were planted seven to eight yards apart on either side of a dead straight road. The distance between them across this track was sixteen yards and the Avenue was approximately a mile long. The 1887 ordnance survey showed exactly 100 trees each side of the road, but presumably this was a map-maker's licence, for there must have been twice that number. The elms were estimated to have been 150 years old. They were depicted as well grown trees on a map dated 1810. The Avenue – then as now – seemed to lead from nowhere to nowhere: merely a link between Ashton village and the Lutton road.

When I was a child of about eleven I was told by someone – I cannot remember by whom – that the Avenue at Ashton was the work of John the Planter (Duke of Montagu), who lived from 1689–1749, and spent not a little of his time planting avenues at Boughton and all over the county. Oddly enough I experienced a feeling of deep disappointment when my father told me he considered this extremely improbable. (The Duke's estates stopped short at the Polebrook/Lutton Road and skirted Ashton Wold.) He added no-one really knew who planted our Avenue, though it could well have been inspired by John's example, but was actually created a bit later. As far as I recall he did not give his reasons for this belief, but I have no doubt my father had researched the matter thoroughly, for he was a tireless investigator, a master of detail and never made careless assertions. Moreover he loved the Avenue. He put up bird boxes on several of the trees, faced with bark from the elms. All were occupied. (Recent evidence suggests the Avenue was planted by Dr William Walcot about 1700.)

About half way along the Avenue crosses a section of the so-called Bullock Track at right angles. The Bullock Track is an old cattle road which can be traced northwards from Ashton Wold as far as the Lynch (near Alwalton) and southwards at various points towards London. It ran roughly parallel to Ermine Street and was used principally to move farm animals to various large southern market towns. Where the two roads meet the Avenue

Oxeye daisy. (RP)

fans out into a large circle and the elms were extended for about 200 yards along the Bullock Track itself, both to the north as far as Stamford Corner and the Warmington Road, and about 50 yards to the south. This large circle of trees and the elms on either side of the Bullock Track are clearly marked on the 1810 map.

Again, during my childhood, I made friends with one of our woodmen, a delightful old man with a bushy red beard whom I remember as Mister Jackson. He seemed to me to be as ancient as the elms themselves but, looking back, I suppose he was in his late sixties. One Sunday morning I met him pushing his bicycle along the Avenue where it crossed the Bullock Track. He stopped and waved a hand towards the circle of trees. 'My grandfather told me, Miss Miriam,' he said, 'that when he was a boy he saw the cattle thieves settling down here for the night. They stayed the night here, did the rustlers, and shod their stolen beasts in this circle. The forges were set up under the trees with brasiers full of red hot coals. Before dawn they upped and drove the cattle southwards to the London markets.' Then Mister Jackson mounted on his bike and rode away.

When my father planted a protective belt of woodland at the northern end of Ashton Wold he extended the Avenue for another 200 yards but these young trees succumbed to the first attack of elm disease. There were also some losses from storms, and the gaps, for some reason I cannot explain, were not re-planted with elms, but horse-chestnut trees. A high proportion of the giant elms were still standing when the recent second wave of disease destroyed them all; those in the circle were the last to go. I left a number of the hollow stumps standing in an attempt to save the fine population of various Hymenoptera which inhabited them. I once peered inside one of these relics and to my surprise found a dog fox asleep at the bottom.

During the Second World War when the American Air Force were installed in camps over the whole area of the Wold, a curious episode occurred. Even before the advent of the elm disease, the trunks of many of these venerable giants were hollow, and rabbits dug holes inside the bark near the ground. Some of the fellows from the camp decided to smoke out the rabbits from a couple of the largest trees. They therefore stuffed petrol-soaked rags into the cracks and put a match to them. Owing to the hollow nature of the trunks they formed wind tunnels for the flames, which roared up these natural chimneys and emerged as flaming torches at the ends of all the larger branches. It was an awe-inspiring sight. 'All we need now,' I thought, 'Is for Moses himself to appear . . .'

Fortunately, the fire fighting equipment on the camp was quickly on the scene and proved highly effective. The wood was saved and the fire extinguished before the Luftwaffe were attracted to the spot.

Today the Avenue is a sorry sight, for not only have the elms gone but the edge of the October 1987 hurricane caught the chestnuts planted to fill the gaps, and twisted the tops off the largest. I have replanted with young limes, but at least half of these must now be replaced because of servere damage inflicted by sika deer and muntjac. I must say these animals are immensely attractive . . . It is a grand sight to see a herd of 30 or 40 against a dawn sky feeding among the moon daisies.

Hawthorn. (BD)

38

LEFT: Green woodpecker drawn at Ashton by F.W. Frohawk. (FWF)
RIGHT: Charles Rothschild. BELOW: Dog's mercury. (BG)

Kings Wood LNR. (BG)

The Changing Vegetation

by *Jeffrey A. Best, School of Sciences, Nene College, Northampton*

Our history is a common thread throughout this book. The influence of the past is now widely acknowledged. Many cherished sites are the product of centuries of exploitation and management by man and are as much a part of the cultural heritage as they are of our natural history. They deserve conservation just as more obvious artefacts such as churches. In some places, fragments of long-established habitat and their associated wildlife are perhaps the oldest features to be seen, going back as far as the Dark Ages or even Roman times. Altered yes, they nonetheless retain much from their ancient descent. Continuing research reveals that much of the countryside is older than previously supposed. Growing evidence points to the hitherto unsuspected extent and intensity of prehistoric man's impact on the land, profoundly altering its nature. In the process, many conventional wisdoms have been exposed as myth, nowhere more so than with regard to the history of our woodlands.

Woodlands We now know that Neolithic farmers were capable of coppice management. Bronze Age and Iron Age farmers were responsible for removal of most of the primeval wildwood. Numerous Romano-British farmsteads then made substantial encroachments into the woodland bastions upon the supposedly hostile boulder-clay. A 'bite' out of the southern edge of Pipewell Woods (SP83-85-) is paralleled by medieval bank and ditch – the field within contains the remains of one such farmstead. Contrary to popular belief, Anglo-Saxon colonists were far from the first to undertake heroic clearance of primary woodland cover. Coming instead to an already developed landscape, much of their effort was devoted to reclearance of secondary woodland, on abandoned Roman fields, before pushing on to the shrunken wildwood beyond. Even in the revered heartland of Rockingham Forest, fieldwalking has uncovered much occupation debris in the soil beneath recently removed 'ancient' woods, showing that most of these woods cannot be older than 2000 years and are of secondary origin. The major thrust of woodland clearance was effectively completed 200 years before the Norman Conquest. The rate of woodland loss actually slowed throughout the Middle Ages. Forest Law was an effective brake, ensuring good conservation of much of what remained and controlling further release and conversion, for genuine local need rather than opportunism.

Tracts of more or less undisturbed wildwood must have survived into this period, but their identification has so far proved elusive. Perhaps this was due to the damaging impact of the subsequent grazing regime within the Forest woodlands. Apart from their secondary origin, this could explain the comparatively species-poor floras of those woods today, compared to

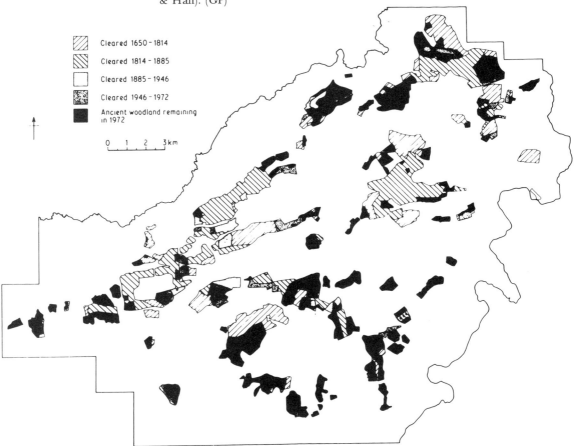

Map of Rockingham Forest showing the changes since 1650 (from *Woodland Conservation and Management* by G.F. Peterken, 1981, Chapman & Hall). (GP)

Cleared 1650-1814
Cleared 1814-1885
Cleared 1885-1946
Cleared 1946-1972
Ancient woodland remaining in 1972

0 1 2 3km

ones outside the Forest bounds. Oak was by no means the only dominant tree in the wildwood; elm, small-leaved lime and others were prominent locally, though cleared first because of the quality of the soils beneath, except from marginal situations like Easton Hornstocks (TF01-00-), where they survive atypically today. Thus the tree so often regarded as symbolic of old English woodlands came to prominence later, in more places than nature intended, because of its value to woodland managers. Moreover, many more so-called 'oak woods' are actually the outcome of deliberate in-planting or replanting as recently as the early 19th century. At Salcey, most of the large oaks were planted between 1831–46. In woods elsewhere, oaks of equivalent stature mark the failure of the timber market in the late 19th century to anticipate demand in the early 20th century.

The 'modern' destruction of ancient woodland is another entrenched view now subject to necessary revision. Although there has been recent loss, of Gibb Wood (SP82-73-) for example, there is no doubt that more serious damage was caused by Victorian landowners, freed from the Forest Law and encouraged by potentially higher returns from cereals, rather than by their mid-20th century counterparts. King's Wood, Corby (SP86-87-) for example, was effectively isolated from its historical context well before 1900, whilst Gretton Woods (SP90-93-) had largely been removed. Before this the inheritors of the, by then, derelict Tudor Forest woods either transformed them into intensively managed coppice woods – something they had rarely been before – or unceremoniously grubbed them up to create fields.

42

Thus fragmentation of the Forest woodlands is not new, the last episode in a process going back some four centuries. Few nowadays mistake medieval Forest as just extensive tree cover. Within its disputed limits were cultivated fields, settlements, pastures and other conventional land uses. It is more like today's National Parks, where there are constraints upon development, but recreation and conservation are by no means the only or even the most important feature. Maintenance of the Royal Forest as a functioning enterprise required an interrelated complex of management and habitat units quite different from the modern sense of the term 'forest'. Not only was the woodland subdivided into a cellular system of parcels – there were no less than seventeen separately identified woods around Beanfield Lawn (SP85-87-) alone – but interspersed tracts of Forest Plain and Lawn were vital for support of the deer and other grazing livestock. It is perhaps the subsequent loss of these associated open-grass habitats, rather than of the woodland *per se* which really ought to be mourned for its reduction of wildlife and landscape heritage. In Salcey the principal lawn has been replaced by waving barley, although geriatric pollards serve to remind us of its historical character. Unenclosed pasture-woodland habitat was present in parts of Rockingham, but what there was has long since given way to other uses because it was the easiest Forest land to convert when the opportunity came. Relict fragments remain at Morehay and an attempt to reconstruct this now nationally rare landscape/habitat for educational purposes is under way within part of King's Wood. The surviving ancient Forest woodland has accommodated a number of other changes in private hands since Tudor times. These include increased emphasis on coppice 'with-standards' (more oak trees again) in place of coppice 'with-grazing', 'enhancement' by block and scatter insertion of alien pines, larch, and genetically consistent oak, trials with sweet chestnut, turkey oak and amenity horse chestnut, before more or less complete replacement by close stands of alien softwoods – all too familiar a fate in most recent times. Apparent persistence of discrete woods with ancient names can be misleading. Upon inspection, the only vestiges of antiquity are found around the margins or, where density and spacing relaxed, as a stubborn field layer flora within.

There has been insufficient appreciation also of substantial phases of 'asset stripping' and equally damaging 'management neglect'. Many woods lost their mature timber due to the pressures of two world wars or shortage of estate cash, whilst almost all have suffered management neglect following collapse of the market for coppice, decline of gamekeeping or uncertainty about the future – be it threat from urban development, quarrying or death duties. Look out for the extensive spreads of hawthorn and blackthorn, mature thorn trees and dense infill by swarms of ash saplings and maidens amongst the labouring, overgrown, multiple-stemmed field maple and hazel in such examples as King's Wood. Changes in climate may have played a part, but neglect of coppice management has also severely reduced suitable opportunities for attractive woodland butterflies like fritillaries and white admiral and consigned colourful 'coppice floor' spring wildflowers to protracted and unaccustomed gloom, within living memory. There is evidence for mismanagement of coppice in earlier times. The letters of Daniel Eaton (Wake and Webster 1971) record less than textbook regularity of the coppice rotation cycle in Corby woods during the 18th century, and there are reasons for doubting the efficiency of the often casual and indifferent – if not downright crooked – servants of the Royal Forest administration.

Controversy attends the resurgence of interest in hunting and shooting, but few can deny that the active pursuit of game conservation preserved some woods which would otherwise have been removed long since. King's Wood and the nationally important suite of woods at Pipewell are good examples, whilst many more entirely new woodlands were added to the landscape. In this county of spires and squires a rash of, usually, small woods made their

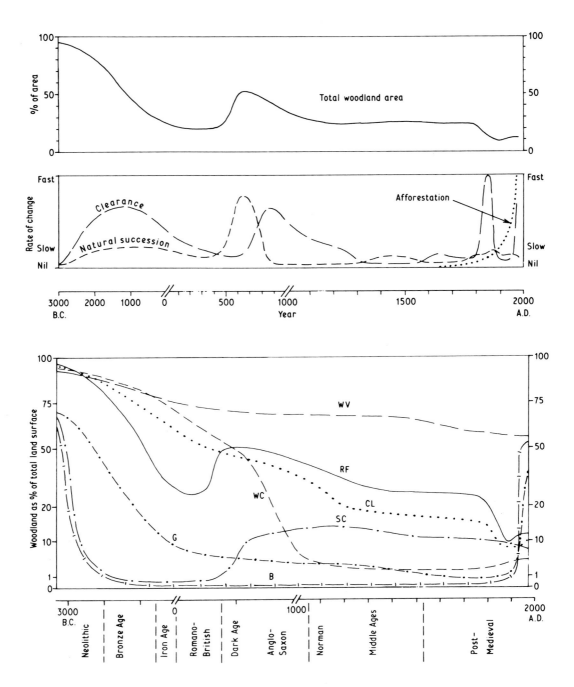

Summary of the long term changes in the amount of woodland in Rockingham Forest (from *Woodland Conservation and Management* by G.F. Peterken, 1981, Chapman & Hall). (GP)

first appearance from the 18th century. These were not only sited to enhance the view from houses and within transformed deer parks, but also throughout the associated grounds of the tenantry. Spinneys, coverts, clumps and plantations – often with evocative names and geometric shapes – bear witness to this fashionable precursor of modern estate planting of 'odd corners' outside the profit margin of conventional agriculture. Predominance of ash, thorn and species-poor shrub layer with plentiful elder, with or without the tell-tale corrugations of underlying ridge and furrow, is the frequent and widespread result. Anciently established parkland, as at Rockingham Castle, did not escape such transformation, although the introduced limes there now support a noteworthy beetle fauna, which contrasts sharply with the general paucity of wildlife conservation value in upstart new plantings elsewhere.

Losses of woodland to quarrying for ironstone and limestone have diminished the anciently established stock of woodland further, but this exploitation of much older resources has been followed in many places by re-afforestation: a cheap and convenient means of 'reclamation' adopted as a private venture within the larger dynastic estates and, more recently, on land controlled by British Steel. Hence the woods of larch, pine, oak, ash, sycamore and beech upon concealed 'hill and dale' around Corby and Kettering, and of course at Irchester Country Park (SP91-66-). Though abhorred by many, it could be argued that – in a county still not short of ancient woodland – these contribute to variety and diversity of opportunity for wildlife. Why else would crossbill come to Newton (SP88-83-) or goldcrest to Stanion Lane (SP91-87-)? Overall, there must be concern that a resurgence of woodland establishment this century masks a continuing and disastrous decline in the area of ancient, semi-natural woodland within the county, which no amount of replanting will properly compensate for because they supported the most interesting communities of associated plants and animals. A wildlife resource of this calibre which cannot be re-created is too rare for complacency.

Grasslands   As to the grasslands of the county, historical investigation again reveals that all is not what it might appear to be. Comparison of present grassland with that displayed by the first land utilisation survey maps (the first in the country) of 1928–29, suggests dramatic diminution of this habitat in modern times. But had we equivalent maps from the 1860s, the situation would be seen in a different perspective, with almost as much arable then as now. The greater proportion of grassland 'lost' in recent times was itself of comparatively recent origin, as a tumbledown or sown down response to the agricultural depression of 1875–1935, and of indifferent quality for wildlife conservation.

Grassland has experienced a particularly volatile history in Northamptonshire, advancing and retreating according to prevailing economic circumstances. Many of the most-valued neutral grasslands today occur on pronounced ridge and furrow and are therefore of secondary origin, developed on abandoned tillage, most often from only the 18th century. Some of the old ploughlands marked excessive expansion onto unsuitable terrain during times of extreme population pressure, never seriously in contention for re-use as arable once that medieval crisis had passed. Much survived beyond the high tide of Victorian and wartime hunger for renewed cultivation, only to succumb to recent profit, rather than population, pressure. A fortunate survival is now a Trust reserve at Great Oakley (SP86-85-) where, paradoxically, urban incorporation secured the site, whereas in the remote countryside of Loddington (SP81-78-) an equivalent site has once again been lost under the plough.

Neutral grassland is the most widespread and characteristic category in the county. In a survey of grassland between Corby and Kettering in 1983 is was found that 'planning blight' around the urban fringe has protected some fields from recent agricultural change. However the 'best' quality, long established sites there, and in other districts today, owe their persistence to remoteness from farmstead, proximity to parish boundary, tenancy or ownership in the hands of elderly farmers with more than wealth uppermost in their outlook, awkward topography – especially multiplicity of facets within individual fields – presence of wetland or watercourses and subdivision and isolation of uneconomic plots by insertion of canal, railway or modern highway. An almost traditionally managed, species-rich hay meadow survives sandwiched thus between railway, road and river, with many of the other site attributes too, at Barford Bridge (SP86-83-) – now included within the River Ise SSSI. Other sites of this kind are still worth searching for 'off the beaten track' in other districts. Perhaps the best example of flood pasture, fen and mire associations, including marsh-marigold, marsh-orchids and cottongrass, was 'discovered' as recently as 1985 within sight of Northampton. Similarly, in the Tove valley, an unimproved riverside meadow, thick with great burnet and other associated herbs and grasses, was found as lately as 1987.

Access to the lower parts of grass fields adjacent to the numerous streams and brooks of the county is not always legally easy, but it is there one is most likely to find the most valuable of all surviving neutral grassland swards. Having defiantly frustrated generations of attempts to drain and convert to more productive grass seed mixes or cereal monocultures, such gems, on ground liable to flooding, probably represent the closest contact we have with ancestral grassland communities. They would be familiar to a returning Anglo-Saxon, or perhaps even Romano-British, time-travelling farmer. Both the reserve at Great Oakley and the meadow at Barford Bridge include stretches of riverine meadow unploughed since Domesday.

Within-field intensification of grassland production has certainly been as important a cause of diminution of wildlife interest as physical destruction of the county's neutral grassland. Acre after acre of tedious rye-grass and white clover is all that the majority of managed farm grassland now has to offer. Herbicides, lime, inorganic fertilisers, let alone drainage, ploughing and re-seeding, have triumphed where centuries of judicious husbandry evidently failed. Even so, it is worthwhile closely examining field margins for any residual 'information content' as to previous character. It is quite surprising how frequently a ghost of the erstwhile flora can be recovered, though now lost from the bulk of the field.

Like undifferentiated woodland, neutral grassland has increased in extent alongside recent destruction of quality sites. The enormous amount of amenity and recreational grassland, together with that associated with motorways and other modern roadsides is at present dull but, if the precedents of railway embankments and cuttings, enclosure road verges and redundant green lanes is anything to go by, ought to have some future potential for colonisation and spread of additional grass and herb species. There are certainly more cowslip banks now thanks to such development in districts where the plant's traditional cow pasture habitat has been destroyed. Grassland associated with old railway lines is a significant conservation element within the Trust reserve at Farthinghoe (SP51-40-) and prospective Country Park near Lamport (SP74-74-). The 'heaths' beloved of Clare, like the fens and meres once within range of the Soke, are largely memories, belated recognition that many of the heaths upon unproductive limestone were probably occupied by grassland and scrub, promises especial significance to the beleagured Kingsthorpe Scrub Field (SP75-62-). Notorious because for the first time in 1984, a Minister of State (William Waldegrave) publicly condemned damage to what was in process of becoming an SSSI there: it has now recovered most of its recorded interest and may yet become the most significant reserve within Northampton Borough.

Water Creation of flooded gravel pits and reservoirs have actually increased the amount and incidence of such habitats; the riparian wildlife associated with segments of canal – particularly the Grand Union – have more than compensated for the inevitable loss of grassland and other habitats occasioned by their construction a couple of centuries ago. The recent Trust reserve, at Stoke Bruerne (SP74-49-), would not otherwise have come into being.

A characteristic feature of the claylands is the derelict remains of medieval fishponds. For many centuries these judicious blends of sophisticated engineering and exploitation of local terrain made effective use of intractable soggy ground. Most of the slight valleys and other low-lying ground on impermeable drift or solid deposits was much wetter than we see it today. At Harrington (SP77-80-) and Braybrooke (SP76-84-) disadvantage was reversed by creating nothing less than commercial fish farms, whilst few manors were without more modest groups of ponds impounded by still impressive earthwork dams as, for example, at Stoke Albany (SP80-87-). Apart from their prime purpose, the many bodies of water and accompanying island and bank habitats must have harboured incidental wildlife interest. Waterfowl, including the ubiquitous 'mere-hen', were undoubtedly exploited for their eggs and flesh long before the arrival of duck decoys and farm duckponds. Following centuries of neglect, the majority of ancient fishponds are now high and dry although a few still hold water, as at Brampton Ash (SP79-87-). Modern farmers seeking alternative enterprise could do well to re-examine their previous 500 years of productive use.

Over the wider landscape the impact of dogged and repeated attempts to drain wetland has only become profound during the last 200 years. Only with the means to manufacture cheap, durable clay 'tile' drains and the machinery to lay them, did the extent and character of marsh and damp grassland begin to change. Subsequently reinforced and extended by plastic pipe and canalisation of the receiving watercourses themselves, widespread field drainage has been one of the most significant developments affecting the countryside in recent times. Throughout most of the county only vestigial fragments of once characteristic habitat and associated communities of plants and animals of wet fields remain.

Corn marigold. (RP)

Loss of field ponds is a negative trend for which there is no obvious substitute, although popularity of garden ponds at least assists amphibians within caring suburbs and villages.

Hedgerows Loss of hedges has been of particular concern to more than one active member of the Wildlife Trust. It has to be admitted that, while the county has shared the rest of lowland Britain's reduction of hedgerow population, significant loss of wildlife interest is limited. The vast majority of hedgerows removed to facilitate industrial agriculture are youthful 'enclosure' features of poor species diversity and only general-purpose wildlife support. Of course their removal reduces food and nesting opportunities for resident and migratory birds of farmland, shelter for mammals and corridors for movement within an otherwise hostile landscape, but nothing of fundamental conservation importance is removed. Loss of any aged hedgerow trees matters more, since it is unlikely that well-meant tagging of emergent saplings will maintain the continuity of the increasingly scarce habitat of dead but standing timber. Of far greater concern is removal of any lengths of anciently established hedgerow. A good population of medieval (and possibly older) hedges survive within the milieu of Moulton Park in Northampton (SP77-65-), but particular vigilance is needed to ensure maintenance of this most valuable sub-set of the hedge habitat type.

Buildings The wildlife conservation value of buildings is regrettably a minority interest. Modern houses are, sometimes irritatingly, attractive to the common species of bat; many village dwellers are ambivalent hosts to nesting house martins and modern roofing materials and 'street furniture' are amenable to colonisation by rosette-forming lichens. Earlier structures, dating from the 'great rebuilding' of the 16th century, post-enclosure dispersal of village farmsteads, 18th and 19th century bridge works, additional or remodelled farms, walls of all ages and even World War II concrete pill-boxes deserve more than passing consideration as valued habitats for various birds, mammals, reptiles and lower plants. Often, as recent Trust surveys in advance of development proposals confirm, the 'old' built structures of a district – especially where made of ironstone, limestone, slate, asbestos and composite tile – are noteworthy refuges in otherwise sterile modern farmscapes. The conversion of redundant barns to dwellings proceeds apace with farm business diversification and barn owls, swallows, other stack and yard-midden domiciles and visitors have quietly disappeared in the process. However, derelict watermills, exemplified by that at Duston, and another in sympathetic human occupation at Upton (both SP72-59-), remain key loci for associated wildlife inherited from the past.

The future The prospects of change for wildlife are both good and bad. Northamptonshire is clearly set on updating its outmoded road system whilst continuing to deal with the impact of urban development. The long-awaited A1/M1 link, with associated and additional bypasses, whilst necessary, is largely detrimental in conservation terms. Abandoned quarries, regarded by many only as wasteful eyesores are rapidly becoming rare features. Cowthick pit (SP92-88-) with its population of tiger beetles and aquatic habitat frequented by migrant waterfowl is threatened by infill, as are the primitive limestone grassland and other features at Cranford (SP93-76-), Lodge pit (SP91-64-) and the few remaining old ironstone gullets elsewhere. Although initially destructive and bringing inevitable dereliction in their wake, such major excavations, once disused, diversified the generally dull landscapes involved, and their eventual passing is now to be lamented. This makes the Trust reserves at Rothwell gullet (SP80-81-), the Plens (SP80-83-) and those encapsulated in Country Parks especially important. Old limestone quarries are habitats for some of our most exciting communities of plants and animals. Gravel pits have consumed valued grassland habitat and continue to threaten established interest in the Nene, and so far neglected Welland, valleys. There may already be too many, but once abandoned and flooded, these features have growing value for aquatic habitats and their associated birdlife.

Urban development will continue to supplant countryside around all the major centres of population and employment. The signs suggest that development will be novel, with numerous 'business parks' and low density workplaces in 'campus' setting, leisure complexes, theme parks, golf courses and hotels amongst well-landscaped residential clusters. Such space-extensive layouts will make huge demands upon land, but there is, reassuringly, a lot of agricultural and reclaimed land of comparatively low conservation value to accommodate them. Attention to detail ought to see both security for established sites of nature conservation value identified by the Trust, in its expanding consultancy role, and designation of additional sites with creative conservation potential, where economics, though not principally concerned for wildlife conservation effectively excludes other, more harmful, forms of development. In many respects the wildlife conservation interest is better served by positive development than by continuing uncertainty.

Country Parks and Pocket Parks – pioneered in Northamptonshire – offer both retention of established wildlife interest and sensitive management of enclosed habitats. Further population growth is to be welcomed where circumstances allow.

What of the diminishing countryside itself? Whether or not the county is successful in obtaining grant-aided development of a 'New Forest' as proposed by the Countryside Commission, the odds are on the appearance of such a feature anyway. The benefits of tourism, rural employment and appropriate use of marginal or reclaimed agricultural land are all in favour of this exciting venture, howsoever the package is assembled and implemented. As envisaged, this would be no more nor less than a repeat of what was imposed upon the county in early medieval times, and all are agreed how beneficial that was for wildlife! New woodlands of appropriate species composition, actively managed along more than simply modern forest plantation lines, with intervening habitats of other kinds and sensitive integration of what survives from the earlier Forest landscape, are all to be welcomed.

Addition of another generation of small woods in odd corners of farmland might be anticipated from current pleas and inducements for diversification and extensification of farm business. There ought also to be sensible return of grassland in many places, as arable once again shrinks in the face of the unfavourable climate for cereal production.

Enforced fallow of 'set-aside' could, on the other hand, prove to be a short-lived and expeditious episode. Unless properly reinforced by truly low(er) input-low(er) output systems of crop or livestock husbandry, or purposeful replacement by woodlands of successional or planted origin, it is difficult to see much positive benefit from a wildlife point of view. Diversification into alternative field crops and unconventional livestock promises less predictable outcomes. A practicable possibility with proven pedigree here would of course be re-appearance of the deliberate farming of deer, whilst in another part of the country there is already an example of 'wild' boar keeping – a spectacular beast not seen in Northamptonshire since the 13th century. Meanwhile, horseyculture is likely to continue to expand. What might be the floristic composition of grassland grazed by llama in a midlands county? Will lucerne, borage, sunflowers or Russian lupins prove attractive to butterflies? Whatever comes to pass it cannot be worse than the present rape. Then there is the possibility of fast-maturing coppice energy crops, the resultant habitat of which is equally uncertain but could not be worse than the conservation opportunities of horizon-to-horizon cereals. Wildflower seed mixes are already widely available, with 'Miriam's mix' enlivening roadsides near Oundle and John Chambers' products leading historical ecologists on many a wild goose chase in response to new sightings of really long-extinct corncockle. Terry Wells' achievements in providing seed mixtures that simulate species-rich grassland associations from the past have yet to be evaluated in the long term but are obviously worth pursuing, especially where the seed has been derived from truly vernacular sources.

Quite independent of these facsimiles, a serendipitous consequence of recent urban development has been the chance afforded for reappearance of genuine arable 'weed' species associations from the past, on ground disturbed by building. Adjacent to the Nene Valley Way, within the Eastern Development of expanded Northampton and elsewhere – especially upon ironstone or other light soils – the spirited flowering of corn marigold, fodder burnet, parsley-piert, bugloss, henbit dead-nettle, wild radish and of course poppies, all too briefly enlivened journeys to the Trust HQ at Lings. Where have they come from? They haven't come from anywhere; they have been there all the time, simply awaiting disturbance to flourish once more. The seed banks sealed beneath low maintenance cost inter-war grassland have served to demonstrate the remarkable capacity of annuals to persist, and remind us again of the floristic appeal of pre-industrial arable fields. Having flowered and set seed, future re-appearance well into the next century is now possible, should inadvertent disturbance recur.

49

ABOVE: Kings Wood LNR. (BG) BELOW: Geddington Chase, like many of the Rockingham Forest woodlands, has been much planted up with conifers in the past. (TB)

50

The Woodlands

(RP)

by Jonathon Spencer, Nature Conservancy Council, Peterborough

Woods are amongst the most enduring features in the landscape, each with an individuality that reflects their long and often complex histories. Though many woods have been planted, some recently, many more have persisted in the Northamptonshire landscape for hundreds, if not thousands, of years. A few will have been part of the county's landscape since its emergence from the icy wastes of the last glaciation.

An important distinction can thus be readily made between two major classes of woodland, based on their origins – ancient woods and recent woods.

Ancient woods are defined as those that are known to have existed since at least the Middle Ages. They are generally richer in wildlife than more recent woods which have arisen, either spontaneously or through planting, in the last 300 years or less.

Ancient woods exhibit a suite of characteristic features. Most have been managed as coppice in the past and many contain large coppice stools, the result of continuous cropping of poles over many years. They usually have distinctive boundary banks and ditches, with the most ancient boundaries tending to be more massive and spread than the slighter and straighter boundaries of recent centuries. A study of such earthworks within a wood can reveal a lot about the history of land-use at the site and consequently contribute to an understanding of its current ecology.

Ancient woods have characteristic associations of plants and animals. They tend to have diverse flora and fauna compared to more recent woods on similar soils and they harbour many species which, because of their poor powers of dispersal, are largely confined to ancient woods or other ancient habitats. A few species, such as the native small-leaved lime and the wild service-tree are now almost entirely confined to ancient woods or ancient hedgerows. These two trees spread throughout England under continental conditions,

51

52

reaching as far north as Cumbria. Neither readily produce offspring from seed in the present cool, wet climate and they have persisted largely because of their strong powers of vegetative regrowth. They persist only where there has been a long continuity of woodland and may be regarded as strong indicators of ancient woodland.

Many other plant species, such as herb-Paris, lily-of-the-valley, and the common wood anemone are similarly restricted in distribution, being almost entirely confined to ancient woodland within the county. Other species of woodland plants and animals (particularly snails and other invertebrates) show a degree of close association with ancient woods arising from their ecological needs – the continuity of damp woodland soils for example, or the presence of dead and decaying wood. This close association with ancient woods also results from their limited abilities to colonise new woodland habitats as they become available.

Recent woods have many plant species whose mechanisms of dispersal and ecology suit them well to the colonising of new habitats. These tend to be the species of disturbed places and woodland margins, producing prolific fruit that is wind or animal dispersed. Wind-dispersed trees such as ash, birch and sycamore, berry-bearing thorns and shrubs such as elder and hawthorn, and herbs such as enchanter's-nightshade and wood avens with their barbed fruits, are consequently all typical elements of the flora of recent woods.

In addition to differences in their plant and animal communities, recent woods also differ in the relative abundance of the plant species present and in their structure and composition. This is admirably illustrated at Glapthorn Cow Pasture, (TL00-90-) a small secondary wood near Oundle, which has arisen over the last 200 years or so on former pastureland and which is now a Wildlife Trust reserve. Blackthorn thickets are extensive, and common hawthorn, alder, spindle and privet are all more abundant here than in the nearby ancient Short Wood, a mile away to the north-east. Ash, maple, goat, willow and hazel are all present, though the frequency of hazel, a rather slow coloniser on clay soils, is markedly lower than in Short Wood. Some areas show signs of past coppicing, demonstrating that this form of management is not confined to ancient woods alone. The few large coppice stools of ash probably originate from trees growing in the former open pasture. The structure and composition of Glapthorn Cow Pasture and its distinctive flora (grassland species are abundant and wood anemone has yet to arrive) clearly reflect its origins as former grassland.

Native Woodland Trees and Shrubs Northamptonshire has a wide range of native trees and shrubs. The principal species, pedunculate oak, ash, hazel, goat, willow, birch, hawthorn and field maple, are widespread and found in suitable situations in most of the older woods. Ash and maple take precedence on the calcareous clay soils, while oak, though present in all ancient woods, reaches abundance only in the drier woods on sandier soils west of Northampton, as at Everdon Stubbs (SP60-56-). Other species have a more localised distribution. Wild cherry, holly, rowan and aspen are distinctive features of the woods of the Northampton Sands along the western fringe of the county, being local elsewhere. This is readily seen at the Northamptonshire Trust reserve at High Wood (SP59-54-) where an abundance of cherry and aspen grows on the wet but sandy soils.

The native small-leaved lime, though a catholic species in its response to soil conditions, is largely confined to the Purlieu Woods of Rockingham Forest, where it is most common on calcareous clay soils. This distribution is similar to that of the wild service-tree, also found in the north-east of the county. Wych elm is similarly only found with any frequency on the limestones of the north-east.

ABOVE: A ride in Buckingham Thicks Copse. (JS) LEFT: Ancient oaks
in Whittlewood Forest. (JS) CENTRE: Bluebells. (RP) RIGHT: The late
Phyllida Rixon in a clearing at Glapthorn Cow Pastures. Phyllida Rixon
contributed a great deal to the knowledge and conservation of the flora
of the county. (FHP)

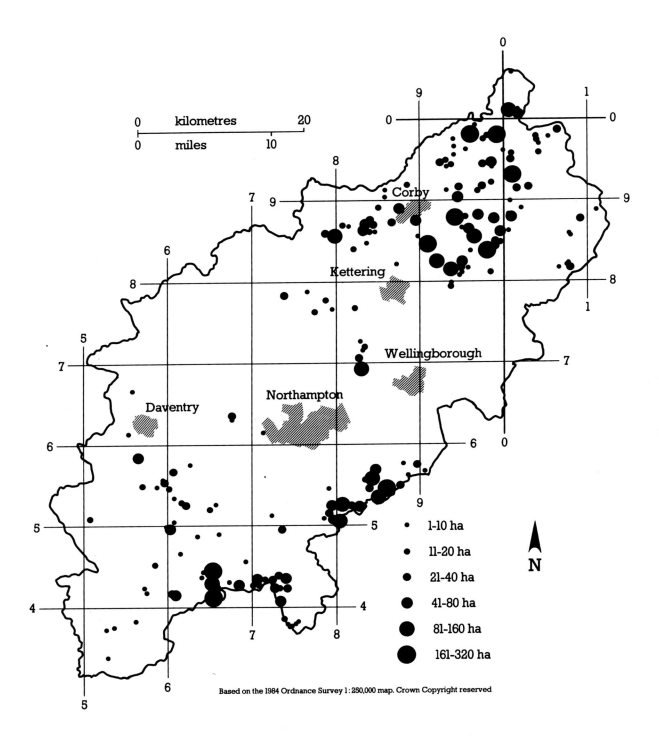

Map of ancient woodlands in the County. (NCC)

Elms of the smooth, small-leaved type (the *Ulmus minor* elms) are locally common in some woods in the north-east, where they also occur as small groves or individual hedgerow trees. Occasionally they may be found in the larger semi-natural woods as part of the coppice understorey or as invasive clones of suckering trees. The English elm, *Ulmus procera,* has all but disappeared from the Northamptonshire landscape because of the spread of Dutch elm disease, though it may readily be found as young suckers in hedgerows and woods. Unlike the wych elm, the small-leaved elms and their related hybrids, the English elm does not seem to have become an important part of the ancient woodland, though several *U. procera* 'invasions' are recorded and many of the smaller woods contain stands of English elm, presumably derived from nearby hedges. A good example of an 'invasive' elm stand can be seen at Short Wood (TL01-91-), though here the elms seem to be hybrids, intermediate in appearance between the *U. minor* types and *U. procera.*

Beech and hornbeam are difficult species to assess in Northamptonshire and their nativeness is questionable. Both are recorded in the late Middle Ages, beech as a parkland tree in Rockingham Forest and hornbeam as growing 'plentifully' in the county. Beech is also recorded as part of the coppice of Bedford Purlieus in the 18th century. The presence of beech pollen in late post-glacial deposits of fen peats in South Yorkshire along with these late medieval records, suggests at least the possibility of a native origin for this species in the limestone districts of north-east England. The huge beech pollard beside Wakerley Spinney,

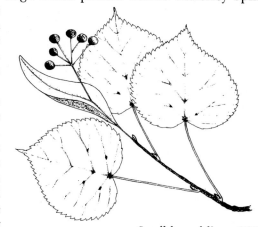

Small-leaved lime. (AW)

which must have germinated some time in the 16th and early 17th centuries, may well be a descendant of this native population. There remains the tantalising possibility that both trees were present as rare or local natives in the county from early times.

Alongside the natives, there are two important tree species that have become naturalised in the county in recent centuries. Sycamore and sweet chestnut are both introductions to Great Britain – sycamore in the middle ages and sweet chestnut much earlier, by the Romans. Both are found throughout the county, though only sycamore has become an important component in many woods, particularly in the wetter west of the county, where its abundant fruiting and tolerance of shade has given it a strong competitive edge over many native species. Badby Wood (SP56-58-) now has significant amounts of sycamore and chestnut, alongside the native ash, oak, cherry and hazel. By contrast, sweet chestnut has not spread widely from those woods on sandy soils where it was originally planted.

Native Woodland Plant Communities The wide range of woodland plants in Northamptonshire combine in suitable situations to form distinctive associations of species known as plant communities. These are far from random, dictated by the ecological characteristics of each wood, in particular the soil chemistry and drainage characteristics of the site.

Within Northamptonshire, the woodland variation can be divided into three broad categories reflecting the influence of the county's underlying geology. Though showing strong geographical distributions, these characteristic woodland plant communities are present throughout in suitable locations.

The woods of limestone and lime-rich clays are characteristically rich in ash and field maple, with a wide range of other trees and shrubs present in what is typically a diverse woodland type. Oak, hawthorn, hazel, wych elm may be present (to varying degrees of abundance), along with spindle, wayfaring-tree and dogwood – understorey shrubs typical of woods on limestone soils. The abundance of these last three species is characteristic of these woods. In the north of the county, in the Purlieu Woods of Rockingham Forest, stands of small-leaved lime are also present, and the rare, generally solitary wild service-tree may be found. Stands of woodland elms are also found in the area in this type of woodland.

Common hawthorn. (RP)

Three distinctive types of woodland stand may be found.

Ash-wych elm woods – on rich soils; these stands are amongst the most floristically rich in Northants. Oak and ash are often present as standards in coppice stands of ash, wych elm and field maple. Ash-wych elm stands are rare, occurring as small areas within other types of woodland, usually the ash-maple-hazel woodland described below. Good examples can be seen at Bedford Purlieus and at Lynn Wood near Fineshade (SP97-97-).

Ash-maple-hazel woods – these stands, with varying amounts of ash, maple or hazel in the coppice, occur generally on clay soils that are calcareous to slightly acidic in nature, on a wide range of soil water conditions from wet to dry. It is one of the commonest types of ancient semi-natural woodland, both here in the limestone region and on the clays elsewhere in the county. Oak and sometimes ash are present as standards in coppice stands that are predominantly ash or hazel, though with frequent maple and both the common and midland hawthorns. Other trees and shrubs – blackthorn, crab apple, birch, goat willow –are common but less frequent. Good examples can be seen at Short Wood, Weldon Park Wood (SP94-90-) and many other ancient woods.

Limewoods – Northamptonshire's few remaining stands are all in the limestone region. The limewoods are characterised by the presence of the native small-leaved lime, even though it is often present only as a few coppice stools. The limewoods occur in two forms, one on the more calcareous soils where it grows in association with ash, hazel and field maple, and the other on more acidic sandy or gravelly soils, where the lime is associated with oak and birch. Both types can be seen by the roadside at Easton Hornstocks, where the limewoods are on limestone soils and acidic, sandy, superficial deposits. The tall standards here are some of the finest native limes in the country. Other fine examples can be seen at Bedford Purlieus, where the complex pattern of undisturbed soils gives rise to a mosaic of stands of lime and other woodland types.

The ground flora of the limestone woods is typically dominated by carpets of patches of dog's mercury, often under dense brambles, with a wide range of other plants such as herb-Robert, primrose, wood spurge, yellow archangel, woodruff and bluebell.

In wetter parts, the mercury, a plant sensitive to soil waterlogging, is replaced by tufted hairgrass, ramsons and, in the more open areas

Midland hawthorn. (RP)

along drains and in glades, by meadowsweet. Bluebells, wood anemone and lesser celandine are all common in this woodland, becoming abundant in the wetter areas away from the competitive shade of the mercury, where they produce impressive displays of flowers in the spring. On drier banks and slopes the dainty grass, wood melick, may become abundant.

The limestone woods harbour many of the county's rare and local woodland plants. Columbine, herb-Paris, lily-of-the-valley, and fly orchid, and a wide range of other woodland orchids are all comparatively frequent here. The woods in this area are also distinguished by being on the limits of distribution for a number of woodland plants. This, combined with the diversity of soils and geology in the limestone region of Northamptonshire, have produced some of the most floristically diverse woods in the country.

The woods on the clays are the most common type of semi-natural woodland and found in the county, with much of the woodland of the former Royal Forests on the heavy clay soils of the boulder clay and the lias.

These vary according to how calcareous or acidic the underlying clay is. Those on the calcareous boulder clays along the eastern half of the county support plant communities similar to the wetter woods of the limestone. Stands of ash, hazel and maple or hazel and hawthorn, with oak standards are found over a field layer of bramble, dog's mercury, bluebell and tufted hairgrass. Primrose, bugle, ground-ivy, violets, wood anemone and other herbs are frequent, with ramsons, meadowsweet and sedges in wetter areas. Wood melick, wood sage and occasionally bracken may be found in drier areas.

On the much less calcareous Lias clays, the frequency of maple, and to some extent ash, declines and hazel, oak, birch and hawthorn become the most frequent species present. The plants of lime rich soils become much less abundant in these woods – dog's mercury, for example, becomes patchy in its distribution. On the poorest clay soils, with little or no lime, a distinctive plant community develops. Oak becomes common, over an understorey of hazel and hawthorn with occasional ash. The field layer is characteristic, consisting of bramble, abundant bracken and much honeysuckle. The ground flora is not varied, with a profusion of bluebells a typical feature. Anemone, broad buckler-fern, ivy, wood-sorrel and creeping soft-grass are all characteristically present on these wet, slightly acid soils.

Woods on calcareous clay soils are most common along the eastern edge of the county, with good examples at Short Wood and Glapthorn Cow Pasture. The more acidic clay woods are found throughout the county with particularly good examples in Whittlewood Forest, Yardley Chase (SP84-55-) and Salcey Forest (SP80-52-). Nutrient-poor clay woodland can also be seen at the Northamptonshire Wildlife Trust reserve at High Wood, near Badby. Here the rich clay soils along the bottom of the little valley in which the wood is situated contrast with the woodland of more acidic sandy soils along the upper slopes.

Two major types of woodland stand may be found. Ash-maple-hazel woodlands is the characteristic woodland type on neutral-to-calcareous clay soils. The more calcareous clays produce the ash-maple-hazel woodland described above under limestone woods, while maple diminishes in frequency on more neutral clay soils with the decrease in soil pH and nutrients. Oak and ash standards, often increased by past planting, are found in former coppice stands in which ash and hazel predominate. This type of woodland can to seen in many woods on boulder and lias clays; good examples are visible from the footpaths through Geddington Chase near Kettering (SP90-84-).

Ash-hazel-oak woods comprise the characteristic woodland on more acidic clays. These stands are not extensive in Northamptonshire though they are present in many of the woods of the former Royal Forests (at Buckingham Thick Copse in Whittlewood for example and at Salcey Forest) and in a few other woods such as Badby Wood in the west of the county. At Badby the stands of ash-hazel-oak woodland have been considerably modified by the widespread invasion of sycamore.

Also on the poorly draining clays, but now sadly lost to the county, were the plateau alder woods. Where drainage from the surface was impeded, the additional waterlogging led to an abundance of alder in the stand, a species typical of wet soils. The remnants of one of these stands, always a rarity in Northamptonshire, survived at Brampton Wood (SP79-85-) until its conversion to plantation in recent years. No other similar stands are known to exist in the county.

The woods of the sandstone represent the extreme end of this trend towards more acidic soils, particularly those on the Northampton Sands in the west of the county. The woods here are floristically quite poor, though they do have certain features – particularly the abundance of wild cherry, rowan, holly and aspen – that distinguish them from other woods in the county.

Woodland on the sandstone has a high frequency of oak in the canopy, over an understorey of birch and hazel. The field layer in these drier woods is dominated by bracken, particularly in the more open glades. It is this and the scarcity of bramble that separates them from the more acidic clay woods. Bluebell is abundant here and along with creeping soft-grass, greater stitchwort and wood-sorrel, makes up the species-poor flora typical of these sandy woods. Common cow-wheat is sometimes found, and the fungus flora is often diverse. Alongside the high frequency of cherry, rowan and aspen the woods of the Northampton Sands also contain much sycamore and, occasionally, sweet chestnut. Sycamore is particularly abundant in the wetter woods, at Badby Wood for example, while chestnut is a feature of drier areas. Everdon Stubbs, one of the best examples of the dry sandstone woods, has some large coppice stools of sweet chestnut on the drier upper slopes, probably planted several hundred years ago, whereas sycamore along with much of the cherry and aspen, is found on the wetter slopes on the south side of this hilltop wood.

Woodland on sandy soils occurs elsewhere in the county. At Buckingham Thick Copse the western edge of the wood is on sandy superficial deposits over clay, which gives rise to oak and birch woodland (with a high proportion of planted chestnut). In the limestone regions of the county there are many small patches of superficial sands in the woods, often readily revealed by stands of bracken and birch. In these woods, amongst the least modified in the county, these sandy patches sometimes support lily-of-the-valley amongst the bracken and bluebells, a situation typical for this rare plant in eastern and southern England.

Two distinctive woodland communities occur on the sands.

Oak-hazel woods on the wetter more clayey sandy soils, have an abundance of oak, hazel, bramble and honeysuckle and are typically species-poor. They are drier than the similar, acidic clay woodlands. Good examples are to be found in many of the western woods, at Badby Wood, Everdon Stubbs and High Wood, in Salcey Forest and Whittlewood, and on superficial sand deposits in the woods of Rockingham Forest.

Oak-birch wood stands occur on the driest, sandiest best drained and infertile soils which do not happily support hazel, ash or any of the more demanding species. Oak and birch, bracken and bluebell are the major components. The oak occurs as both standards and coppice, with birch, rowan and holly making up the rest of the stand. A scattering of hazel may be present, along with sweet chestnut.

This type of woodland of acidic soils, abundant in north and west Britain, is very local in Northamptonshire and confined to the driest hillside situations in a handful of woods. It is best seen at Everdon Stubbs, where its transition to oak-hazel woodland on the better watered, slightly richer soils of the lower slopes is well demonstrated.

In addition to the woodlands of the three broad geographical regions outlined above, there are two more woodland types in the county, both restricted in their distribution.

Alder woods and elmwoods formerly occurred over wide areas alongside rivers and streams and on nutrient-rich alluvial valley bottoms. The clearance of such valuable land for agriculture has meant these woodland types are now only tiny fragments compared to their former extent, and as parts of the agricultural landscape rather than as stands within surviving ancient woodland.

Alder woods can be found in areas of permanently waterlogged soils, along streamsides, in 'sumps' where soil water collects, and in areas where water movement is impeded through the soil, usually as a result of the presence of underlying impervious clays. Alder woods have variable floras, the nature of the flora depending on the nature of the waterlogging. Ramsons, tussock-sedges, meadowsweet, yellow flag and gipsywort may all be found, along with opposite-leaved golden-saxifrage, sedges and buckler-ferns. Some alder woods are more akin to a fen flora, along river edges and brooks for example as at Wadenhoe (TLO0-83-), while others are more typically wet woodlands where drainage is impeded. Alder woods are now rare in the county, with only small isolated patches remaining.

Valley elmwoods are found on similarly wet nutrient-rich, though better aerated, soils where elms, usually of the *Ulmus minor* types, grow alongside ash, sycamore, and occasionally oak and birch. Species typical of nutrient-rich soils predominate in these woods (eg elder, cleavers, ground-ivy and nettles) – alongside those more strictly woodland plants such as ramsons, dog's mercury, wood anemone and yellow archangel.

Valley elmwoods are rare in Britain. The fine stand that follows the narrow valley across the woodland at Bedford Purlieus is one of the best examples in the country. Other tiny stands can be found as small groves alongside streams in the north-east of Northamptonshire. A good example may be seen on either side of the roadside at the bridge crossing the stream to the east of Southwick, at the tiny ancient wood known as Wych Spinney (TL02-92-).

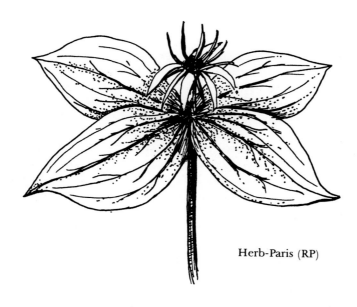

Herb-Paris (RP)

In Bedford Purlieus

I enter into the Green Man's mind . . .

Beneath the towering canopy
butterflies flit like dappled sunlight,
bird-calls echo through the hollow wood.

Time trickles slowly through its glass.
The pulse of Nature slowly ticks away
like a great green clock, broken . . .

Suddenly a squirrel jumps through the branches
chittering like a monkey . . .

(As though a thought had suddenly struck him . . .)

Then, silence.

He muses in a green gloom of trees

Dark shadows from which flower-faces peer.

The snake sleeps in its coil.
The grasshopper measures the empty minutes away.

I enter into the Green Man's mind . . .

Trevor Hold

Appendix

Short Wood – a pocket guide to woodland and ecology.

Short Wood clearly illustrates the wealth of history that can be found in a few acres of ancient woodland. It also demonstrates how this history influences the vegetation that makes up a woodland and how, with practice, the clues from the banks, hollows and ditches and the behaviour of the vegetation may be used to provide an understanding of the origins of a piece of woodland.

Short Wood is a small woodland nature reserve, owned by the Northamptonshire Wildlife Trust, on the crest of a low ridge between Glapthorn and Southwick. It is a relict of the woodland of the old Royal Forest of Rockingham and for centuries contributed to the local economy, providing firewood and timber, and the materials for a range of other products.

The wood lies on fertile but heavy calcareous boulder clay soils and is made up of a complex of ancient woodland and secondary woodland of various origins.

Short Wood, the ancient core of the wood, is bounded by a typical medieval woodbank and ditch along its northern edge. A sunken lane now forms the southern boundary. Until the 17th century this lane separated Short Wood from further woodland to the south. Dodhouse Wood to the east is largely comprised of ancient secondary woodland on the ridge and furrow of medieval arable farmland.

Other small enclosures are found at the eastern end of the wood, some of which are old fields while others, like Hall Close, are parcels of old woodland. Cockshoot Close is the most recent addition to the woodland, having been planted only recently with trees.

The calcareous clay soils give rise to a species-rich ash-maple-hazel woodland with ash, maple, hazel and elm coppice with standards of oak and ash. Both native hawthorns are present (*Crataegus monogyna* and *C. laevigata*), along with dogwood, spindle, guelder-rose and wayfaring-tree. Other tree species – birch, crab apple, goat sallow and wild service – are present as rare trees.

The flora is typical of woods in the clay region of Northamptonshire. Dog's mercury, bramble, bluebell and tufted hair-grass dominate the woodland floor, their relative abundance determined by local soil and water conditions. With these plants are associated a wide range of other herbs such as wood anemone, ground-ivy, herb-Robert, primrose, violets, bugle, meadowsweet and, more locally, common spotted-orchid and twayblade.

Some patches of the ancient Short Wood have a more calcifuge flora of bracken, wood-sorrel, bramble and male ferns (*Dryopteris filix-mas* and *D. affinis*), probably on surface patches of more acidic sandy soil. Such patches are absent in Dodhouse Wood, probably because of the marling effect of ploughing in the Middle Ages.

Several local rarities have been recorded, including bird's-nest orchid, greater butterfly-orchid, violet helleborine and the rare wood barley, *Hordelymus europaeus*. Herb-Paris, a plant that, within the county, seems to be entirely confined to ancient woods, has also been recorded.

The influence of history on the woodland is best illustrated by the elms. Within the ancient Short Wood, there are two large clones of elm poles (apparently natural hybrids between *Ulmus procera* group elms and *Ulmus minor* group elms, now widely regarded as native). These clones are extensive in area and confined to the ancient core of the wood. Their size suggests they are many centuries old. Sadly, they have suffered greatly from Dutch elm disease, though the vigorous growth of suckers suggests that they will recover and continue to spread. In the younger, more recent parts of the wood, elm is present but has not had sufficient time to create the extensive clones of stems found within the ancient Short Wood.

While some species are largely confined to the ancient part of the wood – wild service-tree for example – others are found in abundance throughout. The varied history of the compartments is also reflected in the abundance of some species and in the composition of the coppice. Very large ancient coppice stools of ash and maple are a feature of the oldest parts of the wood, the stools in Dodhouse Wood being generally smaller than those of Short Wood and Hall Close. Ploughing in Dodhouse Wood has also created a more homogeneous soil, and consequently a more uniform field layer than in Short Wood. The ridge and furrow here has also had a marked effect on drainage, reflected in the abundance of tufted hair-grass (a plant of wet clay soils) in the furrows, and the presence of dog's mercury (a species intolerant of waterlogged soils) along the ridges. Even after several hundred years, the coppice here is more uniformly comprised of ash, hazel, maple and hawthorn than in the original wood. Wild service is absent, even after many centuries as woodland.

Of the other compartments in the wood, Cockshoot Close, until recently an area of grassland, is the most different. Under the canopy of planted ash poles, there is a grassy sward, dominated by the coarse tussocks of hair-grass and low bushes of bramble. Only a few of the slower colonising and less competitive woodland plants can be found and these only sparingly.

Short Wood was saved from destruction at the eleventh hour, by the Northamptonshire Wildlife Trust in 1974. It was valued as a splendid bluebell wood and as a site for a number of rare and local plants. Close study of its history and ecology have since shown how complex and instructive Short Wood really is. It clearly demonstrates the individuality of ancient woods and the need for careful research of those that remain.

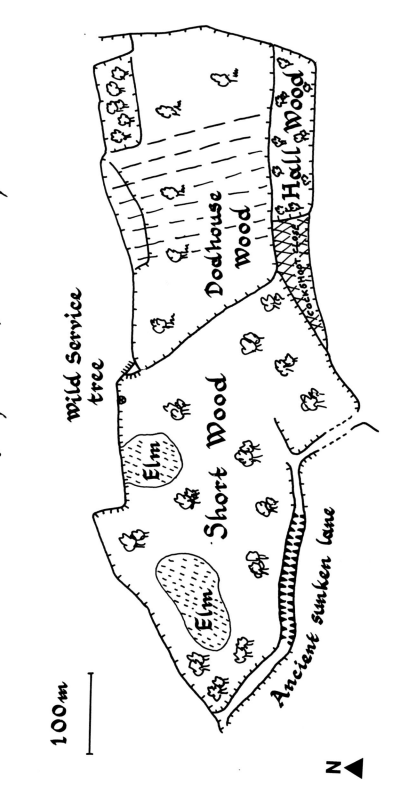

Short Wood near Glapthorn, Northamptonshire

100m

Wild Service tree

Doahouse Wood

Hall Wood

COCKSHOOT

Short Wood

Elm

Elm

Ancient sunken lane

N

Map of Short Wood. (JS)

62

LEFT: Old boundary pollard, Short Wood. (BG) BELOW: Derelict small-leaved lime coppice. (PW) RIGHT: Ramsons under small-leaved lime coppice. (TB)

63

The Birds of Short Wood

by Nick Owens, Head of Biology, Oundle School

A visit to Short Wood on a warm day in late April can be enchanting. The buds of the canopy are beginning to break, but do not yet obscure the woodpeckers and tits searching the ash flowers and oak buds for insects. The shrub layer of hazel, midland hawthorn and honeysuckle is already green, while the field layer at one's feet is in full swing. Here celandines and the first bluebells compete for the attention of the brimstone butterflies and queen bumble bees. Drifts of wood-sorrel, primrose clumps and the unfurling fronds of fern bedeck the rides to greet the first cuckoos and blackcaps. By the third week in May the bluebells carpet the woodland floor to make a spectacle unrivalled in the county. The wood gives a sense of timeless renewal, yet today forms but a small oasis in a sea of intensive agriculture. Over Britain as a whole, only about one tenth of the land surface remains wooded. The Rockingham Forest area is rich in medieval woodlands, yet has been particularly vulnerable to clearance and neglect since 1946 (Peterken and Harding, 1974). Such ancient woodland contains enormous natural diversity, much of it yet to be fully documented and studied.

From 1977 to 1986 I carried out an annual Common Birds Census which formed part of the national programme organised by the British Trust for Ornithology (BTO).

Male birds of many species proclaim their territories by song and, by plotting the positions of singing males on a map, it is possible to work out the approximate boundaries of their territories. Censuses pooled from many regions of Britain indicate population trends and help to elucidate the habitat requirements of birds and their responses to changes in land use or pollution.

Recognition of songs can be tricky at times. For example, I have heard blackcaps imitating starling, whitethroat and nightingale, all within one song sequence! (Blackcaps rank with blackbirds and nightingales as the most accomplished and beautiful British songsters.) Identification becomes easier with practice, since each species has a characteristic voice and song pattern.

Bedford Purlieus, Rockingham Forest. (PW)

YEAR

Species	77	78	79	80	81	82	83	84	85	86	No./10ha
Chaffinch	11	9	10	14	17	21	23	20	16	19	16.0
Robin	17	9	14	16	16	11	13	16	11	13	13.6
Blue Tit	10	9	9	13	14	10	17	22	12	14	13.0
Willow Warbler	10	7	8	13	12	15	13	11	14	13	11.6
Wren	13	15	4	8	12	12	13	12	10	3	10.2
Blackbird	13	7	10	11	13	10	9	10	8	6	9.7
Song Thrush	11	7	7	7	9	6	6	6	1	1	6.1
Blackcap	6	4	4	5	3	6	6	7	5	3	4.9
Great Tit	3	4	6	6	6	4	5	7	4	4	4.9
Dunnock	6	6	5	5	6	4	2	3	1	1	3.9
Greenfinch	2	2	2	4	2	4	3	2	1	*	2.3
Starling	1	0	*	4	3	3	3	4	1	0	2.0
Long-tailed Tit	1	1	3	1	3	2	1	2	2	1	1.7
Marsh Tit	2	1	2	1	2	2	*	2	*	3	1.6
Pheasant	1	*	1	1	*	1	2	2	1	4	1.4
Chiffchaff	2	*	3	2	1	2	0	1	1	1	1.4
Treecreeper	*	*	1	*	*	1	1	3	3	2	1.3
Garden Warbler	1	0	*	*	1	2	3	2	2	*	1.3
Cuckoo	*	1	1	2	1	1	*	3	1	*	1.2
Redpoll	3	1	0	3	0	*	1	*	*	*	1.0
Coal Tit	*	2	0	1	*	*	1	2	2	0	1.0
Jay	2	1	*	1	1	1	1	1	*	*	1.0
Bullfinch	2	1	2	*	1	*	*	1	0	1	1.0
Yellowhammer	0	1	1	1	2	1	2	1	*	0	1.0
Turtle Dove	3	3	2	*	0	0	0	0	0	*	0.9
Tawny Owl	*	1	1	1	1	1	1	1	1	*	0.9
Gt.-sp. Woodpecker	*	1	1	1	1	1	1	1	1	*	0.9
Woodcock	*	0	0	*	2	1	1	*	1	*	0.7
Tree Sparrow	*	*	1	1	*	2	0	0	0	0	0.6
Spotted Flycatcher	*	0	*	0	1	*	0	*	1	1	0.5
Lesser Whitethroat	*	0	*	*	0	1	*	1	*	0	0.5
Whitethroat	0	0	1	*	1	1	*	*	0	0	0.5
Nuthatch	0	0	0	0	0	0	*	3	1	0	0.5
Lr.-sp. Woodpecker	0	0	*	*	1	*	0	1	0	0	0.4
Mistle Thrush	*	*	0	*	0	1	*	*	0	0	0.4
Goldcrest	*	1	0	0	*	1	0	*	0	0	0.4
Willow Tit	0	*	0	0	0	0	0	*	2	0	0.3
Goldfinch	0	*	*	0	0	0	0	*	*	*	0.3
Mallard	0	0	1	0	*	0	*	0	0	0	0.2
Kestrel	0	0	0	0	*	0	*	0	0	*	0.2
Carrion Crow	0	0	0	*	*	*	0	0	0	0	0.2
Sparrowhawk	0	0	0	0	0	0	0	*	0	0	0.05
Stock Dove	0	0	0	0	0	0	0	*	0	0	0.05
Magpie	0	0	0	0	0	0	0	*	0	0	0.05

Table 1: The number of territories of each species breeding in 10 hectares of Short Wood, 1977-86. (* indicates that the species was present but may not have bred in the study area that year). The right hand column shows the mean number of territories in the study area over the ten years.

The Bird Community   The area surveyed in Short Wood covers 10 hectares (25 acres) to the east of Burton Ride, excluding the elm coppice, but covering almost half of the reserve. The census area was relatively small, and the coverage thorough. The estimates of numbers of territories are likely to be accurate to within ±2. The full results are shown in Table 1. Woodpigeons and house sparrows were present, but were not counted in the survey. Woodpigeons were abundant breeders but are difficult to count. House sparrows often fed in the wood, but there was no evidence of breeding.

Forty species of bird bred in at least one year out of the ten. A further eight were regularly present during the breeding season during at least one year, but were not recorded often enough for breeding to be deemed likely (* on Table 1). Woodland is an extremely variable habitat, and many factors influence the bird community. Analysis of the BTO's Register of Ornithological Sites shows that larger woods tend to hold more species than smaller ones, and those in the south and east of Britain often hold more than those in the north and west.

Short Wood supports a bird population fairly typical for its size and location. It is striking that the commonest ten species in the wood – chaffinch, robin, blue tit, willow warbler, wren, blackbird, song thrush, blackcap, great tit and dunnock – make up over three quarters of the nesting birds. Thereafter there is a long 'tail' to the species-profile of birds which are never common. A long tail of this kind is characteristic of habitats such as woodland in which this kind of vegetation is complex both in three dimensional structure and in species composition: there is thus a wide range of specialised niches for birds.

Short Wood's top ten species include eight which were identified by Fuller as 'almost ubiquitous' in British woods (and which also breed at high density), namely chaffinch, robin, blue tit, willow warbler, wren, blackbird, song thrush and great tit. Dunnock and blackcap occurred in 80–90% of British woods, though blackcaps are rare in the north.

Several of the less common birds deserve mention. Both marsh tit and willow tit occurred in the same wood. These species are similar in appearance and closely related, but differ in calls and choice of nesting site. Marsh tits adopt ready-made holes, but willow tits excavate their own in rotting timbers. Both great- and lesser-spotted woodpeckers regularly bred. The lesser- is much harder to see as it feeds largely among the small branches in the canopy. Great-spotted can be highly conspicuous. In early April their high-pitched notes ring out as they make spectacular displays, fanning and twisting their tails to reveal the startling red vent. Both woodpecker species are best seen early in the spring, and drumming can be heard from the first week of March. Green woodpeckers have also nested in the past, but feed largely on pastures outside the wood. Perhaps the most unusual sighting was a splendid male pied flycatcher which stopped on migration to feed in Jackson Ride on 23 April 1984. Birds not seen, but which might occur, include hawfinch and hobby.

Habitat use   By pooling the singing positions of each species over several years, it is possible to discover habitat preferences.

The top ten species show a fairly even distribution throughout the wood. They are woodland specialists that find the whole wood to their liking. It is interesting that the residents among them have adapted so well to living in gardens, whereas the two summer migrants in the top ten, namely willow warbler and blackcap, have not done so. It may well be that the enforced proximity to mans' dwellings induced by hard weather has encouraged these birds to adopt gardens for breeding. Many of Short Wood's 'resident' small birds temporarily desert the wood during cold weather, even as late as March.

The territory sizes required by these passerines is relatively small. Chaffinches and blue tits have both reached a density of more than two pairs per hectare in some years. Blackbirds seem to require a somewhat larger area and averaged about one pair per hectare. Larger woodland birds, particularly those at the top of the food chain, require more room: a pair of tawny owls needed the whole survey area to support it.

Woodcock and great-spotted woodpeckers can both commonly be seen flying between Short Wood and nearby Southwick Wood. Both rely on food with a patchy distribution; boggy ground and rotting wood respectively. They have to cover a wide area to satisfy their needs.

Other species are limited by the distribution of nesting sites. Starlings nested almost exclusively in abandoned woodpecker holes, and tree sparrows relied on the holes in some ancient oaks.

Several of the birds recorded here are not true woodland species. For example yellowhammers prefer short farmland hedgerows for nesting, yet often used the wood's boundary trees as song posts. Likewise whitethroats and lesser whitethroats occurred only along the woodland edge, with their territories lying along hedgerows adjacent to the wood. Mallards occupied the wood in 1979 when all the perimeter dykes were flooded in spring.

The warblers illustrate the kind of data obtained. Figure 2 shows the distribution of singing males of four warbler species consisting of two closely related pairs: willow warbler/chiffchaff and blackcap/garden warbler. Despite the willow warblers' use of the whole of the wood, there are areas where singing was particularly frequent. These coincide with places where there are breaks in the canopy, with birch and sallow taking the place of the forest trees. A completely closed canopy does not suit willow warblers. However, Sharrock (1976) states that 'even the smallest glade or clearing, or the narrowest ride, where the canopy is broken and secondary growth flourishes, will have nesting pairs'. Chiffchaffs by contrast occurred in different regions in different years, but were never so numerous as willow warblers. Chiffchaffs need tall trees as song posts, but again prefer woodland or gardens without a closed canopy. There was little evidence that they preferred a particular type of habitat within the wood.

Blackcaps and garden warblers make an interesting comparison for, while blackcaps occupied the whole study area more or less evenly, garden warblers showed a distinct preference for the southern edge, and seem to have been attracted to the thicker boundary hedge along the southern border. Analysis of the BTO's nest record cards indicates that garden warblers nest more frequently in scrub than do blackcaps, which occur more in high canopy woodland. The territories of all the four species of warbler overlapped, suggesting that they could co-exist despite being closely related. There may nevertheless be some degree of competition between them for food.

Woodland management is likely to have a strong influence on breeding warblers. Parts of the wood which have already been clear-felled in the battle against elm disease will soon yield the thick scrub and secondary growth enjoyed by willow and garden warblers, and might also attract nightingales. Damp areas of ground and rotting wood are also vital in order to maintain bird diversity. Such habitats must, however, be extensive enough to maintain viable populations.

Population changes   A glance at Table 1 reveals that Short Wood's bird population is anything but stable. All of the top ten species except robin varied in number of territories by at least a factor of two over the ten years. The number of species establishing firm territories ranged from 17 in 1986 to 29 in 1982 (mean = 24). The total number of territories held by all species combined ranged from 90 in 1986 to 132 in 1981 (mean = 116).

Some of the changes reflect population trends that occur nationwide. For example, song thrushes and dunnocks have shown a marked decline in the wood over the ten years. In 1987 their numbers in woodlands as a whole were the lowest recorded since the Common Birds Census began in 1962. Tree sparrows ceased to breed after 1982, and have declined nationally along with several other seed eating birds, largely in response to increased use of herbicides and fewer weed seeds on farmland.

Some species undergo long-term cyclical changes in numbers, for example redpolls and starlings, for reasons that are not clear but are probably related to food supply. Numbers in Short Wood are likely to be affected by national trends. Recently both species have declined.

Territorial behaviour places a constraint on the number of pairs occupying the wood, and some species may be more flexible than others in their spatial requirements. Territories

ABOVE: Pitsford Reservoir, important for its large numbers of wintering wildfowl, breeding and passage birds. (PW) BELOW: Swans feeding on riverside grassland. (RWB) CENTRE LEFT: Blue-winged teal, a rare vagrant duck from America recorded in Northamptonshire at Thrapston gravel pits. (RWB) BELOW LEFT: The hoopoe, another rare occasional visitor to the County. (RWB) RIGHT: The osprey is recorded every year at migration time from sites such as Pitsford Reservoir. (RWB)

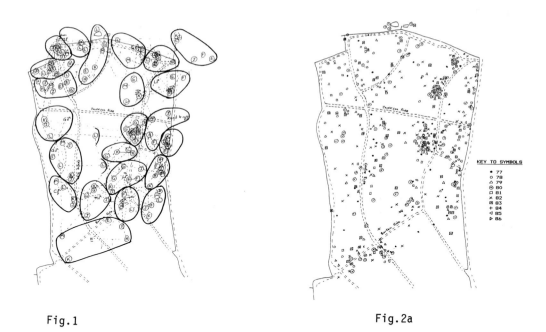

Fig.1   Fig.2a

KEY TO SYMBOLS

● 77
○ 78
△ 79
⊙ 80
☐ 81
✕ 82
⊞ 83
+ 84
◁ 85
▷ 86

ABOVE LEFT: Fig 1 – Species map for chaffinch 1983; RIGHT: Fig 2a – Singing position of willow warbler 1977–83; BELOW LEFT: Fig 2b – Singing position of chiffchaff 1977–83; RIGHT: Fig 2c – Singing position of blackcap; 1977–83; OPPOSITE LEFT: Fig 2d – Singing position of garden warbler 1977–83; and RIGHT: Fig 3 Singing position of chaffinch 1972–82. (All NO)

Fig.2c

Fig.2b

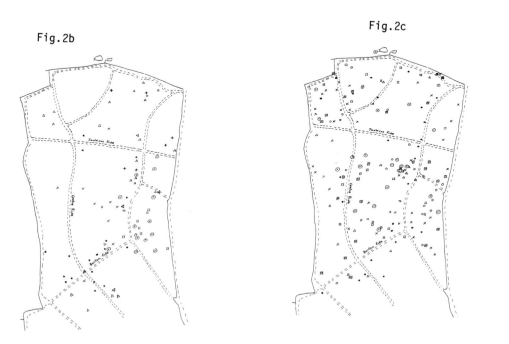

70

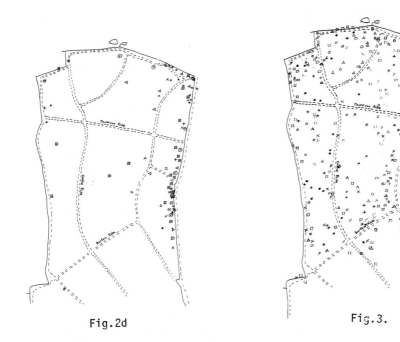

Fig.2d   Fig.3.

KEY TO SYMBOLS

○ 77
+ 78
● 79
△ 80
× 81
□ 82

behave rather like compressible balloons; as bird density increases, so does their resistance. Some species appeared to have a minimum territory size. For example robins seemed to reach a maximum of 16 or 17 territories, willow warblers 14 or 15 and wrens 12 or 13 in the 10 hectares. It may be that above a critical density it becomes more profitable to breed in poorer quality habitats outside the wood. Careful studies of breeding performance at different population densities are needed.

Chaffinch song was recorded rather more frequently near the edges than in the body of the wood (Figure 3). This may have been because chaffinches holding territory along adjacent hedgerows often entered the wood to feed, thereby triggering territorial disputes. Alternatively, woodland edge habitats may be more attractive. The mean density of chaffinches over ten years in Short Wood – 160 pairs per km^2 was above the range for broad leaved woodland of 49–145 pairs per km^2 quoted by Newton (1972).

Cold weather also played a part in controlling some birds. The winters of 1978/9 and 1981/2 were particularly cold, and 1983/4, '84/5 and '85/6 were quite cold. Wrens showed a marked drop in numbers between 1978/9 and 1985/6. In both winters there was a lot of snow cover which blocked up the shrub and field layer among which wrens feed. Other cold winters, such as 1981/2, which involved hard frosts but little snow, did not affect them. After the population crash in 1978/9, wrens built up to their former numbers in two seasons. Clearly they have enormous reproductive potential. As numbers increase, it is presumably territorial behaviour that puts a brake on further increase within the wood. Surplus birds may then fill other habitats such as farmland hedgerows. After the infamous cold winter of 1962/3, it was found that wrens filled woodland habitats first, then spilled over into farmland as woodlands became full (Williamson, 1969). Short Wood's song thrushes may also have been adversely affected by a succession of cold winters in the 1980s.

Chance must also play a large part in the number of birds breeding in a small wood such as this. The populations of isolated woodlands behave in some respects like islands in the sea. The number of breeding species is determined by the balance between the chance arrival of new species and the extinction or emigration of those already there. Nuthatch and mistle thrush may well be such species that arrive by chance and breed, then after an unsuccessful spell become extinct in the wood until a further invasion occurs. Only 22 species either held firm territories or were regularly present in the breeding season in every one of the ten years.

It is clear that Short Wood on its own cannot support viable populations of any but the commonest species. Even wrens were down to three pairs in the study area in 1986 (probably under 10 pairs in the whole wood). The existence of nearby Glapthorn Cow Pasture and Southwick Wood undoubtedly make local extinction much less probable. Adjacent hedges and copses are also likely to be of great importance.

Comparisons with Glapthorn Cow Pasture Glapthorn Cow Pasture was acquired by the Trust in the same year as Short Wood and lies about one mile to the west. Its history is different, formed by a process of succession from pasture land relatively recently and makes a fascinating comparison with Short Wood. Much of the reserve is enveloped in thick blackthorn scrub, largely absent from Short Wood. The dense scrub with occasional large oaks makes ideal habitat for nightingales, of which there are up to five pairs. Turtle doves, magpies and bullfinches also relish the dense scrub and are more common here than in Short Wood. Collared doves are plentiful too. The thick cover encourages small numbers of starlings to come in and roost at certain times of the year. Long-eared owls have bred in the past.

Difficult to observe, but strikingly coloured are the golden pheasants that breed. Feathers with a bright coppery sheen can sometimes be found along the rides. Song thrushes seem to do much better here too. In May 1986 I counted seven singing males at a time when they were down to one or two pairs in Short Wood. Further systematic recording of birds and other species is urgently needed. So far we have only scratched the surface of what is to be discovered in these two excellent reserves. The more we know about their wildlife, the better they can be managed and enjoyed.

Wren

One day you'll explode
and burst your dynamo,
your coiled-up spring will snap,
your bones and feathers scatter
in all directions.

Could we harness such energy,
fifty wrens at full pelt
would drive a power-station,
heat a thousand houses,
light a dozen beacons.

Yet you expend it all
in fury at another tiny wren
who happens to cross your nesting-ground!

Trevor Hold

LEFT: Bluebells. (NO) RIGHT: Hazel coppice and bluebells in Short
Wood. (NO) BELOW: Ride at Short Wood. (BG)

ABOVE: Barnack Hills and Holes in winter. (BG) BELOW: Marshy grasslands, such as this one at Bulwick, were once a feature of the river valleys. (RP)

Grasslands

by Susan Page, Department of Adult Education, Leicester University, Northampton

'Where the Cowslips do unfold,
  Shaking tassels all of gold.'   John Clare, 1793–1864

Throughout John Clare's work there are many references to the wealth of plants which were once so characteristic of this county's grasslands. Although flower-rich meadows and pastures are now much reduced in both extent and variety as a result of modern, intensive agricultural practices, Northamptonshire still retains small examples of unimproved grassland maintained by traditional management methods. These remnants of a past agricultural landscape have a high intrinsic appeal, particularly during the months of late spring and early summer when their colourful, flowery swards contrast strongly with the monochrome monocultures of neighbouring fields.

Grasslands are in fact secondary communities occupying ground which under natural conditions, ie in the absence of man or his grazing animals, would be woodland. Although semi-natural habitats, they may be of high wildlife value, supporting a great variety of plants and invertebrates (beetles, butterflies, spiders, grasshoppers); some grasslands are also of considerable antiquity. But this high wildlife value only persists if they are managed by traditional, low intensity methods which allow a diverse sward to develop – add too much fertiliser and nutrient-demanding, fast-growing grasses dominate at the expense of the less aggressive grasses and herbs.

On the basis of their soils, grasslands may be assigned to one of three broad categories: calcareous, neutral or acid. In Northamptonshire calcareous grasslands occur principally on the oolitic limestones of the great Jurassic ridge which crosses the county. The resultant soils are thin, porous, frequently rocky and rich in lime (calcium carbonate). Neutral grasslands, as their name suggests, have soils which are neither markedly acid or alkaline. These grasslands are widespread in Northamptonshire and comprise flood meadow – areas of

Grassland plants: yellow-rattle, cowslip, greater burnet, quaking-grass
      and meadow saxifrage. (RP)

permanent pasture beside rivers and streams liable to winter flooding; old ridge-and-furrow pastures, usually on boulder clay; and hay meadows. Acid grasslands have a limited distribution in the county, restricted to the acid, free-draining soils overlying Liassic sands in the west of the county. Occasionally, where the soils have a deeper surface layer of acid humus, these grasslands grade into heath.

Calcareous grasslands   Unimproved grasslands on oolitic limestone support some of the most spectacular plant communities in England. The thin soils, although rich in calcium and humus, contain relatively low amounts of the other important plant nutrients – nitrate, phosphate, potassium and iron. This low fertility favours slow-growing plants and the development of a diverse sward – more than 30 different plant species may be recorded from one square metre of turf. The Northamptonshire Heights in the north were once one large expanse of unimproved, sheep-grazed pasture. However, most of this habitat has long since disappeared in the wake of agricultural improvements and is now scarce, both within the county and the larger East Midlands region. Remnants persist by virtue of their low fertility and shallow soils; at Southorpe Paddock (TF08-02-), a Northamptonshire Wildlife Trust reserve near Barnack, an attempt at cultivation in the early 1960s was abandoned because of severe damage to the plough. Two of the best examples of calcareous grassland in the county are, however, not directly derived from limestone pasture. Instead they occupy former quarries where, following abandonment, the uneven topography prevented ploughing, and the bare rock and spoil tips were quickly colonised by lime-loving plants from surrounding pastureland.

Characteristic plants of this county's calcareous grasslands include the grasses upright brome, tor-grass, meadow and yellow oat-grasses, quaking-grass (Clare's 'totter' grass), sheep's-fescue and crested hair-grass, plus two members of the *Cyperaceae*, the small spring-sedge and larger glaucous sedge. Herbs are also plentiful in a spectrum of flower-colours from the yellows of common rock-rose, common bird's-foot-trefoil, vetch (horseshoe and kidney), meadow vetchling, mouse-ear hawkweed and lady's bedstraw, which dries with a scent of hay, to the pinks and purples of clustered bellflower, wild thyme, common and greater knapweed, small scabious, squinancywort, purple milk-vetch, dwarf thistle, salad burnet and the whites of dropwort, burnet-saxifrage and diminutive fairy flax. Around Eastertide (late April and early May) the beautiful, vividly purple, bell-like flowers of the pasqueflower decorate the short limestone turf, whilst later in the season numerous orchids come into flower. Several of these lime-loving plants have a much wider distribution further south in Europe and only extend northwards into Britain in free-draining, chalky soils. A few, including man orchid, approach the northern limits of their British range on the oolitic limestone of Northamptonshire.

Most of the county's calcareous grasslands were formerly managed by winter grazing, usually by sheep, from October to March. This practice produces a short turf, by limiting the growth of tall grasses, notably tor-grass and upright brome. In the absence of grazing, dead plant material accumulates on the soil surface at the end of the growing season, smothering the young sward and suppressing the growth of small, slower-growing herbs. Several plants associated with oolitic limestone are known to benefit from a winter grazing regime, including pasqueflower, horseshoe vetch and kidney vetch. At Barnack Hills and Holes reserve, the recent re-introduction of a winter sheep-grazing regime brought about a spectacular increase in the number of pasqueflower plants – from 1,500 to 15,000 over 10 years. The rise in orchids was also impressive, with in excess of 10,000 spikes of man orchid now appearing annually.

A further consequence of reduced grazing pressure on all grasslands is scrub invasion – part of the natural succession from open grassland to woodland. Although the presence of scrub may enhance the wildlife value of a site by increasing the range of habitats available for birds and invertebrates, the light levels beneath scrub are too low for most grassland species to survive. On all of its grassland reserves in the county, the Northamptonshire Wildlife Trust manages the land for the maximum benefit of fauna and flora and, whilst on several sites limited scrub development is allowed, on other sites the principal feature of conservation interest is the rich assemblage of open grassland plants.

The jewel of Northamptonshire calcareous grasslands is Barnack Hills and Holes National Nature Reserve, near Stamford (TF-07-04-). This site covers some 22 ha of old stone workings just south of the village of Barnack. The oolitic limestone of this area yielded a particularly fine building stone, Barnack ragstone, which was quarried from Roman to medieval times, and used in the construction of most of the great Norman abbeys of East Anglia. The quarries were worked out some 500 years ago, but the evidence of former extraction remains in the extremely irregular 'hills and holes' topography – short ridges, steep slopes, often with bare rock showing through, and deep pits – now clothed in a plant-rich turf of more than 230 species. Although the hummocky landscape was too uneven for ploughing, the area was turned over to sheep pasture and was regularly grazed until the Second World War. Although subsequently burnt on occasion, the reduction in grazing resulted in progressive invasion by trees, shrubs and tall, coarse grasses. Fortunately, the active involvement of both the Northamptonshire Wildlife Trust and the Nature Conservancy Council on the site in recent years has redressed the balance in favour of the grassland flora, which continues to contain many interesting plants.

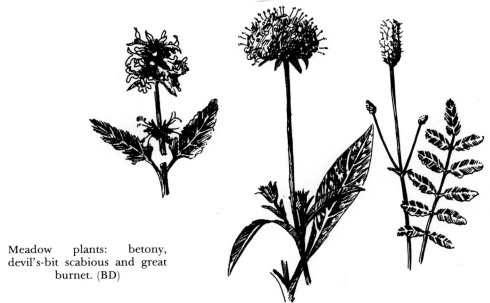

Meadow plants: betony, devil's-bit scabious and great burnet. (BD)

Barnack National Nature Reserve is one of the finest sites in England for the pasqueflower, but there are also large colonies of man orchid (whose yellowish-green flowers open to reveal a floral structure reminiscent of small, cut-out men), pyramidal orchid and sweet-scented fragrant orchid. Early-purple orchid, twayblade and the fascinating bee orchid also thrive here, whilst careful search might reveal the inconspicuous frog orchid. Other noteworthy botanical features of the reserve include a small colony of mountain everlasting, growing at one of the few sites in southern England for this northern species, and large clumps of purple milk-vetch and hairy violet, both of which are predominantly eastern in their British distribution.

77

This diverse flora supports a variety of butterflies – 28 species have been recorded in recent years. Grassland butterflies are numerous, including small white, meadow brown, gatekeeper and common blue, whilst other species like the chalkhill blue, whose larvae feed mainly on horseshoe vetch, and marbled white, are present in smaller numbers and approach the northern limits of their ranges at Barnack. Brightly-coloured six-spot burnet moths are abundant, attracted by the purple flowers of scabious and knapweed.

In the same neighbourhood as Barnack, Collyweston Quarries (The Deeps) lies mid-way between the villages of Collyweston and Easton-on-the-Hill. This Northamptonshire Wildlife Trust reserve is also designated an SSSI. As at Barnack, the species-rich sheep-grazed turf has developed on hummocky terrain of an old quarry site – not worked for building stone but for roofing tiles. When the Northamptonshire Wildlife Trust became involved with Collyweston Quarries, sheep grazing was no longer practised and large areas had scrubbed over with dense thickets of hawthorn, elder, blackthorn and rose. Winter sheep grazing has now been reinstated and sections of scrub removed, whilst the remaining thickets provide nesting habitat for whitethroat, chiffchaff and blackcap. Although the Barnack and Collyweston grasslands are only a short distance apart, their vegetation is not identical. At The Deeps there is an abundance of dyer's greenweed, a close relative of gorse and broom, which in July transforms large parts of the site into a sea of golden blooms. Dyer's greenweed also plays 'host' to one of the county's rarer plants – the dodder – a rootless parasite of heathers and other small shrubby plants, which attaches itself to the greenweed by means of tiny suckers. The leafless, red twining stems of the dodder sprawl over the host plant and in late summer bear small clusters of pinkish flowers. Another abundant parasitic plant at both this and the Barnack site is the knapweed broomrape which, like other broomrapes, attaches itself to the root system of the host plant. Although other species are parasitic chiefly on clovers and other members of the pea family, this broomrape is particularly associated with the greater knapweed. As the young flowering stems of the broomrape appear above ground in May their scaly stems and terminal flowering spike are reminiscent of large brown asparagus spears. Unlike the Barnack grassland, there are no pasqueflowers at Collyweston and man orchids are infrequent. The Deeps is, however, one of only 10 sites in the British Isles for spotted cat's-ear – a member of the daisy family which at first glance resembles an overgrown hawkbit with purple-spotted leaves. The flowers of this rare composite may reach two inches in diameter and the erect flower stems a height of one to two feet.

At both Barnack and Collyweston, the undulating topography produces marked differences in the flora of north- and south-facing slopes. On the warmer, drier south-facing slopes carpets of rock-rose, horseshoe vetch and thyme grow amongst the short turf of sheep's-fescue and crested hair-grass; at Barnack pasqueflowers are most frequent on these sunny slopes. On cooler, north-facing slopes the deeper soils support a more luxurious growth of tall grasses and low-growing herbs are largely absent. Amongst the clumps of tor-grass and upright brome, cowslips, man and pyramidal orchids are frequently to be found.

Neutral grasslands   Neutral grassland is the characteristic, semi-natural grassland of most of Northamptonshire and comprises both pastures (grasslands grazed more or less continuously throughout the year) and meadows (grasslands initially cut for hay during the early summer and then aftermath grazed by stock into early autumn). The floristic composition of these grasslands is greatly influenced by past and present agricultural practices – the frequency and intensity of grazing, cutting and manuring – but soil conditions also play an important role, in particular soil drainage and fertility. Meadowland was frequently situated near streams or rivers liable to winter flooding; the seasonal influx of waters onto the land brought a natural source of fertiliser in the form of nutrient-rich silts which maintained the productivity of the sward. The Domesday record for Northamptonshire shows a concentration of meadowland in the valleys of the Nene and Ise, with particularly large amounts around Kettering and at Billing, on the outskirts of Northampton. Hay making and stock grazing regimes are also important in controlling and maintaining the floristic diversity of meadows. For example, if the hay crop is removed before meadow species have set and dispersed seed the sward diversity will be reduced, with the selective removal of late-flowering species, in particular orchids, whilst excessive grazing, trampling and manuring will encourage unpalatable coarse grasses, rushes, nettles, creeping and spear thistles to assume dominance.

Characteristic meadow and pasture species include a large number of grasses: meadow foxtail, meadow and red fescues, Yorkshire-fog, timothy, smooth and rough meadow-grasses, cock's-foot and sweet vernal-grass, which is rich in coumarin, a natural oil which gives fresh-mown hay its unique fragrance. On dry, neutral pastures which are grazed and not mown, the species diversity is lower and crested dog's-tail, perennial rye-grass and annual meadow-grass are more conspicuous, whilst on calcareous boulder clay tor-grass and upright brome may be present. The herbaceous component of neutral grasslands contributes greatly to the characteristic colour and texture of the meadow sward and seasonal aspects are well marked: early-flowering plants include lesser celandine and cowslip, while meadow and bulbous buttercups, common knapweed, red clover, common sorrel, selfheal, ribwort plantain, oxeye daisy, pignut and yellow-rattle are late spring and early summer additions which flower and set seed prior to hay cut in late June or early July. The presence of other plants, most of which are now declining and rare or local within Northamptonshire, are indicative of old, unimproved grasslands: green-winged orchid, meadow saxifrage, pepper-saxifrage (not a true saxifrage, but a member of the *Umbelliferae*, the carrot family) and the tiny adder's-tongue fern. Unfortunately, two other old meadow 'indicator plants' no longer grow in the county – fritillary and meadow saffron. The former was always rare but in the 16th century the latter was a common sight on riverside meadows in Kingsthorpe and Northampton.

On the ancient grassland of Great Oakley Meadow near Corby (SP86-85-), the influence of localised variation in geology, topography and drainage on the vegetation is well marked. Much of the field bears ridge and furrow and is one of the best surviving fragments of the ancient field system of Great Oakley village. On the drier ridges a species-rich community contains selfheal, common knapweed, bird's-foot-trefoil, bulbous buttercup, cowslip and a variety of grasses, whilst the damper furrows support a less diverse assemblage of tufted hair-grass, meadow fescue, cock's-foot grass and the early-flowering cuckooflower. The lower part of this reserve alongside Harper's Brook has probably never been ploughed and was formerly shut-up during spring and early summer for hay. Here an early yellow flush is provided by the flowers of marsh-marigold and creeping buttercup. Hairy sedge is frequent amongst the rushes, whilst the wettest depressions contain marsh foxtail, floating sweet-grass and brooklime.

In east Northamptonshire, on gently undulating boulder clay adjacent to Sudborough Green Lodge, two hay meadows provide one of the largest and best examples of traditionally-managed neutral meadow grassland in the county. The sward is a rich assemblage of grasses and herbs, with thousands of cowslip blooms appearing in spring; there are also populations of green-winged orchid and adder's-tongue fern, confirming the long continuity of 'traditional' management which the site has received. Where the soil is free-draining and has a higher lime content, upright brome, salad burnet, dwarf thistle and glaucous sedge are locally abundant. This is an uncommon grassland community in the county, composed of species normally associated with more alkaline soils, and is regarded as a botanical 'link' between neutral and calcareous grassland vegetation.

Damp, riparian grasslands on alluvial soils or shallow peats have also been much reduced in extent as a result of land drainage and agricultural intensification. The largest remaining areas are located in east Northamptonshire beside the Nene and its tributaries. These wetlands often support a mosaic of plant communities which reflect the variation in soil organic and moisture contents. Where the water table is close to the surface throughout the year, tall fen vegetation of reed sweet-grass, reed canary-grass, common reed and lesser pond-sedge grows, providing a habitat for common valerian and the delicate ragged-Robin; in mid-summer the air is scented by the fragrant creamy flowerheads of meadowsweet. Further away from the river, fen vegetation grades into marshy grassland, rich in species of rush and sedge and interspersed with shallow depressions where winter floodwater persists. These areas are vital feeding and breeding sites for wetland birds – snipe, redshank, lapwing and yellow wagtail – all of which are now uncommon in the county. Flood-plain grasslands are also the habitat of several locally rare plants – early and southern marsh-orchids with their tall pink and purple spikes, the marsh arrowgrass, a rush-like plant bearing racemes of small, greenish flowers, and the small marsh valerian.

The largest area of riparian wetland in the county lies astride the R.Nene to the south of the small village of Wadenhoe, near Oundle (TL00-82-). This site is notable for its high floristic diversity (over 100 flowering plant species have been recorded) and the wet meadows also provide suitable breeding habitat for redshank, lapwing and snipe. Some distance upstream, beyond Northampton, another excellent example of species-rich flood-plain meadowland and fen beside the R.Nene has also been 'brought to light'. This site has been managed for centuries to provide hay and seasonal grazing for livestock and has probably been in more or less continuous use since Domesday. This long history of 'traditional' management, without recourse to inorganic fertilisers or more productive seed-mixes, is reflected in the flora, which is not only varied but also contains a number of county rarities: sneezewort, southern marsh-orchid, lesser spearwort, marsh arrowgrass and marsh valerian, plus, on soil rich in organic matter, the common cottongrass.

Acid grasslands   In contrast to the profusion of plants associated with neutral and calcareous grasslands, acid grasslands and heaths are floristically poor. In Northamptonshire, unimproved acid grassland is rare, largely confined to a few steeply sloping sites in the west. One of the best examples is High Wood Meadow, between the villages of Preston Capes and Upper Stowe (SP59-54-). The SSSI lies adjacent to High Wood and the whole site is owned and managed by the Trust. The meadow is an excellent illustration of a lowland bent-fescue grassland, maintained by regular grazing. The open sward is dominated by common bent and red fescue; additional grasses include sweet vernal-grass and Yorkshire-fog. Trailing amongst the grasses grow acid-loving plants – heath bedstraw with panicles of numerous, tiny white flowers and the larger, yellow-flowered tormentil. Conspicuous grass-covered mounds, 12 to 18 inches high, are the anthills of the yellow meadow ant. These mounds are a definite indication that High Meadow has not been ploughed for a long time. Where water seeps out to form wet flushes, communities of tall, wetland plants replace the dry grassland: wild angelica, common valerian, ragged-Robin and meadowsweet add colour to the meadow during the flowering season, whilst the softer ground provides feeding habitat for the curlew and snipe.

Heaths   Acid grassland has several species in common with heathland – one of the rarest habitats in the county. Little remains of the heaths around Northampton, although place-names indicate their former extent, *eg* Dallington, Harlestone and King's Heaths to the north-west of the town, and to the east, Billing Lings which, as its name denotes, was another area where ling (heather) once grew. Most of Harlestone Heath is now occupied by a coniferous plantation, but on an area left unplanted to serve as a firebreak, heather, gorse and broom are amongst the shrubs which persist. A small strip of land here is leased to the Trust as a nature reserve which harbours three county rarities – petty whin, green-ribbed

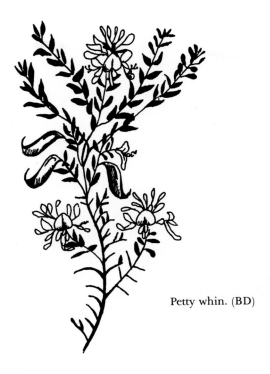

Petty whin. (BD)

sedge and flea sedge. On a summer's night flightless female glow-worms illuminate the heath with a greenish light in their efforts to attract winged, male glow-worm beetles.

In protecting the range of grassland nature reserves throughout the county, the Northamptonshire Wildlife Trust relies heavily on the goodwill of land-owners, land managers and the hard work of volunteers. Traditional grassland management regimes have been maintained or reinstated and, as a result, communities of plants and animals which are increasingly confined to only a few sites in the county, are being conserved. These irreplaceable habitats are a direct link with the agricultural landscapes of past centuries.

Larks

Today the fields are an aerodrome
busy with larks.
Along furrowed runways
they taxi and take off
like miniature aircraft,
the air noisy with their singing:
they rise singing, descend singing,
flutter in mid-air singing,
perch on clods singing,
until the ear is numbed and dazzled,
the world one ceaseless lark-song.

Trevor Hold

The River Nene from Cogenhoe – in the foreground, the channel has been canalised. Top right is the Billing sewage works and the Earls Barton gravel workings; top left is Lings Wood, HQ of the Trust. (PW)

Freshwater

by David Harper, Department of Zoology, Leicester University

The animals and plants of freshwater habitats are often neglected in natural history and conservation simply because they are less obvious than those of the terrestrial environment. This is even more so in Northamptonshire, where freshwaters are widespread but often overlooked because there is nothing big and dramatic in the way of rivers or lakes.

What we have in Northamptonshire is 'a surprising amount', due initially to the mixture of geologies spanned by the county and secondarily to human effects over the last few centuries. Human effects can be both destructive and creative, so we have to weigh the gains of many new types of standing waters, from farm ponds to gravel pits and reservoirs, against the losses of many natural types, from springs and flushes to meandering rivers.

Freshwaters The higher ground in the south and west of the county is a continuation of the limestone-dominated Cotswold hills. Streams flowing off these hills, often once spring-fed because of the porous nature of the rock but now reduced to drainage ditches, are rich in calcium and flow over a stony bottom with such plants as watercress often covering the bed. The valleys in these hills, where the limestone is suitably overlain by boulder clay of glacial origin, were suitable sites for reservoir construction near the larger towns last century. Major rivers start their course here as small brooks and quickly leave in all directions. The Avon rises near Naseby and flows west to the Severn; the Cherwell rises near Badby and flows south to the Thames; the Tove and Great Ouse rise near Sulgrave and flow east into Cambridgeshire.

The county's two main rivers, the Nene, which forms our backbone, and the Welland, which is much of our northern boundary, both rise on the other side of the hill from the Avon, near Naseby and Sibbertoft, the Welland to flow north before turning east and the Nene to flow south and east. These rivers are more influenced by the boulder clay; spatey in character, with eroded grey clay often visible between the gravel shoals in their beds.

Once off the uplands, these streams enter broad, flat, glacier-carved valleys, and encounter settlements which often evolved around convenient crossing places on the floodplain. Market Harborough on the Welland, Northampton on the Nene and Kettering on its major tributary, the Ise, are all stategically located as market towns which once served the hill-farms and grew on north-south crossings. The rivers would have been markedly different, meandering across floodplains several miles wide, channels splitting and changing shape with spates, associated marshes and ox-bow lakes, and long periods of winter floods standing in the fields providing rich silts for next year's crops, together with extensive feeding grounds for migrating waterfowl.

Nowadays, like rivers everywhere in lowland Britain, the flow of the Welland and Nene has been imprisoned within a single channel for all but the most severe floods, in the interests of intensive agriculture, reliable transport routes and safe housing. Their characters are influenced more by this physical control than any natural features, and chemical modification in the form of treated effluents from our homes and factories is the main force determining plant and animal distribution.

The Nene too is navigable from Northampton to the sea, and heavily canalised with only a few of its lock bypass channels retaining their natural character of shallow riffles and deeper pools. It is connected to the Grand Union Canal which winds through the county in the west, itself regulated by several small reservoirs built at Naseby, Sulby and Daventry. Throughout the Nene valley from Northampton downstream, the alluvial deposits of the ice-ages have been mined for sand and gravel. Increasingly nowadays, as extraction progresses, worked out pits are restored for recreation and conservation instead of waste dumping and return to agriculture, so that in places at least (for example around Thrapston) the character of the valley floor is closer to the floodplain of the middle ages than it was just a decade ago.

Scattered throughout the county are small to moderate-sized water bodies created by private individuals through the ages, from farm ponds for livestock watering to ornamental lakes in the grounds of large estates, many of them a hundred years old or more, which have acquired a 'naturalness' of their own.

All these water types, from 'natural' to entirely artificial have been colonised by a range of animals and plants adapted to the peculiar habitat which is water.

The branched bur-reed is a common plant fringing streams and rivers and occurs throughout the Nene and its tributaries. A group of abundant mayfly nymphs in the family *Baetidae,* known to anglers by such names as the Lake Olive Dun and the Large Dark Olive Dun, occur throughout Northamptonshire waters, with different species in ponds and streams.

The distribution of some animals and plants in Northamptonshire is influenced by the physical nature of the waters, particularly the type of bottom and the extent to which the water is oxygenated. For example, animals of fast-flowing streams, which can only live in high oxygen levels clinging to rocks or large stones, are rare because the type of stream hardly exists. Many such animals are stonefly or mayfly nymphs, and one or two of these species can be found in the small headwater streams coming off the Northamptonshire ironstone west of Kettering and the limestone streams in the south of the county. One large species of mayfly, *Ephemera danica,* is widespread but rare in the county because it burrows in sandy gravel but cannot tolerate silt hence it is confined to small stony headwater streams in the south, or the bottom of the river Welland at the north east corner where high flow conditions in parts of the channel keep gravel beds clear of silt.

The effects of the chemical environment are more subtle than the physical, because they cannot be observed except through laboratory analyses. Naturally, the county is fairly uniform, with calcium-rich hard water coming from both limestone and clay streams. This means that freshwater snails are widespread, as are crustacea (which need calcium for their carapaces), leeches and flatworms (which need it for the slime which they secrete to aid their movement). The main chemical effects on animal and plant distribution are artificial.

Human effects The two main human effects, from which no Northamptonshire water is immune, are the input of treated sewage and industrial effluent and of agricultural chemicals. To these we can add the effect of introduced species, which may be locally dramatic, and the continued destruction or modification of sites by development or drainage schemes.

Effluent has a number of effects. The first is to reduce the oxygen concentration of the receiving watercourse so that sensitive species progressively disappear. The effects of pollution on plants are far more difficult to assess.

The second effect is to bring suspended material into the water, which fills up the spaces between stones and gravel, so that species such as the mayfly *Ephemera,* or some fish, cannot survive. Their place is taken by species adapted to living in and feeding on fine silt and mud such as blackfly larvae. These kinds of animals then increase dramatically to take up the available food, and the balance of the food chain changes. A small brook polluted by sewage effluent, for example, would undergo a food web change which would make it more like that of a large river.

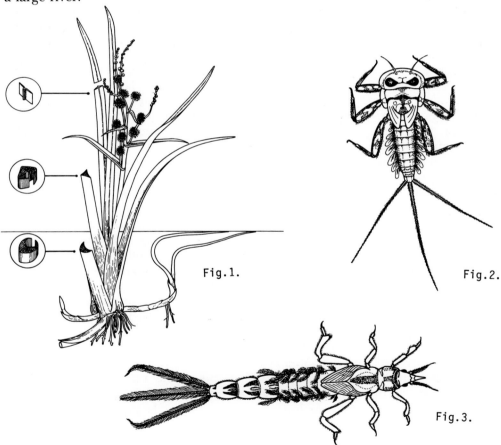

Fig.1.

Fig.2.

Fig.3.

LEFT: Fig 1 – Branched bur-reed combining a streamlined shape with strength and lightness in the stems. RIGHT: Fig 2 – A rare flattened mayfly nymph, confined to stony hardwater streams. BELOW: Fig 3 – The mayfly nymph *(Ephemera danica)* found in sand and gravel streams, adapted to burrowing with a cylindrical shape, stout limbs, and gills protected on its back from sand grains by their feathery structure. (All LA)

The third effect is to bring high concentrations of plant nutrients which stimulate plant growth. There are two plants which dominate the larger streams of the county now, often creating smelly masses in the summer when flow falls and they become stranded. One of these is a large alga, *Cladophora* or cott or blanket weed. The other is a rooted plant, fennel pondweed. These are the most abundant plants throughout the Nene downstream of Northampton, where the combination of sewage effluents and fertiliser run-off from agriculture have created a nutrient-rich waterway. The Nene, because it is regulated by locks, flows slowly enough for dense algal crops to grow in summer and turn the water quite green. The main reservoir – Pitsford (SP78-70-) – is similarly affected at certain times of the summer. To an animal on the river bed, algae are food just like any other fine particle of organic matter, so the net effect of nutrient enrichment on animal communities is often the same as mild pollution.

Biological assessment of pollution in the rivers of the county, using indicator invertebrates, is carried out regularly by ecologists from the water authorities, and maps are published annually by the Department of the Environment. These show pollution 'hot spots' below some of our major effluent discharges with mild pollution (or nutrient enrichment) affecting most of them. However the upper reaches of some streams do achieve the highest quality.

Freshwater conservation   When the Nature Conservation Review was published over ten years ago, there were relatively few wetland sites included and few running water sites – simply because not enough was known about them. What was known was primarily botanical and the idea of conserving sites for fish or invertebrates was then new. However, over the past ten years conservationists have developed new methods for surveying and recognising valuable wetland sites which together with skilled consultations have prevented damaging engineering works to several species-rich lengths of river and some of them have subsequently become SSSIs.

Two medium-sized river sites successfully conserved were the Tove near Grafton Regis (SP76-4-) and the Ise upstream of Geddington (SP78-83-). The latter is now not only an SSSI but an important educational site, with Newton Field Centre on its banks. The value of the Tove lay initially in its flora; being slow-flowing and unshaded along most of its length there is a rich growth of marginal plants which includes the flowering-rush, now rare in the county. The fringing plants are home to breeding water birds including swans, and kingfishers are common. The Ise is of value for different reasons. Its water is clean, particularly since the sewage from Desborough was piped down to a large regional treatment works at Wellingborough, so it contains such rare invertebrates as stonefly nymphs and a rich variety of caddis-fly larvae. It is also physically diverse, with natural meanders, stony riffles and deep pools running all the way from Rushton to Geddington, only slightly damaged by an unnecessary straightening in one place. Alternating riffles and pools are a key component in a natural river's ecology, because riffles are the sites of high invertebrate animal production whilst pools provide shelter for fish which feed on the animals drifting downstream from the riffles. It is no accident that this whole reach is one of the few successful trout streams in the county (although artificially stocked) and the only known natural breeding site of a fish rare in the lowlands, the grayling. Freshwater crayfish too are common, needing bankside holes or tree roots to burrow into for shelter.

The Ise shows clearly one other aspect of a river's ecological role in the landscape – its role as a corridor for wildlife not normally associated with water. Flowing between monocultures of wheat and other arable crops in fields whose hedgerow boundaries were ripped out in the sixties and seventies, the Ise is a narrow green corridor of trees, shrubs and rough grass for birds, mammals and insects to move along safely. Its mature trees with extensive root systems could be resting places for otters if conditions ever allowed them to recolonise the county. There are sadly few long stretches of waterway, as 'semi-natural' as this part of the Ise, left in the county.

On a larger scale the Nene and its floodplain below Northampton were candidates for extensive changes earlier this decade, as Anglian Water examined plans to improve the navigation by upgrading locks and lowering the river bed. This would have had a considerable effect upon the valley water table, as well as the river channel and its backwaters. The plans are at present in abeyance, but extensive survey work was carried out by the Trust and the Nature Conservancy Council to identify those sites and areas most in need of protection and make recommendations, not just to Anglian Water, but also to local authorities in respect of gravel extraction and development. Even though it has been heavily modified, parts of the Nene, particularly backwaters and riverside ditches, are rich in plant species and animals such as dragonflies, whose conservation, for the moment at least, has been achieved.

In the last few years most new river engineering schemes have incorporated principles of conservation, creating new habitats as well as modifying existing ones. Preliminary surveys before the works are started can identify both areas needing protection and areas needing improvement. One recent scheme on the River Ise downstream of Kettering – which can be seen from the bridge near Weetabix (SP88-74-) – has incorporated most of the basic requirements of conservation engineering. Works are carried out from one bank, leaving the opposite untouched and the creation of a berm – a flat ledge at the side of the river just under the water level – enables emergent plants to colonise the banks without impeding flows in the middle. Both the Nature Conservancy Council and the RSPB/RSNC have published guidelines for river engineering.

Conserving standing water bodies is more complicated than rivers. In the first place they are of many different sizes, in different ownership and with different uses. Ponds, more so than rivers, often have a rich history as well; Medieval fishponds for example, can still be seen at Pilton, Rothwell (SP81-80-) and Yardley Hastings (SP86-57-). Ornamental lakes, such as the series of three on the Willow Brook NE of Corby, are important for wildfowl and have a newer, unplanned value as purification lakes for the Brook which is polluted at its upper end by effluents from Corby. Gravel pits have many conflicting uses, some incompatible with conservation, but many with low intensity uses, such as country parks, have a high ecological value. Barnwell Country Park outside Oundle, for example, supports a diverse flora and fauna in a series of pits of different sizes and depths and is extensively used for ecological education. Farm ponds are perhaps the hardest sites to conserve, yet they are one of the habitats under greatest threat due to disuse associated with pasture conversion to arable. They are only partially replaced by new, larger, irrigation ponds increasingly found in the arable prairies in the eastern half of the county.

Conservation The Trust has thirty-six reserves: many were obtained to conserve terrestrial habitats but incidentally contain important freshwater habitats. The main freshwater ones are all primarily bird reserves – Pitsford and Stanford Reservoirs, Titchmarsh – but this last has a length of the clean and ecologically varied Harper's Brook running alongside it, which could be made a more prominent feature becasue of the rarity of such clean, physically diverse streams in the county. Byfield Pool (SP50-52-) and Irthlingborough Newt Ponds (SP94-71-) are the only other two reserves with primarily aquatic conservation in mind; the former with a range of wetland plant communities, the latter with specific animal value. Several others have brooks or ponds; perhaps the best known is Lings Reserve itself (SP80-63-), with two ponds extensively 'dipped' by local WATCH and school groups. Delf Spinney (SP69-66-), Great Oakley Meadow (SP86-85-), and Harlestone Heath (SP72-64-) are bounded by, or are close to, streams which enhance their value. To these reserves must be added the range of freshwaters in Country Parks, the Barnwell gravel pits (which also contain a diverse backwater of the Nene), Sywell and Daventry reservoirs, ponds in Irthlingborough Park, and the increasing numbers of small ponds (and other ecological features) conserved as 'pocket parks' by Parish Councils and village groups.

88

Kingfisher

Appears suddenly round
the bend of the stream,
sapphire-cut air, banking orange.

I wonder how such tropical splendour
can survive these greens and duns,
more fit for the drab cleric-heron.

Shouldn't so dainty a jewel
be locked away in a glass case,
protected from tarnish of muck and mud?

Until I see it vanish, a final flash
of blue, into its nest-hole
ouzing black slurry like a sewage-pipe.

Trevor Hold

OPPOSITE ABOVE: Titchmarsh from the air, showing the heronry and gravel extraction (NCC) LEFT: The River Ise, one of the least polluted stretches of river in the county. (PW) ABOVE RIGHT: Pond at Glapthorn Cow Pastures (NWT) CENTRE: Flowering-rush, now an uncommon riverside plant. BELOW: Freshwater crayfish only survive in the least polluted rivers, such as parts of the River Ise. (JLM)

LEFT: Titchmarsh – the former gravel workings becoming vegetated. (PW) RIGHT: Pond at Brigstock Country Park. (BG) BELOW: River Ise – near Burton Latimer (PW) and OPPOSITE: the Ise with lush emergent vegetation near Geddington. (PW)

LEFT: Pollard willow beside the River Nene at Denford. (BG) RIGHT:
The Willow Brook, one of the major tributaries of the Nene. (RP)
BELOW: Pools in old limestone quarries often become colonised by
dragonflies and amphibians, as well as occasional little ringed plover.
(RP)

The Welland Valley

by Oliver Maxim, Chairman, Northern Region

For thirty-four miles the infant river Welland meanders its way along the boundary between Northants and Leicestershire (and part of the old county of Rutland) then finally, for a short stretch, it separates our county from Lincolnshire. Any self-respecting crow would complete this journey in twenty miles, which just emphasises the tortuosities of this dreamy stream as it falls a mere foot or so per mile on its slow journey to the Wash. Left to its own devices there would be ox-bows and swamps every few miles - but the vigilance of the Water Board and the advent of modern dredging machines, keep the waters to their prescribed confines. Even so the Welland has its moments for, although in summer there are places where it can be forded without the water topping one's walking boots, yet in the winter, after the melting snows it becomes a roaring torrent up to half a mile wide, and farmers have to rush the sheep and cattle to safety.

Old Northamptonshire 'Boys' – a term of endearment applied to anyone under the age of ninety – will tell you how they skated 10 miles from Harringworth to Weston-by-Welland, or vice versa, and over the top of the hedges at that. Whilst I suppose we must accept a modicum of exaggeration, confirmation of this flooding can be seen by studying the map. Most of the valley villages are placed well back and then usually perched on some minor contour. And again, if one studies the location of the water mills (there used to be one every 3–4 miles) it can be seen in most cases they are well isolated from other habitation.

Geologically the river has carved its course through the boulder clays deposited by the ice ages. To the south, the land rises, often quite steeply as on the Rockingham escarpment, to a height of over 300 feet. Above the clay but beneath the limestone, there is a spring line, which has always provided plentiful water for forests, and also attracted man to build. Man also found the ironstone and it was for this ore that, first Iron-Age man, then the Romans, and finally (we hope) the big-diggers of Stewarts and Lloyds (later British Steel), have worked their patterns on the landscape, and it is due to this disruption that we now have considerable areas of conifers and mixed woodlands; for in the 1930s great areas of land were left as hill and dale, with perhaps thirty feet from trough to peak. These were thought to be only fit for planting trees, and were not returned to agricultural use. Now we have woodlands over fifty years old, which we hope will remain as permanent forest.

Bewick's swans flying along the valley. (RP)

93

Not a great deal is known of man's pre-Roman activities in this area, but the Jurassic Way, an ancient track dating back to the Bronze Age, entered the county in the region of Stamford and, keeping to dry high land overlooking the river, turned south somewhere in the region of Rockingham and thence to Desborough where one of the finest Bronze Age mirrors was excavated.

In contrast the Romans left many marks – their road from Huntingdon runs through high ground and a satisfactory excavation was carried out by the Corby Natural History and Archaeological Society in 1958. Earlier a team from Durham University had excavated and documented the extensive village at Weldon – sadly this site had since disappeared in the search for ironstone. Then the road, on its way to Leicester, breasted the escarpment above modern Middleton-cum-Cottingham and plunged down to cross the marshy valley. It must have been a wild place and we know from excavated bones that the bear, the wolf, beaver, deer, boar, the spoon-bill and many other wild creatures lived there. But the Romans found it acceptable enough and built another fine villa at Medbourne (SP79-92-) across the river.

We must pass swiftly through the Dark Ages of the next six hundred years with just a mention that it is said the Viking long ships were able to navigate the Welland as far as Ashley (SP79-91-). They had a shallow draught and, as we do know, had larger vessels sailing as far as Peterborough eight hundred years later – the theory is feasible, if not proven.

Then came William and his Normans but, even after winning the Battle of Hastings, he had his problems, such as Hereward the Wake. He stripped the Saxon earls of their power and began an intensive building programme of vast 'impregnable' castles, of which Rockingham remains one of the finest examples. One of the reasons why it has remained in such excellent order is its superb situation as a functional hunting lodge on the edge of the great Rockingham Forest and above the vast Welland marshlands. Whether the King hunted for the deer with his hounds, or the heron with his falcons, they were always here in plenty – and so they are today. But change had to come, the Fens were drained – or at least partially controlled – and the Welland ran more smoothly to the Wash.

Rockingham Forest was gradually cleared and farming communities thrived in the clearings. The farmers gazed with envy on the fertile valley. Oh what a great following of cattle and sheep could be harvested here – to complement the pigs that rooted about in the woods! It was just a question of more draining, and for two centuries the Valley was famous for its lush water-meadows – under water in the winter – but with the grass fertilised by the rich residual sediments of the floods, with marvellous grazing to fatten the beasts in summer.

The Welland still meandered. From the rising ground the observer could easily determine the course of the river as great pollarded willows, alders and other water-loving trees mapped its path. There were even small areas of 'fen carr' where the land between the ox-bows and the river was unsuitable for cultivation. The products of the pollarding were used for wooden bundles, baskets and many other articles of agricultural usage. In the hollows of the old trees owls nested, and in the roots the secretive otters made their holts.

This was the scene up to the Second World War. Prior to this, farming was a depressed industry. There was little money to 'improve' the land. The *status quo* produced a living. Agricultural methods were adequate, but primitive by modern standards. Not until the thirties did mechanisation have any real impact. Teams of great shire horses could be found in all farms of stature.

But following the war came the greatest and most rapid change that had ever hit the valley. Britain had never been self sufficient in food production. Although our great manufacturing tradition produced great ships and exported countless articles to all parts of the world, we could not, or would not grow enough food to feed ourselves. We probably lost more ships carrying food than any other commodity. It put a great strain on our war effort. And so there came about 'the big three improvements'. Drainage, chemical control of weeds and pests, and clearance – which encompassed hedges, headlands and previously unprofitable rough areas.

The Welland was dredged, straightened, deepened: the vast majority of the trees that lay in its course disappeared. The secret places where the otters bred were destroyed. Reports of their return usually turn out to be mink. The new, powerful machinery ploughed right up to the river banks and gone were the scrubby corners where the linnets, yellowhammers and whinchats nested, together with a great variety of flowers and small creatures. The grey partridge dwindled alarmingly. The rabbit population plunged as a result of myxomatosis and the avian predator population plunged. The sparrowhawk disappeared – not one was seen for over ten years. Tawny owls and kestrels held up well and the brown hare filled the niche vacated by the rabbit, until it too became a pest. The barn owl slid more slowly into decline. Fifteen years ago perhaps ten pairs nested within a five mile radius of Gretton (SP89-94-) and were frequently seen, either hunting by daylight or in the car headlights at night. Now a single sighting is a great event.

However, the changes were absorbed. Many good 'natural history' areas remained and, although not all the lessons that we should have learned were heeded, there were nevertheless considerable changes of thought and attitude by those who either owned or used the land. Many more landowners and farmers 'thought conservation' and tree planting was noticeably increased. The hunting, shooting and fishing fraternities have, in many cases, lent their considerable financial and influential weight to conservation. Their respective magazines bulge with articles concerned with enjoyment of the countryside and its denizens, and although this is no place for a forum on the morality of field sports, there is little doubt that the association between conservationists and the sporting public can create a strong lobby which will hasten those material advances of benefit to wildlife. Let us consider the fox. The Welland Valley has always been a great haven for this species: although the numbers killed by game conservators, the hunt and on the roads is considerable, they are always there. And if you doubt me, buy yourself six chickens and neglect to shut them up at night – you will soon entertain a nocturnal visitor to a good meal – probably of all six. The countryman has an affection for the fox and in spite of the horrible oaths and threats of retribution that follow some of his excesses, the vixens are normally left to breed in peace. Or perhaps they are too clever for us!

Muntjac. (RP)

So here in the north of our county we still have this beautiful area bordering this relatively small river. Because the old flooding habits pushed man's habitations to higher land, we still have large areas without houses – areas only disturbed by the occasional tractor or stock man. Here there is much for the naturalist, a wide variety of ducks and wading species. The migrating Bewick's swans have their favourite meadows where they can be seen every year – evidence that the Welland is part of an ancient fly-way.

The woods on the slopes are the home of healthy herds of deer which are sensibly culled by experts who leave the best specimens. Fallow and muntjac are most commonly found. Here is one of the most thriving concentrations of badgers in the county. The hobby nests and the kingfisher is found in satisfactory numbers. And much of this is on land that is extensively used for field sports.

What of the future – have we seen the worst of the changes; or are there modifications that would either detract from, or benefit, the valley's natural inhabitants? Looking at other parts of the county one can easily see that gravel extraction, although unsightly and disturbing during the actual working, can create habitats that are of enormous benefit to wildlife.

Fallow buck. (RP)

Stag

Proud young stag
tilts its antlers back disdainfully,
points a wet nose to the sun.

Like a high-bred lady
stranded on a muddy road
its prinking hooves scarce deign to touch the ground.

It seems annoyed, this latent Pegasus,
at being bound to earth:
"If only I could, I would fly!"

Trevor Hold

96

ABOVE: The Welland Viaduct. (BG) BELOW: The Welland at Harringworth. (BG)

98   ABOVE: Pond management, CENTRE: footpath renovation and BELOW: children planting shrubs. (All RM)

A Parish in the Western Uplands

(RP)

by Ruth Moffat

The Boddingtons lie at the western edge of Northamptonshire on the watershed between the R.Avon and the R.Thames. The population of 640 lives in two villages: Upper Boddington where the land rises in the north-west to 600 feet above sea-level, and Lower Boddington a mile south at 350 feet. The parish covers 3150 acres, mainly on flat or gently undulating Lower Lias clays and includes a third of Boddington Reservoir, built in 1833 to supply the Oxford Canal.

Boddington is recorded in Domesday Book as Botendon ('a habitation on the downs'), the two townships having separate common field systems with two fields in Upper and three in Lower Boddington. In the upper township these huge open fields and meadows appear to have been surrounded by hedgerows, while in the lower village the area of meadowland can only be estimated from the lack of ridge and furrow, traces of which exist over almost the whole parish. It seems likely that by the 13th century, when the rural population was at its peak, cultivation was so intensive that only unworkable land was left as meadow, protected by hedges; no woodland or common land remained and both wood and hay would probably have been imported.

Boddington would have undergone little change, with 92% of the land cultivated, until 1758 when both townships were enclosed. This resulted in a vast increase in the number of hedges and a decrease in field size to an average of 11.4 acres, with the parish remaining much as in Map 1 for the next 200 years, although by 1871 only 50% was arable and the rest pasture (*Kelly's Directory* 1877). Of the one hundred ponds and watering places that existed at the turn of the century, most would have been dug after enclosure but one fifth may pre-date this.

The next change in land use began in the Second World War when pasture and meadow were ploughed up. While much of this land was subsequently returned to grass, more intensive grain production led to an increase in field size by removal of hedges, and more recently to the infilling of ponds. Drainage of meadowland also led to a reduction in the number of ponds, while the provision of piped water in 1950 removed the need to maintain ponds for stock. From 32 pre-war farms, all milking, the number has fallen to 12, from 50–450 acres; only two produce milk, four are stock farms, three are entirely arable and the rest mixed. More than one third of the land is occupied by the three arable farms while grassland, comprising permanent pasture, ley, silage and hay, now covers only 40%.

The modern parish appears as in Map 2, with an average field size of 16.7 acres, an increase of 50% since 1900. Although the area of many plots has not changed since enclosure, there are now some enormous fields, the biggest being 168.9 acres in the south-

99

MAP 1

THE PARISH OF
BODDINGTON
IN 1900

LEFT: Map of the Parish of Boddington showing field boundaries – 1900, and RIGHT: the boundaries in 1988. (Both RM)

100

east where nine fields have been combined; here one looks for nearly a mile over unbroken grain to the boundary with the next parish. Ridge and furrow remains conspicuous, particularly on the 245 acres that were never ploughed, but also shows clearly on pasture not ploughed since the war. Hedges are still a feature of the landscape but over one sixth have gone in the last 20 years, including at least two miles of pre-enclosure hedges; these form the county, parish and township boundaries as well as bordering the medieval meadows and open fields of the upper (and possibly the lower) village. They could be many hundreds of years old and are generally the richest in species, although some dispersal to adjacent, more recent, hedge has occurred; the loss of nearly 1000 yards of county boundary between Northamptonshire and both Warwickshire and Oxfordshire is regrettable. Equally unfortunate is the halving of the number of ponds since 1900, with most lost after the War. The loss of 94% of the meadowland has left only seven and a half acres in Upper and six acres in Lower Boddington, this latter only an approximation of the original herb-rich meadow owing to fertilisers and partial drainage. There is no doubt, however, that the most dramatic change in the parish is the loss of hedgerow trees. The mature elms that once lined the roads into both villages have gone, killed by Dutch elm disease in the 1970s and never replaced, since farmers have preferred to plant small woodlands rather than put trees back in the hedges.

Horse drawn plough. (DJW-P)

It was with these losses in mind that in 1984 a group in Boddington decided to carry out a Parish Appraisal, the aims of which were three-fold: to record, act and inform. Whilst recognising that wildlife has to co-exist with high productivity farming, it was agreed that action was needed to prevent further unnecessary loss of the natural resources of the parish. Two years of surveys have led to an on-going programme of pond restoration, the purchase of one of the remaining meadows by the Northamptonshire Wildlife Trust and the renovation of the rights-of-way. The result is an increase in public awareness of the plants and animals that mark the progression of the year.

The first wild plant to flower on the wide verges of Boddington's post-enclosure roads is the winter heliotrope, in two fragrant clumps so noticeable in January when there is no other growth. This is succeeded by cowslip and red campion, goat's-beard and crosswort, lady's bedstraw and common knapweed, in patches often so small that the average passer-by misses them. Russian comfrey and horse-radish are more obvious, the latter probably a garden escape as is some gooseberry. Plants with more specific needs are wild mignonette on recently disturbed ground by the canal feeder and meadowsweet wherever the verge is wet; on a steep hedgebank, once probably more wooded, primrose, violet and bluebell delight the walker in early summer. The field verges are much narrower but nevertheless in a few places grow cowslips, red bartsia, hemlock and raspberry, with violets tucked beneath the hedges.

In February a spot of colour is provided by the odd brimstone butterfly that floats across the gardens; its caterpillar feeds on buckthorn, rare in the parish until the establishment of three shrubberies, one with the help of schoolchildren in National Tree Week 1986. Towards the end of the month the heron visits gardens with 'froggy' ponds, and offers of excess spawn are made to restock field ponds where farmers report none for years. Although consistent with national data, the reason is obscure, since newts breed in over half these ponds, but in 1988 frogspawn was found in four field ponds and introduced to 10 more where there are no predatory newts or fish. In contrast the frog occurs in half of Boddington's 28 garden ponds, and also the smooth newt, but the crested newt remains almost exclusively a species of the larger field ponds. Although abundant in some parts of our county, the toad is scarce, with only one record.

Good weather in March is helpful as it is time to visit the 50 field ponds. Half are breeding sites for the crested newt, not uncommon in Northamptonshire but a national rarity with special protection under the Wildlife and Countryside Act 1981. The species has declined dramatically in the last 30 years owing to the loss of ponds, removal of fringe vegetation on which the eggs are laid, or lack of maintenance leading to an inadequate area of open water for its courtship displays. The animal is rarely seen and only at night but its eggs are obvious because they are often laid on blades of floating sweet-grass, the ends of which are turned under to protect the egg. If the grass is sparse, many eggs may be laid on one blade, which is then folded like a concertina; in 1988 the introduction of bunches of plastic grass increased egg-laying enormously. The number of individuals at each pond is not great but this concentration of breeding sites in about 2.5 sq miles is unusual; the majority are in Upper Boddington where, on one farm, six out of the eight ponds, maintained traditionally for stock, contain the crested newt. Although the animal will breed in ponds surrounded by both grassland and crops, its most important requirement is a wide border of rough ground in which to forage after leaving the water in May.

The return of migrant birds in April heralds the summer, with house martins checking last year's sites before disappearing for a few weeks, presumably to replenish their food stores before starting to repair or build new nests; from then on their continuous activity shames those relaxing in the garden. The farmers are particularly fond of the swallows, leaving barn doors open for them, while the imminent return of the swifts speeded up restoration work on the church roof in 1987. Bats, swooping almost unnoticed through the church at evensong, return at this time of year to the the roofs of houses to give birth. In 1986 the Women's Institutes' County Bat Survey produced the first record of a Natterer's bat for this part of the county and also saved two roosts from eviction by unenthusiastic householders. Although the decline in numbers of butterflies is notable, 20 species are recorded, comprising five browns, six whites, six vanessids, small skipper, small copper and common blue. They are particularly abundant on a stretch of old railway line in Lower Boddington, while at the end of April several areas of wet grassland are a mass of cuckooflower, the larval food of the orange tip butterfly. From one wet field in Upper Boddington snipe used to fly up but have not been seen for some years, possibly because the current higher stocking rates increase the likelihood of nests being destroyed by trampling.

Visitors to Boddington in May comment on the frequent occurrence of another returning migrant, the cuckoo, often heard and seen around the hedgerows on which it depends for nests to parasitise, probably those of the dunnock. The countryside is now at its best with hawthorn, true to its old name 'may', now in blossom. The rarer midland hawthorn, a woodland species flowering a little earlier, grows in many pre-enclosure hedges and also in more recent hedges adjacent to the old, as do those other indicators of ancient hedgerows: hazel, dogwood and field maple. Wayfaring-tree, guelder-rose, holly, privet, pear, lime and hornbeam are uncommon, with oak and ash the most numerous trees; elm is suckering profusely and not yet showing signs of disease. One especially rich hedge with 21 species in one 1000 yard stretch borders the road from Upper Boddington to the reservoir, part of the original route of Banbury Lane; dating by Hooper's method gives its age as 675 years. A short stretch of 'green lane', remnant of an old road and now a grassy track, is one of three natural sites of the aspen; its hedgerow trees have been mapped by the schoolchildren in the hope that a Tree Preservation Order may be placed on them, the only way the lane itself can be protected from incorporation into the adjoining farmland. The Welsh Road, running south through the parish, was once a drove road for cattle going to markets in London and the midlands. In parts its flanking hedges, rich in species and probably dating from before the enclosures, are vastly overgrown, in others trimmed by flail cutter but at its southern end the hedges are being laid. This ancient craft is still practised by several elderly men but here the work is done by a young farmer, who has left a number of saplings to mature, while in the newly laid hedges of the cricket field some trees have been planted.

In June 1985 all the field ponds were surveyed in great detail as part of the Women's Institutes' County Pond Survey. Ranging from hollows that dry up in summer to 800 sq yards of open water, many are too closely bordered by trees and crops, lacking the surrounding rough ground essential for a variety of wildlife. An overhang of hawthorn often provides a fox-proof nest site for the moorhen, which can stay beneath the water for long periods with only the red frontal shield giving it away unless it chances to emerge covered with weed. Pond-dipping has produced an impressive list of invertebrates, including the larvae of many insects, the great diving beetle, three species of water-bugs and molluscs and two kinds of shrimp. In flight dragonflies such as the broad-bodied libellula and the brown aeshna are seen and a brilliant blue damselfly, while swimming across the water on one memorable occasion was a grass snake, not uncommon in the parish and known to breed here. The plant life of the ponds is equally rich, each with its own unique composition of submerged, floating, emergent and marsh species. Water-plantain, water mint, common spiked-rush, greater pond-sedge, branched bur-reed and three species of pondweed and crowfoot occur at several locations, while recorded from single sites only are marsh yellow-cress, bulrush, water horsetail and the liverwort, *Riccia fluitans*. The marsh-marigold now flourishes at four ponds, having been transferred, with the farmer's permission, from drained grassland nearby.

Marsh-marigold (BD)

Boddington Meadow, which was bought by the Trust in 1986, is at its most spectacular in July when the betony is in flower. Local interest in the meadow, and the ponds, is reflected in a sampler designed and embroidered by WI members in 1985 to celebrate the 70th anniversary of the WI movement. Boddington's other old meadow has never been drained or fertilised, with the lower wetter part, unploughed even during the War, exhibiting the richest flora. A species list of 50 has been compiled, including 15 grasses and four sedges; most notable are ragged-Robin, great burnet, pepper-saxifrage and sneezewort, the latter occurring nowhere else in the parish. An animal of open grassland such as this is the hare, seldom seen and possibly scarce. In the churchyard the main botanical interest is the 80 or so lichens, which include several growing on a wall where the substrate is nutrient-enriched from the neighbouring farmyard. This is only the second known site in the county of

Psilolechia leprosa, previously thought to occur solely in copper mines and here growing beneath a copper window grill. Covering the lower third of the north wall of the church is a commoner but striking species, *Haematomma ochroleucum* var. *porphyrium*.

A favourite walk is around Boddington Reservoir, for this can be accomplished, at least in part, in all weathers. Great crested grebes are present throughout the year, and also the occasional kingfisher, but in August the birdwatcher will see many geese, ducks, gulls, terns and waders. Following the rebuilding of the dam in 1982–3 there appeared a brilliant display of wild flowers and it seems that the sainfoin, crown and kidney vetch, salad burnet, wild parsnip and carrot and chicory, that grows nowhere else in Northamptonshire, had been introduced in surfacing material. Unfortunately the British Waterways Board cannot be dissuaded from mowing the area to look for cracks in the dam before the flowers have set seed and when skylarks and partridges are nesting. Since the restoration of Boddington's rights-of-way in 1986, with the co-operation of the farmers and support from the County Highways and Planning Departments, many other walks can now be enjoyed; new stiles, bridges, waymarker signs, finger posts and a leaflet describing the walks facilitate access.

In September excess vegetation can safely be removed from ponds since young amphibians have already left the water; the lack of such maintenance is the main threat to aquatic wildlife as weed will gradually cover the pond and build up litter, eventually converting it to dry land. Following the 1985 survey, a pond management programme was started which has increased the area of open water at all but one of the crested newt sites. In ponds polluted by leaf litter from overhanging trees there is little plant growth and animal life is reduced to species tolerant of low oxygen levels. Some have been opened up by the farmers and a Community Programme Team and restocked with plants, while an old farmyard pond was dug out for school projects. Half the field ponds have now been improved, without losing their individuality, although many of them need enlarging and deepening.

Early October is a colourful time to look at the woodlands which have almost doubled in area this century to 19.1 acres, largely due to grants from the Countryside Commission and the County Council. Since the 1960s the farmers have planted over 5,000 trees, mostly native species, in field corners, along the canal feeder, around new and restored ponds and to infill stream meanders. Under the new set-aside incentives another 2.6 acres of woodland will be established on previously cultivated land and will include 10% of native shrubs, sadly lacking in earlier plantings. Although the mature woods do not appear to be more than 200 years old they contain an impressive number of species including wych elm in two places, while an area of even more recent woodland has some massive hawthorn trees. Muntjac deer are seen, most commonly near Fox Covert, the largest wood in the parish covering about 7½ acres and roe deer have been recorded twice since 1987. Also associated with this habitat is the badger, rarely seen unless killed on the road; in contrast foxes are often observed in early summer when food must be found for the cubs and their footprints may be found near to houses during prolonged periods of snow.

In November more migrant birds arrive, reminders of oncoming winter. Distinguishable from other thrushes by their flocking habits, the redwings and fieldfares enter gardens only in severe weather, heavily laden *Pyracantha* bushes being common targets in forays from a suitably distant perch. The bird table now attracts resident species not seen in the summer garden, such as the long-tailed and coal tits and the reed bunting; 39 species have been recorded in my 11-year-old garden, including green and great-spotted woodpecker, while lesser-spotted woodpecker, nuthatch and treecreeper visit the more mature gardens. Raptors

OPPOSITE ABOVE: Detail of Women's Institute sampler showing the NWT reserve, Boddington Meadow. (BG) BELOW: Cowslip (at Barnack Hills and Holes). (FWW) LEFT: The marbled white butterfly has recently returned to the county, and RIGHT: the wood white is common in some of the woods in the county. (Both JLM)

105

seen most frequently in the parish are kestrel and little owl with the less common sparrowhawk more conspicuous in winter as it skims along the hedgerows in search of prey. Reports of 'large owls' are usually tawnys but barn owls have been seen since 1986; farmers are keen to encourage the bird's return by installing nest boxes, but its recovery ultimately depends on a network of rough grassland strips along streams and around fields to maintain links between neighbouring communities of barn owls.

Orders placed early with the County Council Parish Tree Planting Scheme has ensured delivery in December, and planting at this time has given minimal losses without watering. In the last 15 years the Parish Council has put in over 250 trees, mostly native species, singly and in groups on verges and in the cricket field. These attempts to make good the losses from Dutch elm disease have suffered little damage and have been augmented by the tagging of a few hedgerow saplings. The protection of mature trees is as important as the planting of new ones, but existing Tree Preservation Orders have failed to halt the loss of many. Plans have been drawn up, marking 30 individuals in both villages, plus five groups of trees, in addition to the 'green lane', which residents would like to see protected. The current District Council village-wide survey, aimed at increasing the protection, gives some cause for optimism that this may be achieved.

Looking back to the start of Boddington's Parish Appraisal it is startling how much has been accomplished in four years, especially the increase in awareness within the community of the value of wildlife. Most important of all is the involvement of the schoolchildren in conservation through their use of local habitats for study, while a request from the Young Farmers' Club for a talk on the pond restoration programme was rewarding. As one of only five parishes in the county to carry out an appraisal, the team's advice has been incorporated by the County Planning and Transportation Department into their recent pack 'Parish 2000'. The publicity given to Boddington's conservation work on local radio and the recognition it received by its recommendation in the 1987 Ford Conservation Awards may encourage other parishes to do similar work.

It is hoped that, for Boddington at least, the words of the poet will not come true: that the heritage of this small part of the English countryside will not just 'linger on in the galleries' but will remain and thrive for future generations to enjoy.

'And that will be England gone,
The shadows, the meadows, the lanes,
The guildhalls, the carved choirs.
There'll be books; it will linger on
In the galleries; but all that remains
For us will be concrete and tyres.'

Philip Larkin 1974 – from *Going, Going*
(reprinted by permission of Faber & Faber Ltd)
from *High Windows*, by Philip Larkin.

(The author is grateful to the farmers of Boddington for their assistance in the preparation of this chapter and also to the following who have contributed information: T. Chester, M. Clugston, D. Hall, S. Hood, M. Lane, A. Rawlings and J. Sadler.)

Great crested newt. (RP)

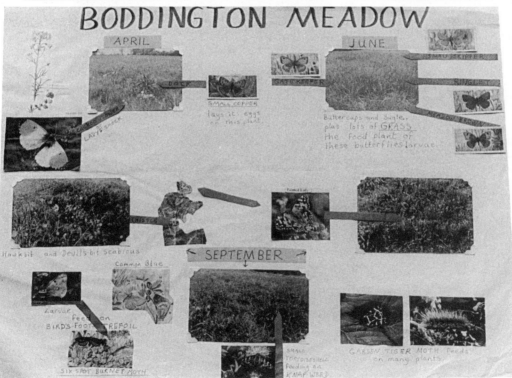

ABOVE: Hedgerow tree planting. BELOW: Children's meadow study.
(Both RM)

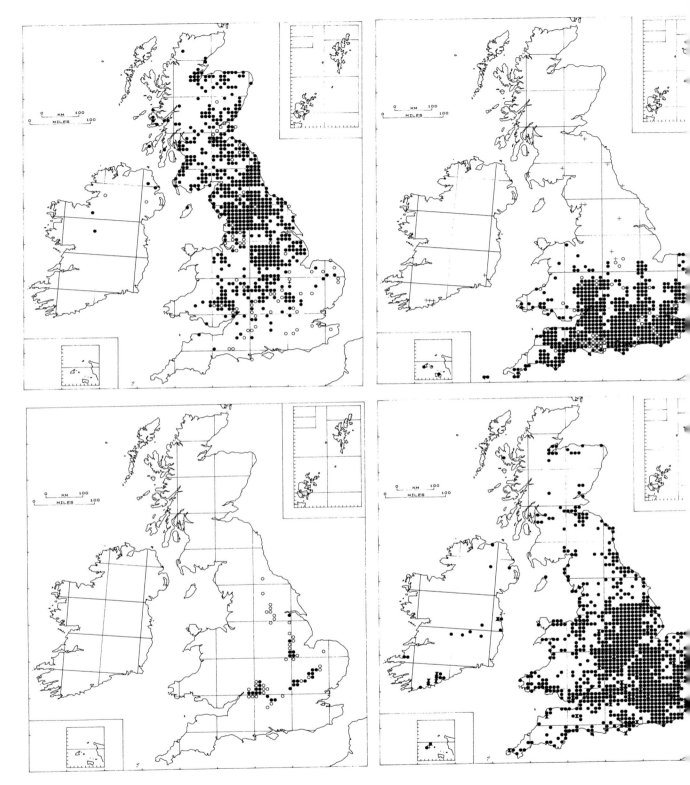

10 km square distribution in Great Britain and Ireland of some Northamptonshire wild flowers.
ABOVE LEFT: Giant bellflower *Campanula latifolia*   ● 1950 onwards O Before 1950
RIGHT: Wood spurge *Euphorbia amygdaloides*   ● 1950 onwards O Before 1950
                                                            + Introductions

BELOW LEFT: Pasqueflower *Pulsatilla vulgaris*   ● 1950 onwards O Before 1950
RIGHT: Oxford ragwort *Senecio squalidus*   ✶ Before 1900 ● Other records
We gratefully acknowledge the help of the Biological Records Centre, Institute of Terrestrial Ecology,
Monks Wood in supplying these maps and allowing them to be reproduced here.

Wild Flowers

by Gill Gent, Botanical Society of the British Isles Vice-County Recorder

The starting point for an account of the wild flowers of our county must be *The Flora of Northamptonshire* by the great George Claridge Druce published in 1930. This work includes records made by various authors, such as John Morton, over the previous 200 years as well as his own, though it is apparent that the majority of his field observations were made before he moved to Oxford in 1879.

The county has changed much since 1930; many fields were ploughed up during the Second World War never to return to pasture. Increased mechanisation has decreased the number of rough habitats on farms and marshy areas are now being easily drained. These factors, and the planting up of many woodlands with conifers, have all helped in the decline of many of our native species of plants. Northamptonshire is still well endowed with woodland and, in areas which are fragments of the once extensive ancient Forests of Rockingham, Salcey and Whittlebury, there is still a rich selection of species, at least in areas which are not densely planted with conifers. One such plant is herb-Paris, sometimes to be found with other indicators of ancient woodland, such as yellow archangel, and the attractive yellow star-of-Bethlehem, which is recorded from a few areas, particularly in the north of the county. These woodlands are on calcareous soils and have a number of species at the limit of their range.

Mountain melick is an attractive grass which occurs sporadically in Beford Purlieus (TL03-99-) the only place in the county. This northern continental species is at its southern limit here. Another plant which is also at its southern limit is giant bellflower which can be quite common in woods north of Kettering. In contrast wood spurge, a continental southern species, reaches its northern limit in the same belt of woodland.

Here also can be found an interesting parasitic plant, toothwort, growing on the roots of hazel, and the uncommon fly orchid which is often shy of flowering and difficult to find. Stinking hellebore with long-lasting green flowers, columbine, lily-of-the-valley, and caper

Uncommon wildflowers of Northamptonshire: stinking hellebore, yellow star-of-Bethleham, lily-of-the-valley, wild columbine, purple milk-vetch.
(RP)

Opposite-leaved golden-saxifrage. (BD)

spurge are all truly native species here in these woods, as is deadly nightshade. The rather sinister purple-green bellflowers, and shiny black and poisonous berries make this species quite a spectacular plant, often growing to four or five feet

Common woodland orchids, such as early-purple, broad helleborine, and common spotted-, are fairly well distributed, but the uncommon birds-nest orchid, although recorded from many of our woods, is seldom noticed. It grows in deep shade and in a good depth of leaf litter; being a saprophytic species it possesses no green leaves for the manufacture of its own food.

The county is not particularly rich in woodland ferns: male-fern and broad buckler-fern are the common ones, but recent surveys have shown that both species of shield-fern, hard and soft, are commoner than they were once thought to be.

The lighter sandy soils in the west have plants not to be found in the rest of the county. Here in woodland, foxgloves, slender St John's-wort, and the attractive wood vetch with cream flowers delicately marked with mauve streaks, may be found. Where the woods are damp enough opposite-leaved golden-saxifrage makes large green-gold patches of flowers in early spring. Moschatel or Town-hall-clock is another early flowering species found commonly in this area, whilst the more uncommon, attractively drooping, wood horsetail is restricted to a couple of localities.

True heathland is a habitat lacking in our county, although there are two places, now well planted up with trees, which may once have qualified for such a title. Harlestone Firs, (SP71-63-) still has an area of heather grasslands and the light sandy soil favours such species as broom and bird's-foot, and in areas where recent tree-felling has taken place, the reappearance of species, once thought to have disappeared, such as wood sage and heath cudweed, is encouraging.

The limestone belt in the north of the county is the home of many of Britain's rarer plants, such as pasqueflower. This beautiful plant was known in past years in many areas in south and east Britain, but now farming practices have all but eliminated it. It is, therefore, important that it is now protected within the National Nature Reserve at Barnack (TF07-04-). This area is of great interest botanically being one of the few places where limestone plants may be seen at their best. One of the most interesting species is a parasite, tall broomrape, which grows there with its host plant, greater knapweed. This species, along with other limeloving plants, is only found in areas untouched by agriculture, which indicates what a rich heritage of plants we have all but lost, such as purple milk-vetch, horseshoe vetch, dyer's greenweed, and several orchids including pyramidal and man orchid.

Water plants have, in many cases, been affected by infilling of ponds, and the canalisation of many streams. With the opening up of vast areas for gravel extraction, we have an increase in certain species and there is still a fairly rich flora to be found alongside our canals. Species such as marsh and golden dock were considered to be quite rare before the War, but now are to be found commonly along the Nene valley, and around our reservoirs, along with the pink water-speedwell. Plants which are unusual in this part of Britain, floating water-plantain and mudwort, have also been found in such areas as new gravel workings and reservoirs. A fairly recent newcomer to the county is orange balsam. This species has spread over the last twenty to thirty years and is now very much at home along our canals, and other waterways. A plant which is not quite so welcome is an alien from Australasia which has made an appearance in a couple of ponds; the New Zealand pigmy-weed, *Crassula helmsii*, first introduced into the wild in southern England has now become quite a pest as far north as Scotland, smothering out the native aquatic vegetation, as a cast-out from aquaria.

In contrast to those wetland species which have spread into our county there are others which we have nearly lost, namely those which once grew along fen ditches in the north east.

110

Water-violet, frogbit and bogbean have virtually disappeared due, no doubt, to extensive drainage, weed-killers and increased use of chemical fertilisers. Small marshy areas too, have nearly disappeared where species, such as common butterwort, an insectivorous plant, grass-of-Parnassus, and many other local species grew.

During the period of ironstone extraction in the county in the latter half of the last century, and first half of this, vast areas of the overburden, ie the calcareous clays etc, which lay over the Ironstone Beds, were dumped. These have in themselves provided habitats for many interesting species. In particular, the open nature of the terrain favours plants such as common centaury, fairy flax, blue fleabane, and ploughman's-spikenard. The beautiful flowers of bee orchid are often present in large numbers in suitable areas in these quarries, and one or two uncommon hawkweed species are recorded. One, *Hieracium flagellare,* was only previously known near the county boundary from the mainline railway at Hanslope (SP78-46-) but has now been found in two quarries. The calcareous nature of the soil favours some of our more showy thistles, both carline and woolly, whilst the deep quarry workings provide habitats for many aquatic plants. Quite recently fern pondweed, *Potamogeton coloratus,* which is only in eastern England, has been found in one such quarry.

Disused railway lines are now important for many plants and, indeed, the railway network itself has played a part in the distribution of many species. Oxford ragwort was distributed mainly by the railways from the Botanical Gardens in Oxford from which it escaped at the end of the 18th century. In 1930 it was considered rare by G.C. Druce in his *Flora,* but in the intervening years it has spread rapidly. Another species which has spread along the railway is the grey mouse-ear, *Cerastium brachypetalum.* This small plant was formerly only known from disturbed areas alongside the main line at Sharnbrook in Bedfordshire. It has now spread further north into Northamptonshire where, however, its appearances are somewhat intermittent.

Wood sage. (RP)

Other plants have been introduced and dispersed by means of motor traffic. Great lettuce, a rather strikingly tall member of the dandelion family, has spread onto the verges of many new stretches of roads, including the A1 near Wansford (TF07-00-). One strange introduction was the continental broad-leaved ragwort, *Senecio fluviatilis,* on a roadside far away from any obvious possible source, and not on a ditch side which would have been more likely. Even more bizarre was the discovery of holly fern in Wellingborough, the nearest sources being North Wales, or the Lake District.

Recent extensive gritting of our main roads has led to the spread of saltmarsh plants onto the edge of their verges. One species, in particular, reflexed saltmarsh-grass has become widespread alongside our main roads and the appearance of dittander in one area may also be linked to this practice. As we have seen the flora of the county is changing and although some plants may be lost, new ones are being introduced in various ways. The overall picture is never stable, but changes continuously due to a multitude of factors.

Churchyards, for the most part, have never been ploughed, artificially fertilised or been subject to chemical sprays. They consist mainly of the original turf and grasses which would have been present when the churchyard was enclosed. These reflect the native flora of the area which was once present in meadow and pasture surrounding the village.

Realising that these areas were in many cases of great conservation value, in 1981 the Botanical Society of the British Isles set up a monitoring scheme to collect information on churchyards and other burial grounds which would be passed to the Wildlife or Conservation Trusts, who could then draw-up a management scheme. Special recording sheets were issued. This is an ongoing scheme, and by 1988 about three-quarters of the churchyards in Northamptonshire had been surveyed. A similar but simpler scheme was also launched by the Women's Institute.

The survey has shown that the average number of species occurring is between sixty and eighty flowering plants, trees and ferns. Some churchyards may have a count of forty or less where mowing has controlled most flowering plants and the grass resembles a well-cut lawn. In other churchyards the count is much higher; those with the richest flora have over 100 species.

Typically churchyards in the county have a complement of grasses which are present in old hay meadows with the buttercups *Ranunculus bulbosus* and *R.acris,* sorrel, bird's-foot-trefoil, oxeye daisy, salad burnet, and burnet-saxifrage with cuckooflower in the damper places.

Common hedgerow species such as cow parsley, common nettle, cleavers and hedge woundwort, are also present, and sometimes typical woodland species such as goldilocks buttercup. Cowslips and primroses can also be in abundance, but in many cases introduced to the area originally as grave plants.

In several of the county's churchyards meadow saxifrage is quite a common plant. As this species has all but disappeared from our meadows now, this is an important area for its survival. Along with the more common grassland species, a number of churchyards have fiddle dock growing. This appears to be most frequent in the central region and seems to be fairly resistant to mowing. The characteristic leaves, with the fiddle-type waist, are easily picked out in the mown grass, along with the rosettes of hoary plantain – another plant obviously also resistant to mowing. Some species one associated with limestone grassland only occur in churchyards now; wild clary and common calamint are two which have been discovered during the survey. Wall lettuce is quite at home in many churchyards. This plant, which was once considered scarce, was recorded from eighteen.

One important discovery was a rare crucifer, tower cress, *Arabis turrita,* on one churchyard wall, a plant only known from one other place in the British Isles. Many plants spread in from surrounding areas but others result from grave plantings. Snowdrops, aconites and even such species as dusky crane's-bill and the pink flowered *Cordydalis cava* are well established in some of our churchyards, the former making a wonderful show in the spring.

The walls too can have quite a rich flora, with ferns such as maidenhair spleenwort, wall-rue, common polypody and other species, along with such wall-loving plants as the white and yellow stonecrops, *Sedum album* and *S.reflexum,* and the tiny rue-leaved saxifrage.

The churchyard walls of one or two villages in the far west of the county have wall pennywort and shining crane's-bill, plants more associated with the west and unusual in this part of Britain.

Since 1983 there has been a competition, inaugurated by the Trust, for the churchyard most competently managed for conservation of wild life; plants, insects, birds etc. Although it started slowly with only five entrants in the first year, about a dozen churchyards now regularly compete. The winners are presented with a trophy in the form of a lectern, which stands in their Church for the next year.

To qualify, each churchyard must show that it manages a mowing regime within the area, which leaves parts as long grass and attractive species of flowering plants for butterflies and other insects. In many cases bird boxes have been erected and re-seeding of wild-flower mixtures carried out. One burial ground is being turned into a wild flower garden: in another an ecological survey is carried out from year to year.

Altogether the idea of churchyard conservation is growing, and one hopes that more and more Parish and Parochial Church Councils will follow suit and help conserve their own village churchyard as a refuge for our dwindling wildlife.

Cuckoo-pint. (RP)

Cuckoo-pint

Come rain, snow, frost or drought
it rarely fails,
the first green leaves of spring,
and every year like a seasoned magician,
it shows off its amazing conjuring trick.
In April it points,
half-sheathed in a green glove,
a rude brown finger. In August
glove and finger have disappeared
and it offers,
equally impertinently,
a fist of orange berries.

Trevor Hold

113

LEFT: Nettle-leaved bellflower. RIGHT: Woolly thistles are especially showy in late summer. (PW/NCC) BELOW: Wild daffodil – still found in a few Northamptonshire woodlands. (TB)

Lichens

by Tom Chester, British Lichen Society Vice-County Recorder

The earliest known reference to lichens in our county is to be found in Morton's *The Natural History of Northamptonshire* published in 1712. Two lichen species are described and it is probable, although by no means certain, that these are *Usnea articulata* and *Collema crispum*. *Usnea articulata,* a beard-like plant usually draping the branches of trees and festooning hedges, was once widespread in Central England. It is, however, particularly sensitive to SO_2 pollution and is now confined to the extreme south and west of the British Isles. In 1712, it was growing on an oak in Sholbrook Lawn (SP73-42-), Whittlewood Forest. A close relative, *Usnea subfloridana,* is occasionally present in the less polluted parts of the county, growing on trees and fences. *Collema crispum,* a brown-black gelatinous lichen, still frequents the crevices of churchyard walls. In 1712, it was found in old, grass-covered stone-pits around Clipston (SP71-81-) and Oxendon (SP73-83-).

In the first part of the 19th century, as a result of the fieldwork carried out by three reverend gentlemen – Miles Berkeley, Andrew Bloxam and Churchill Babington – a few additional species found their way into herbaria now held at the British Museum (Natural History). In the 1880s a collection was made by Robert Rogers, mainly from Castle Ashby (SP85-59-), Yardley Hastings (SP86-56-) and Culworth (SP54-47-) and around thirty species were later deposited at Kettering Museum. In 1888, a further nine species, including *Usnea barbata* and *Usnea florida,* were collected by W.H. Wilkinson on a botanical expedition to Fawsley Park (SP56-57-) organised by the Midland Union of Natural History Societies.

In the first half of the present century, there appears to have been little lichenological activity. Watson in a *Census Catalogue of British Lichens* published in 1953 listed only 49 species for the vice-county, although other records suggest that the total was around 66. The next decade saw a dramatic change. A young naturalist from Kettering, J.R. Laundon, took up the study of lichens and subsequently has gone on to gain an international reputation, particularly in the fields of taxonomy and nomenclature. He has worked at the British Museum (Natural History) for the past thirty years and has been both secretary and president of the British Lichen Society formed in 1958. By 1960, another 100 species had been located and identified, a third on stone, a little over a third on bark or decorticated wood and a quarter on soil.

F.A. Adams became recorder for fungi and lichens and was active in the field in 1960 and 1961 while Dr F. Rose visited Fawsley Park in 1972. In April 1975 a Monks Wood Symposium on Bedford Purlieus (TL03-99-) was published. Dr O.L. Gilbert carried out the lichen survey, extending the number recorded to 60, of which 35 were on trees and the remainder occurred 'in accessory man-made habitats such as around the army huts'. Two years later, the British Lichen Society held a joint field weekend with the Kettering Natural History Society again visiting Fawsley Park, as well as Clipston, Pipewell (SP83-85-), and the churchyards at Old (SP78-73-) and Cottingham (SP84-89-). By 1981, the beginning of the present era of recording, the county total had been advanced to 179 species.

A new checklist of British lichens was produced in 1980, listing 1701 species. Field identification has advanced over the past decade and a new flora is being prepared. It is also possible to have critical species determined by thin-layer chromatography. As a result of this new knowledge and much fieldwork, the species list for vice-county 32 had reached 240 by October 1984, when a second British Lichen Society field meeting was held in the south-west of the county. Eighteen sites were visited in four days and no less than 225 species were seen, of which over 60 were new records. Since this meeting, the current recorder has been helped considerably by Dr C.J.B. Hitch of Suffolk and the grand total at the time of writing is 350. It is interesting to compare this total with the most recently available figures from some neighbouring counties ie Bedfordshire 133, Lincolnshire 224, Warwickshire c240, Buckinghamshire 267, Leicestershire 329 and Oxfordshire 343. In the absence of herbarium material, some early records from most of these counties must be considered doubtful. It is clear that figures such as these tend to reflect the activity of lichenologists as much as the abundance of lichens.

The main lichen habitats   In the article published in 1956, J.R. Laundon summarized the lichen ecology of Northamptonshire, pointing out that 'several habitats where lichens would grow abundantly are absent or rare in the County. For example, Northamptonshire has no natural outcrops of rocks, although this is compensated for to some extent by quarries and some stone walling, and again, there is only one heath of any significance and this is now largely planted with pine trees, which exclude lichens. The County also has no shore-line, so that species characteristic of sand dunes and shingle beaches are absent'. There are few ground lichens of note on Harlestone Heath (SP71-63-) today and these species are more often found around disused quarries or in disused railways where other vegetation is sparse. In all, 45 species belonging to nine families have been found on this substrate.

Laundon begins his article by describing Northamptonshire as 'predominantly a county of quiet unspoilt villages set in arable and meadow land, with elm and ash trees adorning the hedgerows and country lanes, and damp oakwoods in abundance, for much of the forests of Rockingham, Whittlewood and Salcey remains'. Since then, the elm, its high pH encouraging lichen growth, has sadly disappeared from this landscape and only small patches of the ancient oakwoods remain. Of these, East Ashalls Copse (SP73-41-), a remnant of Whittlewood, is the richest in tree-bark lichens with 64 recorded so far. Most of the huge old oaks have a disappointingly meagre lichen flora, although one has four old-forest indicators – *Arthonia vinosa, Enterographa crassa, Lecanactis premnea* and *Thelotrema lepadinum* – growing on its massive bole. Sometimes a combination of factors such as illumination, humidity, bark pH and nutrient-enrichment result in a single tree being especially well endowed. A field maple in the nearby Say's Copse (SP72-43-) carries over 20 species, as do hedgerow ashes near to Evenley (SP58-34-) and Farthinghoe (SP53-39-) respectively. An ancient hollow oak in a clearing adjacent to the A43 in Lodge Copse, Hazelborough Forest (SP65-42-) has 33 species, including another old-forest indicator *Rinodina roboris*. But the best tree is an ash at Trafford House Farm (SP52-48-) on which 36 species were recorded in August 1988. Altogether, 136 corticolous species have so far been identified.

WHERE DO LICHENS GROW?

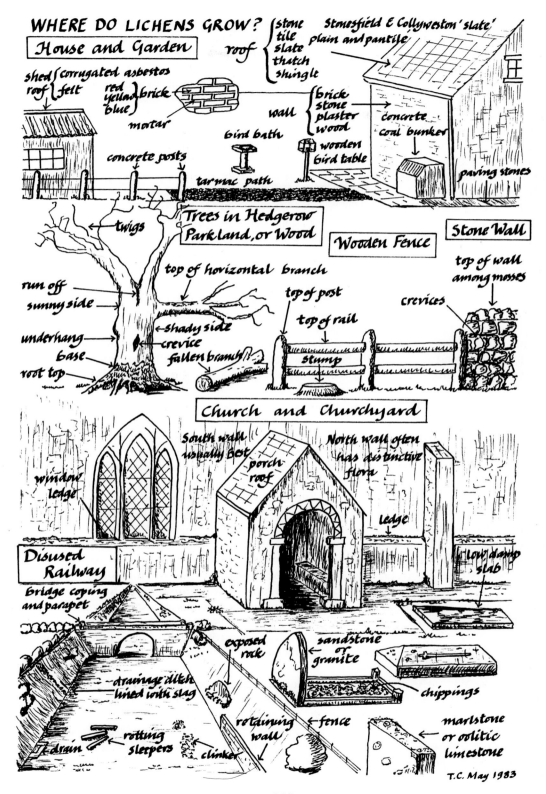

House and Garden

roof { stone / tile / slate / thatch / shingle

Stonesfield & Collyweston 'slate' plain and pantile

shed { roof { corrugated asbestos / felt

brick { red / yellow / blue

mortar

wall { brick / stone / plaster / wood

concrete coal bunker

bird bath

wooden bird table

concrete posts

tar mac path

paving stones

Trees in Hedgerow, Parkland, or Wood

Wooden Fence

Stone Wall

twigs

top of horizontal branch

top of post

top of wall among mosses

crevices

run off sunny side

top of rail

underhang

shady side

crevice

base

fallen branch

stump

root top

Church and Churchyard

window ledge

South wall usually best

porch roof

North wall often has distinctive flora

ledge

Disused Railway

low damp slab

bridge coping and parapet

exposed rock

sandstone or granite

chippings

drainage ditch lined with slag

retaining wall

fence

marlstone or oolitic limestone

drain

rotting sleepers

clinker

T.C. May 1983

Other species show a preference for decorticated wood and are found on dead trees, stumps and fences. Sixty species have been found on such substrates. Certain common lichens can often be found growing on more than one substrate. For example, the yellow leafy rosettes of *Xanthoria parietina* colonize a variety of surfaces dusted with nutrients and can commonly be seen on walls and roofs, trees and fences especially near to farms.

In recent years, lichenologists have become more aware of fungi allied to or associated with lichens in a variety of complex ways. A key to these fungi has helped considerably with identification and so far 15 such species have been recorded in the county. In the autumn of 1987, high winds caused a tile to be dislodged from the author's bungalow in Evenley. On the tile was a common leafy lichen, *Phaeophyscia orbicularis.* The lobes were covered with tiny black dots which were eventually identified as a parasite *Buelliella physciicola* – a new genus for the British Isles previously recorded only from Czechoslovakia, Austria, Italy and Japan.

Despite the fact that, as Laundon points out, the county has no natural outcrops of rock, there are more lichens growing on stone than on any other substrate. Currently 176 such species have been identified. They are largely to be found on man-made structures: posts, paths, bridges, boundary walls or buildings. The first British record of *Polyblastia albida* was found on a limestone, roadside, wall at Easton Hornstocks (TF01-00-) by J.R. Laundon in 1955.

The richest sites of all are those which have a number of the above-mentioned habitats in close proximity and are well away from the main sources of pollution. The large country estates, for example, are usually blessed both with an abundance of stonework and a wide range of broad-leaved parkland trees. Where they are not affected by chemical sprays, these trees can attract many different lichens. The trunks are often well-illuminated and enriched by nutrients from grazing animals. Steane Park (SP55-38-) in the south of the county has 118 species within its dry-stone boundary walls. Two species of *Peltigera* first found by J.R. Laundon in 1959 are still abundant on the lawns in spite of many mowings.

The lichens of churchyards Somewhat surprisingly Laundon in his 1956 article made no mention of the churchyard as a major lichen habitat. Visits were made to churchyards in the 1950s and 1960s and Cottingham and Old were on the British Lichen Society itinerary in 1977. It is in the last seven years, however, that this habitat has received its most detailed scrutiny. The reasons for its importance are not difficult to envisage. A typical churchyard has a variety of stone surfaces relatively undisturbed over a considerable period of time and exposed to the elements in a variety of ways. A single such site may include surfaces of limestone, ironstone, sandstone, marble, granite, slate, brick, concrete, mortar, plaster, pebble-dash, flint, even corrugated asbestos. These may be vertical, horizontal or sloping; smooth or rough; facing north, south, east or west; damp or dry; exposed or shaded. Some are affected by the nutrients from bird droppings; others by the run-off from metal inscriptions, window grilles or lightning conductors. The combinations are almost limitless and each niche or mini-habitat may have its own distinctive flora. There may also be ground species on the paths or close-mown grass, bark-loving species on the trees, dead-wood species on the fences, seats, notice-boards or wooden crosses, as well as species which grow on mosses on walls or on the lichens themselves. A number have been found growing on rubber dustbin lids!

It was this awareness of the richness of the churchyard as a habitat for lichens that led the present county recorder to begin a special survey in 1983. Quite by chance, he discovered that south of the 60 northings grid line on the ordnance survey map, there were exactly 100 churchyards in our county. The line slices through the southern outskirts of Northampton and runs a little to the north of the churches at Catesby, Newnham, Flore, Kislingbury, Little Houghton, Castle Ashby and Bozeat. If every site was to be visited a wealth of information would be built up and the percentage distribution of individual species would not present

COMMON LICHENS ON CHURCHYARD HEADSTONES

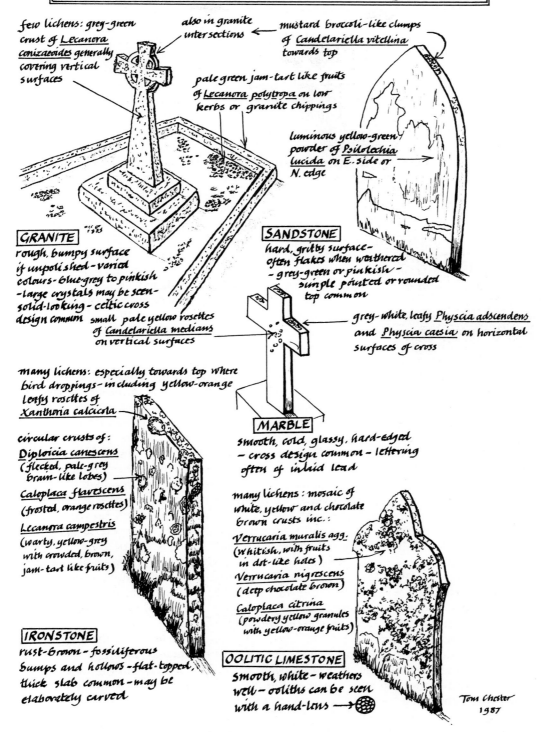

few lichens: grey-green crust of <u>Lecanora conizaeoides</u> generally covering vertical surfaces

also in granite intersections ←

mustard broccoli-like clumps of <u>Candelariella vitellina</u> towards top

pale green jam-tart like fruits of <u>Lecanora polytropa</u> on low kerbs or granite chippings

luminous yellow-green powder of <u>Psilolechia lucida</u> on E. side or N. edge →

GRANITE
rough, bumpy surface if unpolished - varied colours - blue-grey to pinkish - large crystals may be seen - solid-looking - celtic cross design common

small pale yellow rosettes of <u>Candelariella medians</u> on vertical surfaces

SANDSTONE
hard, gritty surface - often flakes when weathered - grey-green or pinkish - simple pointed or rounded top common

grey-white, leafy <u>Physcia adscendens</u> and <u>Physcia caesia</u> on horizontal surfaces of cross

many lichens: especially towards top where bird droppings - including yellow-orange leafy rosettes of <u>Xanthoria calcicola</u>

circular crusts of:
<u>Diploicia canescens</u> (flecked, pale-grey brain-like lobes)

<u>Caloplaca flavescens</u> (frosted, orange rosettes)

<u>Lecanora campestris</u> (warty, yellow-grey with crowded, brown, jam-tart like fruits)

MARBLE
smooth, cold, glassy, hard-edged - cross design common - lettering often of inlaid lead

many lichens: mosaic of white, yellow and chocolate brown crusts inc.:

<u>Verrucaria muralis agg.</u> (whitish, with fruits in dot-like holes)

<u>Verrucaria nigrescens</u> (deep chocolate brown)

<u>Caloplaca citrina</u> (powdery yellow granules with yellow-orange fruits)

IRONSTONE
rust-brown - fossiliferous bumps and hollows - flat-topped, thick slab common - may be elaborately carved

OOLITIC LIMESTONE
smooth, white - weathers well - ooliths can be seen with a hand-lens →

Tom Chester
1987

119

too much of a problem. The first thing was to draw up a checklist which could be carried on a clipboard. Such a list is invaluable because it prevents the recorder from overlooking common species. It has since undergone three revisions. The first covered 76 species; in the current edition this has been increased to 150 with room for additional species and other notes. An initial survey takes about one and a half hours, although some have lasted twice as long. It is necessary to make at least three circuits of the area of ever-decreasing size to examine first the perimeter wall or fence (if there is one), then to look at the gravestones and, finally, the walls of the Church itself. Ideally, one needs a ladder to examine the roof and tower, although generally one has to make do with binoculars. The trees, of course, must not be overlooked (nor the dustbin lid!).

The first phase of 'The Hundred Survey' is now complete, each site having been visited once and some in the south on numerous occasions. As might be expected the poorest churchyard is St Mary's Northampton, which not only lies within the town boundaries beside the main access road from the south, but is also without a single gravestone. Nevertheless, it contains 28 species. The average is much higher – 54.14 in fact. Thirteen sites each have more than 70 species and Helmdon, a large country churchyard, has no fewer than 117 – 95 of which are growing on stone, four on soil or over moss in wall crevices, six on lignum, nine on the bark of trees, while three are parasitic on other lichens. Some grow on more than one substrate. Northampton churchyards compare favourably with those in other parts of the country. Whereas some more coastal counties have lower pollution levels and a higher humidity, few have such a rich variety of stone. Churchyards in the Scottish Highlands may be unpolluted, but almost every gravestone is carved from granite – a somewhat uninviting substrate for lichen growth.

The Hundred Survey will continue for some time to come, with the results fed into the data base of a computer. A further 28 churchyards have been surveyed north of the 60 grid line and, in all, 160 of the county's 176 saxicolous species have been discovered in this habitat. Thirty-four species have also been found on churchyard trees and thirty on lignum. A further 17 species have been found on mosses, soil, or parasitic on other lichens.

While surveys such as this produce valuable statistical information, much of the thrill of lichenology comes from the discovery of a particular lichen in a particular place. When one first peers at it through a hand-lens, one may be puzzled by its precise identification, intrigued as to why it grows where it does, or simply delighted by its sheer beauty. Like some churchgoers, certain lichens are catholic in their tastes. Others have much stricter requirements and are confined to a particular substrate or prefer the shaded north wall to the sunny south. A recently discovered addition to the county list – *Psilolechia leprosa* – occupies a particularly special niche. The first British record was found only two years ago in three Cornish copper mines. It was subsequently found on Ben Lawers in Scotland, and a mudstone outcrop in Lancashire. More recently still, it turned up on a church wall in Warwickshire on stone heavily stained with copper from grilles protecting stained glass windows. In January 1988, this lichen was found in a similar situation on the south-facing wall of Culworth Church (SP54-46-) and an east-facing transept wall at Upper Boddington (SP48-53-). It is probably present but overlooked in many other churchyards. Its close relative, *Psilolechia lucida,* a luminous-green powdery crust, is equally fascinating in other ways. It occurs in every one of the 128 churchyards so far surveyed in the county. It prefers a somewhat shaded acid stone and is frequently found on the east-facing side of a sandstone headstone or the north-facing ironstone wall of a church. The north side of Culworth Church is thus illumined in spectacular fashion. It may also pick out a single acid stone in a wall or occupy the damp recesses of the lettering on an acid gravestone. The only site where it was difficult to locate was Furtho (SP77-43-), a tiny deconsecrated church now used as a farm outbuilding and with few headstones still standing. It was eventually found on an iron door hinge low down on the north wall.

120

Other individual species are no less fascinating. One thinks of *Rinodina calcarea* discovered at Grafton Underwood (SP92-80-) by Dr C.J.B. Hitch in 1982: another British first. It was found again in 1987 at Barnack (TF07-05-), and has also been located in a single Suffolk churchyard. Then, there is the ancient shrubby lichen *Anaptychia ciliaris* first found a century ago on a tree at Fawsley and still hanging on, now on stone, in six churchyards all within 12 miles of the original site. There is a much more recent discovery, *Sarcopyrenia gibba,* consisting of one or two black pear-shaped fruiting bodies which, in some mysterious way, manage always to make themselves a small clearing in the midst of the other lichens on the flat upper surface of a calcareous chest tomb or headstone. The grey-green leafy species *Parmelia mougeotii* often finds a niche humbly at ground level on the granite gravestone chippings, whereas the orange rosettes of *Xanthoria calcicola* proclaim themselves from the tops of headstones (it is said that a few bird-droppings a year keep them in good spirits). Rarely does a rarity shout out its presence in this way. One which did was *Rhizocarpon geographicum,* the map lichen, common on highland outcrops but not on lowland gravestones. Its single location to date is in the middle of a churchyard without a church: Upper Catesby (SP52-59-). Its vivid yellow-green crusty thallus was positively identified from more than the length of a cricket-pitch away.

Perhaps one reason why churchyard habitats were largely ignored in days gone by is that early lichenologists, like their colleagues in other branches of natural history, were great collectors and, while one can happily chip away at a hillside boulder without feeling too guilty, one cannot attack a headstone in this way. Some would hold the view that the lichens themselves disfigure gravestones and ought to be removed. This brings us to the whole question of churchyard conservation. It is true that some species do, in certain instances, obscure the inscriptions; on the other hand, it is equally true that others, like *Psilolechia lucida,* can pick out and almost illuminate the lettering. It is true also that there is evidence that some species can, over a period of time, contribute to surface damage of stone, although this is probably minimal compared with the general effects of weathering, and especially frost damage. One hopes that not too many of your young naturalists are influenced by the following claims in a children's reader: 'there *is* something that does travel round eating glass and lots of other indigestible things as well. It is a vegetable, the hardiest vegetable pirate known. It is called *lichen.*' Fortunately, this 'vegetable' is not too speedy a traveller and, as the article admits 'it is very slow eater, taking perhaps two hundred years to have a church window for breakfast'. No one is suggesting that 'God's Acre' should go completely untended. Some churchyard jungles, where the headstones hardly show above the grass or are obliterated by ivy or brambles, are sad, unsightly places. But equally uninviting are the sterile swards where the headstones have been removed to the boundary walls for the sake of easy mowing. Neither neglect nor fastidiousness serve the lichen well. They are extremely sensitive organisms and suffer not only from the competition of more vigorously growing plants, but also from the less obvious effects of a change of aspect. It is not without significance that the churchyards with the greatest wealth of lichens are those managed more imaginatively. The sheep of Slapton (SP63-46-) and even the goats of Litchborough (SP63-54-), while providing a nutrient-rich environment, thankfully have not yet acquired a taste for these fascinating and attractive colonizers of stonework.

ABOVE: Warkton churchyard. (RP) BELOW: Lichens growing on the
wall of the deer park at Althorp Park. (BG)

Mammals, Reptiles and Amphibians

by Phil Richardson, Northamptonshire Bat Group

Mammals can be found in all areas of the county but, unlike birds, are rarely seen: the mammal enthusiast has to rely on locating the signs that mammals leave behind. Nevertheless, a stroll in the countryside should result in the sighting of a few mammals, particularly late in the evening. The diversity of habitats provides food and shelter for a wide variety of species – 36 mammals and nine species of amphibians. Rarer species tend to be restricted to just one habitat type in a particular area but our more common species can be encountered on a long walk almost anywhere in the county.

Of lighter soils The undulating sandy soils of central and south-west Northamptonshire provide an excellent habitat for numbers of badgers, foxes and rabbits, all of which required banks or raised ground for tunnelling. The well-worn paths of the badgers in the neighbourhood of the setts provide an easy way of locating their feeding and living areas. Some setts have been in recorded use for half a century. Badger-watching is a favourite pastime for many naturalists and there is an active county Badger Group which was set up to help conserve these delightful animals. Unfortunately some persecution does occur each year where setts are blocked or badgers dug out. Too often casualties are found beside the increasingly busy roads which cut through our countryside. Some main roads are responsible for tens of badger deaths each year. Some of these unfortunate animals have been tested for bovine TB. However, the disease has not been found in this or neighbouring counties so there is no excuse for persecuting badgers on health grounds.

Rabbits find the high intensity crop production much to their liking, so the population level is high and now completely recovered from the myxomatosis epidemic of the 1950s. Small outbreaks of the disease are still recorded but the overall population remains healthy. In 1987 over 400 were seen in one small field beneath a wooded ridge that was honeycombed with their warrens, but smaller numbers can be found in almost all areas. Sandy and black-coloured varieties are seen occasionally. Such a large population provides ample food for foxes, weasels and stoats. Foxhunting on horseback is still prevalent but accounts for the deaths of only a small proportion of the population of foxes. They are hated by many farmers and shot or snared. Nevertheless they are far from scarce and are found in all suitable environments. They are most common around farms and villages although they are becoming more commonly recorded in our towns.

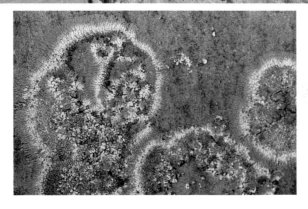

ABOVE LEFT: Dormouse caught at Stoke Wood as part of the dormouse survey. RIGHT: Daubenton's bats in a cluster. (Both PWR) CENTRE: Barnack Hills and Holes from the air. (FWW) BELOW LEFT: Lichens on a headstone at Culworth churchyard. RIGHT: The lichen *Caloplaca flavescens* on a headstone. (Both TC)

Of meadowland   Meadowland provides an excellent habitat for the brown hare. Hares have favourite, traditional fields where they can be seen each year, particularly in spring when they are courting. Hares are also found in fields of crops, but the greatest numbers occur in the large meadows by rivers or streams, such as along the Nene or Tove. Unlike some other parts of the country where there is concern over their decline, hares are fairly abundant and the large numbers that are killed on the roads in the north of the county do not seem to reduce their population dramatically; in fact many farmers still consider the hare a pest. A pack of Basset hounds are used for hare-hunting in winter but few are killed by this technique. Shoots on large farms and country estates have accounted for hundreds over a weekend, yet hares are still found in those areas in the following months. Numbers may be regulated more by the availability of suitable habitat.

Moles also favour meadowland. Regularly ploughed fields disrupt their tunnel systems so permanent pasture holds the greatest numbers. The tunnelling activities are most apparent in January when large numbers of mole hills are cast up. In a local study 7489 hills were counted in 31 acres of pasture in March – equivalent to 57 tons of soil! Moles are widespread and common throughout the county: in a sample 10 km square every one km square within it showed signs of moles, although the density varied greatly.

Rough grassland is found along the edges or corners of fields where farm machinery cannot go, and around flooded gravel pits and reservoirs. Such areas are havens for some of our small mammals – voles, mice and shrews. They make their tunnels beneath the rough tangle of vegetation and so try to stay out of sight of the numerous predators that rely on them for survival, in particular kestrels, owls and, to some extent, foxes. Field voles are particularly numerous and their tiny pathways can be seen leading from their grass tunnels in winter when the vegetation is quite low. The attractive harvest mouse, although now rarely found, uses the longer tangles of grasses for nest building. Reservoir edges, such as at Pitsford (SP78-70-), are the most productive places to find them. Grass snakes can also be found in number at such sites. The uncut and ungrazed grasses provide ample cover and shade for them.

Of woods and copses   The larger tracts of woodland provide shelter for fallow deer, the largest mammals of the county. They roam in small groups, sometimes of up to fifteen animals, between neighbouring woodlands and farmland. Scent-marked patches on woodland rides mark out territories and the rutting season brings the woods alive with the bellowing calls of males. A more common deer is the dog-sized muntjac which can be found even in small copses, some living on rough areas near town centres. Their small pathways criss-crossing our woodlands are a common sight. Usually seen singly, they are often overlooked as being dogs.

A common resident of the woods is the grey squirrel, red squirrels having died out many decades ago. They are regularly shot or trapped by foresters as they can damage or kill trees, yet the numbers remain high in all areas. They have spread into our parks and gardens, often feeding on scraps put out for birds. The scattering of chewed fir cones on the woodland floor give an observant naturalist a hint as to their abundance. The woodland floor is the domain of the wood mouse and where it searches for food. Although numerous, it is rarely seen: its nervous nature helps to ensure its survival against many predators both on the ground or from the air. A much rarer inhabitant is the dormouse. Until recently few if any had been found for many years; then in 1986 one was found in a bird box in Stoke Wood End Quarter, the Trust reserve. This prompted the warden, Mike Miley, to begin a reserve programme, to find out more about them. Dozens of specially built dormouse boxes have been built and erected in the wood. Dormice rely on an abundant supply of hazel nuts and honeysuckle and, as a result, the management of the wood and the adjacent Woodland Trust reserve has been amended to encourage this uncommon animal. Further searches in other woodlands in Rockingham Forest also began, and to date over a dozen new locations have been found, many of them on Forestry Commission properties. Efforts are now being made in these woods to conserve and encourage dormice. The discovery has been exciting and is a success story for the Trust. Other mammals such as moles, weasels and foxes also use woodlands extensively; the ample ground cover provides safe havens. As dusk falls bats may be seen flitting along the woodland edge or along a ride. These are mostly pipistrelles, but a few brown long-eared bats may be seen gleaning insects from the trees and high bushes. Summer roosting places may be behind ivy covering a tree or inside a narrow crack or crevices on the trunk. Bats are becoming rarer in our countryside but they are not alone: the adder used to be found over much of our county but is now restricted to two localities in woodlands in the north.

Dormouse. (RP)

Copses and coverts have often been left on farmland for pheasant rearing (for shooting) or for foxes (for hunting). Even small patches of woodland or scrub within a prairie of crops provides a useful home for wood mice. Spilt grain for the pheasants provides ample food, and a quiet wait near such a pheasant feeding station may be rewarded with excellent views of these endearing little creatures. Predators such as weasels and stoats are also attracted, some of the latter obtaining full white coats in winter. Gamekeepers make short work of them and gibbets of squirrels, stoats and weasels may still be seen in some keepered woods. Occasionally a hedgehog may be seen hanging up as well, perhaps caused by the mistaken belief that they are a major predator of game-bird eggs. Recently a few sightings of roe deer in small woods give hope that this elusive animal may be moving into our area. While corridors of woodland exist, then movements of mammals remain possible. Isolated woods contain mammals that are unlikely to be replaced by outside stock if disaster hits them.

Of water   Northamptonshire is well-endowed with water sites – lakes, reservoirs, flooded gravel pits, rivers, ponds and canals. Canals are the easiest places to observe water voles, a common resident of such places. A slow walk along the towpath will be punctuated by the 'plop' as a vole leaps for safety into the water. The most obvious signs of their presence are the holes in the canal banks, not appreciated by the maintenance crews from British Waterways. Lakes and ponds provide the best places for frogs and toads to breed and even small ornamental ponds in gardens are proving attractive. Toad migrations can be seen in spring as hundreds of them head for a favourite site. At night roads may become covered in them as they continue on their slow but steady path. At busy places they are helped across the roads by conservationists on 'toad patrol'. The great crested newt, quite a scarce newt, is found in some ponds and is given plenty of protection. As village and farm ponds are drained or polluted then garden ponds may become of increasing importance for these endangered animals.

A rarely-recorded mammal in our cleaner streams is the water shrew. It dives to the bottom of small pools and streams, hunting for food. Pollution will reduce the food supply and the water shrews will not survive for long. Pollution does not seem to hold back the mink however. This successful predator moved into the county in the 1970s and is now found in all our waters as well as in neighbouring woods and gardens. It will catch and eat most things, from ducks and eggs to fish and small mammals. Initial glimpses can fool the naturalist into thinking of otters, but the mink is smaller and can be any colour, reflecting their origins as captive-bred animals for the fur trade. Otters no longer breed in Northamptonshire although an occasional sighting does still occur. However, these are likely to be young animals wandering from neighbouring counties.

The greatest number of mammals at the waterside can be seen at dusk. This is the time that bats leave their roosts in nearby towns and villages and come to feed on the high

126

densities of insects over the water and along the water margins. First out are the tiny pipistrelles and they can be seen at canal and river bridges and around borders of some reservoirs and gravel pits, particularly where the vegetation is high. The noctule bat soon follows: these fly very high and are our largest bat species (as big as a swift). Far more scarce than pipistrelles, they are found at particularly good feeding sites such as the canal at Stoke Bruerne (SP74-50-) and over reservoirs at Pitsford and Ravensthorpe (SP67-70-). Bat identification is not easy since most species look the same size and colour and it is not surprising that whiskered bats can be easily overlooked. They prefer the old and mature bodies of water where the trees around the edge give plenty of insect variety. Fawsley Lakes (SP56-56-) and Barnwell Country Park (TL03-87-) are two such sites and few others have been found for this scarce species. Much more widespread and easy to identify is Daubenton's bat. It is found feeding over most waters, catching aquatic insects as it skims low within a few centimetres of the surface at all times, looking like a miniature hovercraft. The county Bat Group have tracked Daubenton's bats flying many miles along canals.

Of roadside verges   Grass verges at the edge of our numerous roads throughout the county provide homes for a large population of shrews, mice and voles. The verges are even more productive if bordered by a hedgerow. Most hedges in Northamptonshire are hawthorn mixed with ash and some blackthorn and often a drainage ditch runs along their length. The bank provides excellent sites for burrowing creatures such as rabbits and rodents. A walk along any road will give the observant naturalist many signs of the local mammal life. Rabbit burrows under the hedge will be marked by their currant-like droppings; smaller holes will have been produced by rats or mice or moles. Tiny tracks of flattened grass in the verge are produced by voles and the shrill squeaks that are heard will signify the frenzied activity of shrews. Occasionally corpses on the road can be found, mowed down by the increasing volume of traffic as the mammals try to cross to the other verge. Sometimes at night an owl will be seen sitting on the road waiting for just such movements. Hedgerows are still commonly found bordering fields, although less in number and much shorter in height than the days before mechanization. The land beneath remains relatively undisturbed so mammal populations can flourish. Recent studies have shown that hedgerows are important markers for flying bats which follow their line as they head towards feeding areas at night.

Of parkland   Parklands, of permanent pasture interspersed with a scattering of mature deciduous trees, play host to large populations of rabbits and moles. Some fallow deer are kept in parks such as at Althorp (SP68-65-) and a herd or red deer are farmed at Whittlebury (SP69-43-). Parks in towns are often the remnants of privately-owned parklands, such as Abington Park (SP77-61-) in Northampton. Many of the features attractive to wildlife remain, and grey squirrels are a common feature, but the huge numbers of people who visit the site

Toad. (RP)

127

for recreation have resulted in a reduced mole and rabbit population. An early morning visitor may still glimpse a muntjac deer, however. The mature deciduous trees provide holes large enough for squirrels as well as suitable cracks and crevices for bats to roost in. Noctule bats only live in such places and as the numbers of suitably old trees have diminished so the population has declined.

Of farmyards   Modernisation of farms has reduced the numbers of mammals that are to be found on them, yet a visit to any farmyard will still yield signs of mice and rats, although usually in small numbers. House mice are, amazingly, not often found – most mice here tend to be wood mice. Battery farming of hens often produces a healthy population of house mice that benefit from the warm conditions and ample food supplies. Brown rats on farms will form tunnels under concrete floors of barns and feed on spilt or stored grain as well as anything else lying around. Mice and rats may burrow into stacked, baled hay and straw where they remain undisturbed until spring when the last of the bales are used. Farm cats, some living ferally, can survive completely on the small mammals found around the farmyard. Farmers will often provide access holes for cats in storage sheds to help reduce the mice and rat numbers. The farmyards and nearby muck-heaps produce high densities of flying insects at night and bats will come and feed. In exposed areas the insects are quickly blown away by the slightest breeze so a high walled farmyard will enable the density of insects to build up. Brown long-eared bats catch large moths and then look for somewhere to hang up and eat them. Dutch barns, hay lofts, stables and even silos are used. The moth's wings are rejected and fall to the ground below. After a few nights quite a pile of wings has developed and this is the easiest way of locating the night roosts of this attractive bat.

Of towns and villages   Towns and villages provide us with our largest numbers of mammals. The wide variety of buildings and huge quantity of food we provide on our rubbish tips, bird-tables or vegetable gardens attract these large numbers. Unfortunately our rarer mammals are not attracted in this way; many have not learnt how to live alongside man. Perhaps the most obvious and widespread visitor is the hedgehog. These delightful animals visit gardens as they hunt for pests such as slugs. Some householders put food out for them at night. They are great wanderers and will visit many gardens in a night. In daytime they find ample shelter under garden sheds, piles of wood or other structures. Garden ponds can be hazardous to hedgehogs – when they lean forward to drink they can fall in and then drown unless there is an easy way out again. Old bonfire and piles of leaves are excellent hibernation sites as long as they are left undisturbed. Compost heaps are good places to find grass snakes and voles and mice: the warmth and ample food is much to their liking. Mice are often noticed in villages in autumn: this is the time when they move into warmer sites for the winter. They will be found in outbuildings and attics and even in kitchens. The wood mouse is the usual culprit but house mice are also found as well as other small mammals. Mouse-traps set in Northamptonshire kitchens and pantries have also caught shrews, bank voles, and rats. In some areas of towns and villages foxes and badgers will wander through the gardens at night looking for food. Some people love to watch them and will put food out to encourage them to appear. Plastic refuse sacks are sometimes torn open to get to food scraps, which causes a lot of mess for the householder, but domestic cats are also offenders. A wire-mesh guard solves the problem.

Wood mouse. (RP)

128

Modern design houses with wide, wooden eaves are the favourite summer roosting sites for pipistrelle bats. The shelter provided behind the soffit is ideal and they will happily raise their single young in such places. A second favourite site is behind hanging tiles on a house wall. The huge expansion in building in the county has provided large numbers of potential bat roosts; it is a pity that rarer bats will not use such sites. Long-eared bats also live in houses but tend to prefer older, larger places where they enter the attic and roost from the ridge beams. Much scarcer than pipistrelles, long-eared bat roosts seldom exceed 30 individuals.

Churchyards provide a peaceful and fairly safe environment for small mammals. Some parishes deliberately allow the grasses to grow up and so provide plenty of cover for the shrews and mice (a short-cropped lawn is of little use to wildlife). The shelter of mature trees provides high insect densities, and bats will regularly feed around the churchyard at night. Some will even live in the nave of the church (rarely the belfry!) if the feeding is particularly good. Natterer's bat, one of our rarest bats, is found at only five ancient churchyards in isolated parts of the county. A survey of all churches by the local Bat Group in 1981 discovered that a third of the 285 church porches were used by bats.

A look at any village from the air makes it easier to understand why so many mammals live within its confines. The area taken up with gardens is large and consists of a wide variety of shrubs and trees which produce a good variety of insects for bats and shrews. Many sheds and outbuildings give shelter for mice, voles and hedgehogs. Mature trees in the churchyard and neighbouring vicarage garden are excellent for squirrels and bats and the grounds of the attached country estate are havens for moles, foxes and muntjac. A village pond or artificial lake on the estate ensures still more mammals and amphibians frequent the area. An unfortunate effect of our mobile human population is that some recent residents in our villages are still thinking like town-folk. The first sign of wildlife in the garden or house causes panic and results in drastic action, but our wildlife is part of our heritage and if we choose to live in their habitats we should not be surprised to find them close to us. Watching mammals is to begin to understand their complex ways: tolerance and a desire to help conserve them whenever possible will surely follow.

Hare

Just watch that moonstruck pair!
They run in tandem, linked
like railway trucks,
follow each other
each swerve and curve
of the way,
stopping together,
continuing together,
caught up in a
strange eccentric dance,
till suddenly
springing into the air,
they land on their hindlegs
and start to spar like boxers.

Bigbum, dewhopper,
turpin, fast traveller,
waybeater, clumsy one,
scutter, grass-nibbler,
furze-cat, lurker,
stag of the stubble,
the springer, the skulker,
the slink-away, flincher:

no wonder they say you're mad!

Trevor Hold

Disused railway lines frequently become havens for wildlife. This section
is to disappear under the A1–M1 link road. (PW/NCC)

Birds

Hobby. (ME)

by Robert Bullock, County Bird Recorder and Cliff Christie

From the swollen rivers carrying glacial melt waters, to the spread and subsequent destruction of natural forests, the Northamptonshire landscape has undergone dramatic changes over the last 10,000 years or so but, increasingly, man's influence has dominated the changes which have affected our birds.

Neolithic man introduced pastoral farming gradually. The addition of open grassland increased the potential for many bird species. Perhaps this was when skylarks first sang over Northamptonshire fields. The vast wetlands to the north-east of the county attracted an impressive array of water birds and the trackless forests by then housed all the woodland species. Then, as now, a great many species bred locally and moved south for the winter.

Through the Bronze and Iron Ages, the speed of change increased: man's ability to determine successful species was gradually refined and the mould was cast. More recently, his grip on the environment has tightened; nowhere has escaped his influence. Sophisticated chemicals, machines, wholesale drainage and urban development have all been major factors in reshaping the countryside for birds. Gravel extraction, and freshwater reservoirs have partly redressed the loss of natural wetlands. Their importance is clear from the huge numbers using them. A hundred years ago, great crested grebes had been persecuted to near destruction for their 'grebe furs' but a count of 111 at Thrapston gravel pits (SP99-79-) in 1972 showed their recovery. In late 1977 a flock of 200 was reported at Pitsford reservoir (SP78-70-) and that was topped in August 1981 when 300 were seen. Tufted ducks have also shared the exploitation of man-made waters – 471 represented a maximum count at Thrapston in 1972: seven years later over a thousand were counted at Stanford reservoir (SP60-80-) and in February 1980, a flock of 1,500 was recorded at Ditchford gravel pits (SP94-68-). By the mid-1980s, Pitsford reservoir was rated the 13th most important wintering site in Britain for this species.

The old, water-filled gravel workings at Thrapston have produced a complex of 11 main lakes over an area of about 210 acres and can boast a great variety of breeding birds including little and great crested grebes, mute swan, Canada and greylag geese, mallard, tufted duck, shoveler, moorhen, coot, ringed plover, little ringed plover, lapwing, redshank, snipe, oystercatcher, yellow wagtail, sedge, reed and grasshopper warblers, nightingale, the largest colony of common terns in the county as well as the second largest heronry, in the old Titchmarsh duck decoy, occupied since before 1928. In areas where sand and gravel extraction continue, opportunist sand martins colonise the ever-changing banks and cliffs and, in some recent years, between 100 and 400 nest holes have been excavated.

In the winter, large numbers of wigeon, teal, mallard, pochard and tufted duck occur, with a total count of more than 3,100 wildfowl in January 1986 and an average winter monthly total of more than 2,100. Fewer, but regular gadwall, shoveler, goldeneye and goosander can be seen, but a count of 202 of the latter in February 1987 was the second highest for any site in Britain that winter. Thrapston has now become nationally the sixth most important site for goosander over the 1982-1987 winters. Thirty species of waders have also called in whilst on passage to or from northern breeding grounds; rarities attracted here include little egret, night heron, American wigeon, blue-winged teal and both whiskered and white-winged black tern, the latter on more than one occasion.

Another important link in the chain of gravel pits traversing the county is at Ditchford, alongside Higham Ferrers. In fact 12 nationally rare birds have occurred, twice as many as elsewhere in Northamptonshire. These include penduline tit and sooty tern, respectively the

Purple heron. (RI)

132

Savi's warbler. (RI)

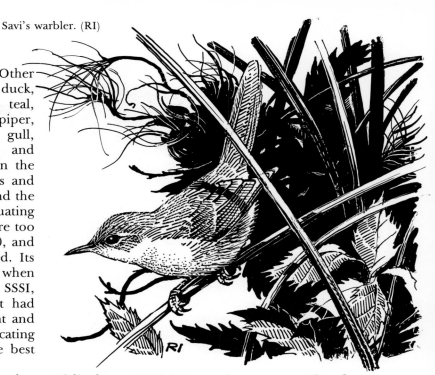

eighth and 25th British records. Other first county records are ring-necked duck, blue-winged teal, green-winged teal, marsh sandpiper, broad-billed sandpiper, red-rumped swallow, ring-billed gull, bluethroat, yellow-browed warbler and Cetti's warbler. The attraction lies in the valley location, the range of habitats and the large area of water margins around the 11 lakes, some with regularly fluctuating water levels, favoured by waders. Here too shelducks first began nesting in 1980, and over 200 species have been recorded. Its importance was finally recognised when part of the complex was made an SSSI, but not before part of the best pit had been lost to a new road development and the diversion of the River Nene, indicating the pressures to which many of the best sites are constantly subjected.

From Tansor (TL05-90-) in the north, to Kislingbury (SP70-59-) on the western side of Northampton itself, gravel has been extracted in the Nene valley, establishing an interesting variety of habitats to complement major rivers.

Large freshwater reservoirs have been constructed to satisfy the ever increasing human population and the County Bird Reports, with their growing number of contributions, bear witness to the importance of such sites as Stanford (SP60-80-), Naseby (SP66-77-), Hollowell (SP68-72-) Ravensthorpe (SP67-70-), Daventry (SP58-63-), Boddington (SP49-53-) and Pitsford reservoirs.

Pitsford, in the centre of the county, was flooded in 1955/6 and holds pride of place as the most important bird-watching site in Northamptonshire. Comprising up to 750 acres of open water and 390 acres of surrounding countryside within the perimeter fence, it is a major attraction for birds. No less than 220 species and four sub-species have been recorded. Along with the more common birds, many rarities to the county drop in: black-winged pratincole, sociable plover, Caspian tern, Pomarine skua, Iceland and glaucous gulls and, with increasing regularity, ospreys pause to fish on their way to and from breeding haunts in Scotland and Scandinavia. The reservoir is on one of the inland flyways crossing south-east Britain from the Wash and each year some 170 species are recorded, including many passage migrants. The surrounds, which include a variety of mixed woodland, have matured sufficiently to attract about 70 breeding species, including nine warblers.

The breeding success of waterfowl depends dramatically on water levels. When high in spring, there is much emergent and semi-submerged vegetation around the edge, particularly on the ungrazed areas inside the Wildlife Trust Reserve, providing suitable nesting cover for great crested and little grebes, mallard, gadwall, shoveler, tufted duck, ruddy duck, coot, moorhen, mute swan and Canada goose. In 1975 there were scores of coots' nests providing ample food for local crows, which robbed the nests of disturbed birds. In contrast, the water level was low in the spring of 1974 and few, if any, coots nested. A sudden drop in water level in early summer can leave many nests high and dry and some rebuilding may take place.

The water level is equally important for migrant waders, which require a low level and exposed mud if they are to stay and feed. Usually the fine, drier summer weather leads to a lower water level in the autumn, just right for the return passage. The Walgrave and

Wigeon. (ME)

Scaldwell arms on the north of the causeway, being shallow, can becomes acres of mud, ideal for wading birds: 38 species of waders have been recorded, including five American vagrants – dowitcher, Wilson's phalarope, buff-breasted sandpiper, pectoral sandpiper and lesser yellowlegs, the latter the first proved ever to over-winter in Britain.

Winter is the season when ducks gather at Pitsford in their thousands. The change in numbers over the years is interesting. Wigeon, which peaked at 4,000 in December 1960, and pochard, at 3,500 in December 1966, have decreased considerably, possibly due to the flooding of more gravel pits and the construction of the huge Grafham (TL15-67-) and Rutland Waters (SK90) not far away, as the duck flies. In contrast, goldeneye and goosander have increased, finding deeper water near the dam to their liking. Nevertheless, the total wildfowl water near the dam to their liking. Nevertheless, the total wildfowl count for December 1987 was 5,599, with an average winter monthly total of more than 3,500; 32 species of ducks and geese have visited this water. The large concentrations of birds at all times of the year have attracted 11 species of birds of prey including peregrine, marsh, hen and Montagu's harriers, red kite and osprey.

Quite how the drainage of some natural wetlands, and the introduction of other man-made habitats has affected birds is difficult to determine accurately but, with the River Nene and its associated flood meadows dominating the central and north-eastern side of the county, and the Welland forming the northern boundary, water birds have always been well represented.

Perhaps the most important tool used by man in recent years to re-shape agriculture has been the application of chemicals. The possibility of chlorinated hydrocarbons being stored in subcutaneous fat of small birds, to be passed on up the food chain to aggregate into lethal doses for birds like sparrowhawks, was either not predicted or considered outside the concern of agriculturalists.

Covering 80% of Britain as a whole, with Northamptonshire being fairly typical, farmland as a bird habitat is of vital importance. The mosaic of woods and copses, hedgerows, streams and fields for stock or crops, has traditionally housed the majority. Many of the woodland and open scrub species still find a niche, alongside some of the more specialist farmland birds – the partridges, lapwings, barn and little owls, skylarks, yellow wagtails, the whitethroats, rooks, goldfinches, yellowhammers and corn buntings. Some of the neglected corners and old hedgerows, which support a rich small mammal fauna, benefit the kestrels and owls, whilst providing nesting cover for many passerines, including wrens, dunnocks, robins, blackbirds and thrushes, several warblers, jays and magpies, linnets and bullfinches.

Until the fairly recent drought in the Sahel region, south of the Sahara Desert, caused the decline of some trans-Saharan migrants, whitethroats were common summer visitors and redstarts nested in many of the streamside pollarded willows. Whitethroats suffered a dramatic decline in 1969 (probably as much as 70%) and a similar reduction in redstarts occurred in the early 1970s, the few returning to breed now occupying the more traditional woodland sites like Badby (SP56-58-), Salcey Forest and Whittlebury Forest, with some in more 'open forest' areas such as Yardley Chase (SP84-55-) and Fermyn Hall Park (SP95-86-).

The fate of these two species does emphasise that some birds are highly mobile, and vulnerable to changes hundreds, and often thousands, of miles from Northamptonshire. The dramatic decline in corncrakes, which nested in the old hay meadows was, of course, much earlier, and the reasons also much nearer machine cutting of hay. Another former breeding species, the red-backed shrike, probably declined because of a climatic deterioration, for suitable habitat still exists in former breeding sites.

The chats have faired little better; most stonechats recently appearing only as passage birds or winter visitors and whinchats reduced to one breeding site in 1986, compared with 1956, when 16 nests were located in the north of the county alone. Their decline is less easy to explain but nationally, whinchats have become increasingly an upland bird with strongholds in the north and west.

Not all birds have suffered recently, however, and the spectacular spread of the collared dove from the mid-1950s to reach pest proportions in some places within 30 years, indicates what can happen when a new species finds a suitable ecological niche. Perhaps less well appreciated has been the expansion in numbers of stock doves and, until recently, turtle doves. Both increased quite dramatically from the mid-19th century, probably benefitting from the increase in arable farming then.

Hawfinches – breed in some Northamptonshire woods. (ME)

The bomb sites of the Second World War, forming inland cliffs and crevices, helped the black redstart colonise Britain from mainland Europe, although it has never become more than a rare nesting species. Breeding was first recorded in the county in 1967 and it was not for another 19 years that a couple of pairs bred again in the centre of Kettering and on a farm near Silverstone (SP67-44-) this time raising three broods.

Other new colonisers include firecrest, which first bred in Britain in the New Forest in 1962. Breeding was suspected in Norway spruce trees at Hazelborough Forest (SP65-42-) between 1973 and 1975 and also at Souther Wood (SP97-83-) in the latter year. In 1979 breeding was confirmed in Maidford Wood (SP61-52-) and strongly suspected at Fineshade (SP98-98-) and Souther Woods in 1984, when a total of 11 singing males were present, but only one in 1985. The similarity of this species to goldcrest, with which it frequently co-habits, may lead to it being overlooked.

In April 1984, a Cetti's warbler was seen at Ditchford gravel pits and the second and third county records were obtained there in 1986 and breeding strongly suspected in the county in 1987.

On a national basis, redpolls have increased substantially in the latter half of this century, possibly aided by afforestation, and this has been reflected in the county records: scattered winter records reported in the *Journal of the Northamptonshire Natural History Society and Field Club* for 1960, whilst the *County Bird Report* for 1972 referred to them as 'well distributed and abundant in the county throughout the year'. There have been ups and downs in the population but generally their future looks secure.

In a dynamic environment, successes and failures are bound to occur. The reduction in coppice management for many of our woods has almost certainly been an important factor in the decline

Cetti's warbler – rare resident. (ME)

of nightingales since the 1950s. Song can still be heard in some suitable woods and Ashton Wold and Glapthorn Cow Pasture reserve (TL00-90-) in the north of the county, and Salcey Forest in the south-east, still support stable populations.

Nightjars have experienced a similar decline in the second half of the century. In 1956 there were at least five county sites where these birds bred, but they were totally absent for the first time in 1986.

Of all the changes, the introduction of Canada goose, ruddy duck, red-legged partridge, golden pheasant, little owl; the spread of gadwall, collared dove and firecrest; the local fluctuations of sparrowhawks or the extinction of nightjar and wryneck, probably none has been greater than the increase in certain gull numbers, exploiting refuse tips for food and using large inland reservoirs to roost. Ironically, black-headed gulls suffered a serious decline in the mid-19th century, when there was fear of their extinction. Since then, numbers have steadily increased until, by the 1980s, roosting flocks of up to 40,000 and regularly more than 10,000 occur in winter at Pitsford reservoir, with many other waters carrying between 2–10,000.

None of the other gulls have reached such numbers, but totals of 4,820 common gulls at Pitsford in January 1983, 4,500 lesser black-backed gulls at Stanford reservoir in September 1984, 1,000 herring gulls at Ravensthorpe reservoir in January 1983 and great black-backed gulls reaching 940 at Ditchford gravel pits in December 1985 indicate the measure of their

Little gulls, sand martins and swallows feeding over gravel pits. (ME)

success. Increasing numbers of kittiwakes, little, glaucous, Iceland and Mediterranean gulls since 1980, ring-billed gull in 1984, and Sabine's gulls at three sites in 1987 all point to the success of this group.

Many recent changes in the countryside have had a profound effect. Anyone driving around Northampton itself, with houses, roads and industrial development rising from the earth like autumn fungi, can see their environmental impact. For all that, the county can still boast an impressive avifauna, with 294 species recorded by the middle of 1988.

From the north-east corner only 21 miles from the sea, with fenland traditions maintained until a few decades ago in places like Borough Fen Decoy, to the extreme south, where the River Cherwell flows towards the Oxfordshire clays, as far from the sea at it is possible to get in Britain, birdlife flourishes.

Mixed woodlands ring to the sound of many birds each spring: spotted woodpeckers drum, nuthatches, robins, treecreepers, goldcrests, chaffinches, wrens, tits and a great many more join the morning chorus, while the night is given to tawny owls and the occasional woodcock. Skylarks rise from the open farmland where yellowhammers, dunnocks, blackbirds, song and mistle thrushes, chaffinches and perhaps, a score more, vie for food and space to raise a family. Each spring and autumn birds moving to and from breeding grounds farther north add variety and interest. Well over 200 species are reported annually within the county, which should not only satisfy the avid bird watcher, but give heart to the dedicated conservationist.

Little Owl

Twin headlamps glare at you indignantly:
What are you doing here?
Though no bigger than a thrush
he defies your presence,
would defend himself to the last feather,
this Jack Russell of Owls.

Trevor Hold

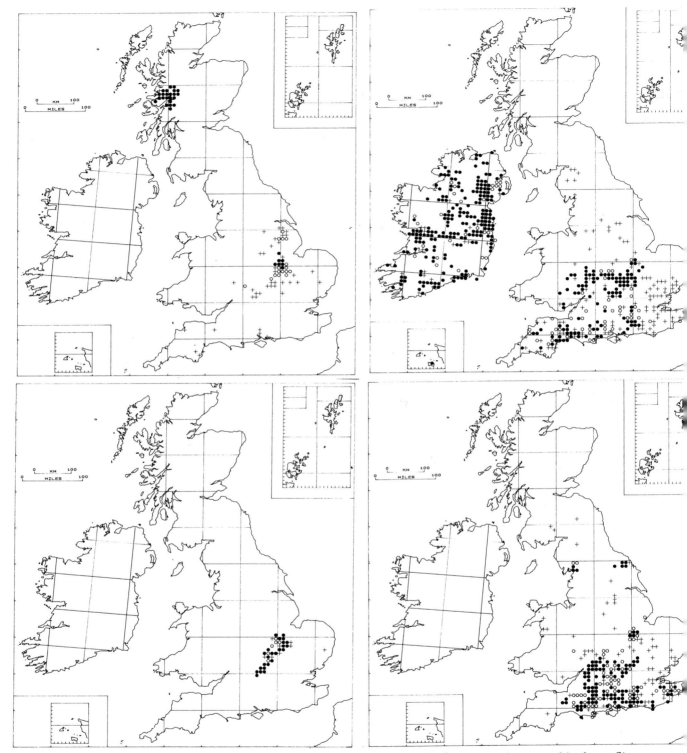

10 km square distribution in Great Britain and Ireland of some Northamptonshire butterflies.

LEFT: Chequered skipper   *Carterocephalus palaemon*
RIGHT: Wood white   *Leptidea sinapis*
BELOW LEFT: Black hairstreak *Strymonidia pruni*
RIGHT: Duke of Burgundy   *Hamearis lucina*

138   • 1970 onwards   O 1940–1969   + Pre 1940

We gratefully acknowledge the help of the Biological Records Centre, Institute of Terrestrial Ecology, Monks Wood in supplying these maps and allowing them to be reproduced here.

Butterflies and Dragonflies

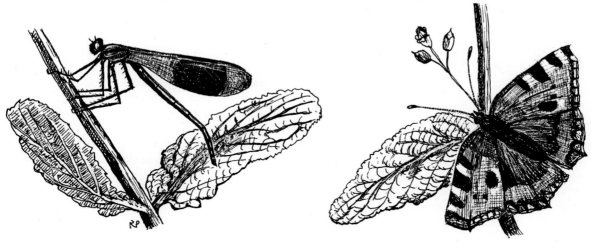

by Peter Gent, Past President, Northamptonshire Natural History Society
and Richard Eden, Vice-County Dragonfly Recorder

Butterflies   Miriam Rothschild has given a detailed account of the changes in the butterflies at Ashton Wold from 1900–1989. During a six-year period 1976–1981 a study on a 10km square basis was carried out on their present distribution in the county as a whole, coordinated by the County Recorder, Ian Flinders. The study period embraced extremes of weather conditions, including 1976 which was unusually warm and dry, and 1979 which was unusually cold and wet.

37 species were recorded in the county over the six years, of which ten were not at all common. The maximum number seen by one observer in a day was 22 but most good days produced 16-19 species, with late July apparently the optimum time for abundance as well as numbers of species.

The 10km square around Yardley Chase (SP85), which has a relatively high area of broadleaf woodland content, produced the highest number of species (32), and six of our 34 10km squares had 25 or more.

From these and earlier observations it appears that 16 species resident in the past can no longer be found in the county, including chequered skipper, black-veined white, large heath, brown hairstreak, Duke of Burgundy, purple emperor, small blue, silver-studded blue, brown argus, chalkhill blue, large blue, large tortoiseshell, small pearl-bordered fritillary, pearl-bordered fritillary, high-brown fritillary and marsh fritillary.

The most outstanding recent loss was, without doubt, the chequered skipper, which had gone into rapid decline by about the 1960s and is now to be found only in Scotland. It was always of local distribution but could be found in quite a number of small and restricted areas, usually in the larger woods. It was also recorded from other adjacent Midland counties. In the mid-sixties it was known at Ashton in the north of our county, where it was restricted to one wide ride which bordered an area of Forestry Commission conifers. This was sprayed from the air and the chequered skipper was not seen again. The false brome grass, its food plant, still flourishes and is not uncommon. It is not easy for single-brooded species like this to withstand set-backs and difficulties of this nature.

Banded demoiselle and small tortoiseshell butterfly. (RP)

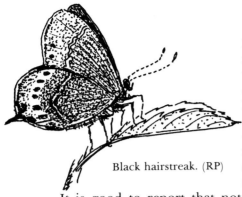

Black hairstreak. (RP)

Another species which seems to have disappeared in the last 20 years is the Duke of Burgundy. This was moderately frequent in open woods in the north of the county, where the caterpillars fed on cowslip and primrose but, apart from one unconfirmed report, there are no recent records. Our loss has been reflected in the decline nationally.

The purple emperor has also almost certainly become extinct in the county since the 1960s. There are occasional records but these are thought to be of recent introductions and, so far, there is no evidence that a self-perpetuating colony has been re-established.

It is good to report that not all is gloom. The wood white, which was once in decline, possibly because of over-collecting, has increased recently and is spreading northwards. It is double-brooded and favours woodland rides where its larval food plants, bird's-foot-trefoil and other leguminous plants, grow.

Today our most celebrated butterfly is perhaps the black hairstreak. This species is restricted to the central counties of England: Northamptonshire, Buckinghamshire, Oxfordshire, Cambridgeshire and Huntingdonshire. It inhabits the borders and rides of woods where the larvae feed on blackthorn. It was particularly to protect this species that the Trust bought Glapthorn Cow Pasture (TL00-90-) in 1974. From early July the adults are on the wing and can be observed quartering the blackthorn tops on which their eggs are laid, or else feeding on privet flowers along the rides. Much work has been done by the Trust to keep the rides open and create clearings over the last decade. This has undoubtedly been of great benefit to these attractive but unobtrusive butterflies, which require open sunny conditions to display and bask. In July 1986 over 80 specimens were counted.

Dragonflies The recent rapid growth of interest in the study of dragonflies nationally has been reflected in Northamptonshire. Distribution maps produced only ten years ago show the county as an area almost devoid of records of even the commonest species. The publication of a number of new guide books, and the formation of both the Odonata Recording Scheme and the British Dragonfly Society, have stimulated interest in this neglected branch of entomology. Before long every 10km square in the county will have at least some records, and most will have a complete list.

The county list now stand at 22 species. Of these, 12 are dragonflies (Order *Anisoptera*) and 10 are damselflies (Order *Zygoptera*). This is typical of a lowland English county with no coastline, but there is some scope for finding new species. This is illustrated by the discovery in June 1986 of a female scarce chaser at one of the gravel pits in the Nene valley. This was the first and, so far, the only record of this nationally rare species. It has a few colonies at gravel pits in neighbouring counties and may well expand its distribution to include the many similar lakes in our county.

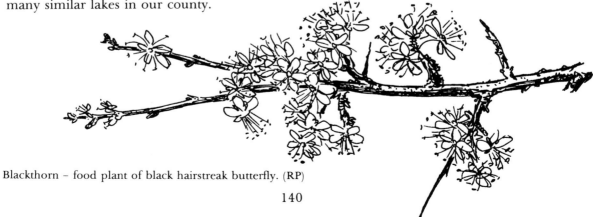

Blackthorn – food plant of black hairstreak butterfly. (RP)

LEFT TO RIGHT: Black hairstreak butterfly, a county speciality; (JLM) a female Emperor dragonfly laying eggs; (RE) the chequered skipper, sadly now extinct in the county, (NCC) and a male common darter dragonfly. (RE) BELOW: Pond at Brigstock Country Park, an excellent site for dragonflies and damselflies. (AC)

The flooded gravel pit complexes of the Nene valley are probably the most important habitat for dragonflies in Northamptonshire. The river itself is used as a corridor for colonisation of newly flooded gravel pits. The commonest damselfly species such as blue-tailed damselfly, common blue damselfly and azure damselfly are found all along its banks and rapidly establish themselves around newly flooded lakes. Adults of dragonfly species like brown hawker and common darter have the power to fly long distances, and a visit by only one egg-laying female can lead to a healthy new colony in just a few years. As the lakes become more mature and established, and the variety of aquatic plants and animals increases, then more species of dragonfly can usually be found. Locally uncommmom species found at sites like this might include emperor dragonfly, large red damselfly and emerald damselfly. In areas where beds of bulrush occur, the four-spotted chaser should be present. It persistently returns to settle on the top of a stem, after flying out to catch passing insect prey. One species particularly favours gravel pits, and has only been found at very few sites away from them. This is the black-tailed skimmer which swarms in hundreds at sites like Thrapston (TL00-81-) and Ditchford gravel pits (SP94-68-). Although superficially similar to the chaser dragonflies in size and shape, it has an interesting behavioural difference. Skimmers, particularly the males, rarely perch on vegetation – instead they almost always settle on the ground.

The majority of rivers in Northamptonshire are quite slow flowing and have a muddy bed. This is the typical habitat of the banded demoiselle, the familiar large damselfly with a dark blue band through the wings of the male, and it has been well recorded throughout the major river systems of the county. This species seems quite susceptible to involuntary, wind-blown dispersal away from its typical riverine habitat. Individuals have turned up in such unlikely locations as wasteground near Northampton 'bus station, and the woods of Yardley Chase (SP84-55-). Its near relative, the beautiful demoiselle, which has all-dark wings, is much rarer in lowland England. It is restricted to narrower, faster flowing rivers with a shingle bottom. This species is found in good numbers along the Tove, upstream of Towcester, where the river exhibits these characteristics, and it has been recorded on the Cherwell near Aynho (SP49-33-). Patient searching of the upper reaches of other rivers in the county may reveal new colonies of this spectacular damselfly.

The canals of Northamptonshire do not maintain the variety of species found in rivers, but they are the only known habitat of another scarce species, the white-legged damselfly. It has been found at eight sites and is certainly under-recorded, because no survey of all the county canals has been undertaken. Observers walking canal banks in early summer should look out for a medium-sized blue damselfly, with large, almost feathery, white legs dangling down from its body as it flies around the towpath vegetation. The increase in water traffic on the canals has not so far shown any effect on the population.

The habitat in which the largest numbers of species are recorded is mature ponds, either in, or next to woodland. Northamptonshire has two excellent examples of this in Yardley Chase and Brigstock Country Park (SP95-85-). Vegetation floating on the surface of the water, such as lily-pads, is favoured by the red-eyed damselfly. This robust damselfly is almost always found within a few inches of the pond surface, because it specialises in capturing insect prey just after they emerge from the water. The smaller dragonfly species, such as broad-bodied chaser, common darter and the nationally scarce ruddy darter hunt over the ponds and settle on waterside plants. Males of the larger hawker dragonflies (*Aeshna* spp.) establish hunting territories along woodland edges and rides, by repeatedly patrolling a stretch of airspace.

Survey work carried out in the last few years has established a fair idea of dragonfly distribution in Northamptonshire. The foundations for further study into populations at known sites have been laid, but there is still scope for work in identifying new localities to fill gaps in the distribution of even the commoner species. With so many good guide books available, field identification of adult dragonflies should be within the **grasp** of most patient observers. For this reason, all naturalists should be encouraged to **take** up the study of dragonflies.

Reflections

The mirror of the pond presents
a rimpled version of the world above.
Sky, clouds and passing birds,
though shown the wrong way round,
are accurately pictured there.
Swallows dip to meet themselves;
two anglers fish at each end of a line;
leaf drops to leaf and a demoiselle
alights upon approaching feet.
But then, with a sudden splash, a chubb
springs up to snap a fly. The mirror's smashed,
revealing in the depths a darker world.

Trevor Hold

Pastoral landscape at Deene. (RP)

So Shall We Reap

by Rosemary Cockerill
Farm Conservation Adviser, Northamptonshire Farming and Wildlife Advisory Group (FWAG)

(RP)

Most of the area of Northamptonshire is farmed, but farmland cannot be regarded as one wildlife habitat. It is a matrix of cropped land which, in these days of intensive agriculture, is unlikely to have a high conservation value, and uncropped areas which contain most of the semi-natural, permanent vegetation to be found on farms and are thus much more valuable to wildlife. Hedges, woodland, ponds, grassland, road verges, old railway lines – these are all found on farms and managed by farmers.

The pattern of farming in Northamptonshire has gone through dramatic changes, not just in the last few years but over the last century. In the 1870s two thirds of the county was under arable farming, with wheat the main arable crop. Then the removal of the protection of the Corn Laws, allied to poor harvests and such distant events as the opening up of the American Mid-West had a disastrous effect on Northamptonshire farmers. The corn land in the county was only marginally suited to corn and, as profits and farm prices fell, so more and more land was turned over to permanent pasture. This continued for several decades, with a slight reversal at the time of the First World War. According to the official returns of the Ministry of Agriculture in 1939, arable land accounted for under one-fifth of the area of the county, permanent pasture for half, woodland for a twenty-fifth and rough grazing for less than one per cent. The remaining area was taken up with housing and industrial land.

In *The Report of the Land Utilisation Survey of Britain* (1943) Stamp said 'The most outstanding feature of Northamptonshire farming is the amount of land laid to grass. It is usually interrupted by patches – individual fields or groups of fields – of arable, which in some areas become relatively important. There are nowhere, however, such sharply marked boundaries as occur on the margins of the Fens, where grassland gives place suddenly to arable – as along Carr Dyke in the Soke of Peterborough. On the other hand there are several parishes in the north-west, e.g. Clipston, Stanford, and Sutton Bassett, in which the agricultural land is entirely laid down to permanent pasture'.

To some extent these differences between parts of the county remain today, but anyone who would like to have a glimpse of how most of the county would have looked in Stamp's day would do well to visit one of the Northamptonshire Wildlife Trust's reserves, Bucknell Wood Pastures (SP64-45-). This is a remarkable area of about 25 ha of unimproved grassland which has been managed for grazing and hay at least since the beginning of this century.

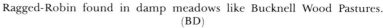

Ragged-Robin found in damp meadows like Bucknell Wood Pastures.
(BD)

Once common plants surviving in the meadows include pepper-saxifrage, pignut, adder's-tongue fern, common spotted-orchid and ragged-Robin. The ten meadows, divided by ancient hedgerows, are owned by Mrs Joyce Sansbury and Mr David Barford. In 1984, their father, the previous owner who had farmed the land, died. They approached the Northamptonshire FWAG to find a way of retaining the character of the area, which is surrounded by arable farms. FWAG introduced them to the Northamptonshire Wildlife Trust to whom they now lease the land for a peppercorn rent. In this way it is possible for us to step back briefly into farmland which had many benefits for wildlife but which is now largely lost, because it cannot compete economically with more modern systems.

In 1943 Stamp welcomed the changes which were obviously coming to farming in the county: 'Now a second war has caused the county's agriculture to be rejuvenated, new capital is being put in, and the whole area is being planned by joint committees of practical farmers and college-trained technicians. It must be the wish of all that common sense will prevail afterwards and that the haphazard old order of the thirties will never return again'.

These changes, the need for more efficient food production, mechanisation, advances in plant breeding, and the financial stability given to agriculture first by the UK Government and then the EEC, have caused a dramatic swing back to arable farming in Northamptonshire.

We think of the traditional farmland landscape of Northamptonshire as the enclosed landscape of small hedged fields, small spinneys and an abundance of hedgerow trees. Historically arable farming predominated to the east of a north-south line through the county, more pastoral farming to the west, although few farms were completely specialized in either direction. Since the War and particularly since the 1970s the proportion of arable farming increased in the county as a whole. Farms also became more specialized, and changes in farm machinery meant that arable farms in particular could be run with much less labour. This could only be done, however, if the small fields previously needed to allow stock rotation were enlarged to make the most efficient use of machinery. Thus modern arable farming has resulted in removal of trees and hedges.

The changes in our farmland landscape and wildlife habitats since the war are illustrated by the *Northamptonshire Farmland Tree and Hedgerow Survey* published by Northamptonshire County Council Planning Department in 1983. The survey looked at hedgerows, free-standing trees and small groups of trees (below 0.25 ha) in 1982 and compared this with aerial photos from the immediate post war period (1946–1950) and from 1971–1972.

There has been an average of about 15% loss of hedgerows since 1946, leaving 6km/km². About half of this loss occurred before and half after 1972. The losses have been greatest in the upper Nene and Brampton valleys, around Corby and in the Yardley Chase area and in the west. This is largely the result of change from pastoral to arable farming. In the east of the county there has been a low density of hedgerows for longer because the area has been mainly arable for longer. Changes in hedgerow management are also important: over 70% of hedgerows were mechanically trimmed by 1982, and many of these were less than 2m in height and depth. Only 20% of hedges were of the high, dense type which is more valuable for nature conservation.

The survey found that, on average across the county, there had been a loss of 14% of individual trees since 1947. Changes in farming were responsible for some of this loss but

146

Adder's tongue-fern – found in old unimproved meadow. (RP)

Dutch elm disease has also been a major factor; in 1972, according to a Forestry Commission survey of hedgerow trees, elm was the most common, accounting for 41%. In the 1983 survey, live elms accounted for only 2% of all hedgerow trees. Ash is now the commonest hedgerow tree (51%), followed by oak (12%). About a quarter of hedgerow trees were dead or in poor condition in 1982, suggesting that they could disappear over the next ten years (to 1992) with a further 25% in the medium term due to the natural ageing process, and with a similar loss from the small groups of trees which are such an important feature of our landscape. These predictions were among the reasons for the importance which the County Council gives to its tree-planting schemes.

Farmland can be changed sympathetically for wildlife as these case studies show.

Woodland

Monastery Farm is about three miles south east of Towcester and six and a half miles south of Northampton. It is a sheep farm of about 200 acres, but this area includes 45 acres of woodland, Stokepark wood (SP73-49-). The wood is an ancient semi-natural woodland left unmanaged for many years. All the useful timber trees had been taken out during the Second World War so the owner, Mr Bill Capell, was faced with overgrown and neglected hazel, ash and field maple coppice, and with no decent standard trees. In most of the wood there was no ground flora to speak of because of the heavy shade, and what rides existed were badly shaded and wet.

From the winter of 1984/5 about ⅔ acre of the wood each winter has been coppiced and any healthy standard trees left standing. As there are so few standards, oak is being replanted within the coppiced areas at a 5–6m spacing in tree-shelters. Although there was originally no hedge marking the boundary, the coppice regrowth beside the road has now been, layered to form one.

Reasons for wanting to bring the wood back into management were to improve pheasant shooting and to stop it from degenerating into a dark, wet wilderness. Mr Capell was alerted to the wildlife benefits of managing the wood when in 1984 he allowed Northamptonshire FWAG to use Monastery Farm for a farm walk.

The objectives were to produce the variety of coppice heights, open spaces, and wider rides which make traditionally managed old woodland one of the most valuable habitats for wildlife and also to improve the wood for pheasants.

The coppicing, planting and hedgelaying have been done when there is time to spare from other farm work by Mr Capell's brother-in-law, who works on the farm and a pensioner who sometimes does casual work. They use a chainsaw and hand implements. The cost is about £1,000 a year but Mr Capell recoups some in grant aid from a scheme run by Northamptonshire County Council and the Countryside Commission.

Cherry plum – common in hedgerows, flowers before blackthorn. (RP)

The benefits to wildlife at this early stage include a big increase in spring wildflowers and in the variety of birds using the wood. Letting the light into the woodland floor has caused a flush of flowers such as primroses, violets and even early-purple orchid in the recently coppiced areas and there is a greater variety of nesting cover, feeding sites and sunning areas for birds. Mr Capell has noticed an increase in woodcock.

Bill Capell is complimentary about the way County Council/Countryside Commission grants are making conservation work possible. Although the wood is already holding pheasants better, it would take a long time to get a return from shooting and he would not have begun the scheme without grant aid. Having someone already working on the farm who was interested in shooting and conservation has also helped the project.

Lesser celandine – early flowering plant along the bottom of hedges.
(RP)

In 1985 Mr Capell allowed MAFF to use the wood for an open day on woodland management for local farmers. He feels that he has learned a lot about nature conservation at the same time as local conservationists have learned something about the practicalities of fitting woodland management into farming.

Hedges Rectory Farm, owned by Simon Marlowe-Thomas, is a 240 acre mixed arable/ livestock enterprise. It is just south of the Northamptonshire/Leicestershire border about 2½ miles south-west of Market Harborough (SP69-85-). It lies in the flat bottom of the valley of the river Welland whose source is two miles to the south-west near Sibbertoft. Although there are still spinneys and coverts in the locality there are few large areas of woodland. Hedges are important here, as one might expect in an area traditionally known for its hunting, and where livestock farmers appreciate their value as stock-fencing and shelter. The proportion of arable crops has increased in this part of the county in recent years but hedge maintenance is still regarded as an important routine farming operation.

A 350 yard long stretch of hedge along the drive to the farm house was laid during the 1985/1986 winter as the start of a programme of hedge improvement. When Mr Marlowe-

Thomas bought this land a few years earlier the hedge had been unmanaged for many years. It was growing tall (30–40 feet) and straggly, and was shading both the hedge bank and the adjoining field.

Mr Marlowe-Thomas' reason for wanting to lay this hedge was to bring it back into routine management before it was too late. If left unmanaged it would have grown into a series of tall, leggy thorn bushes with no natural regeneration or ground flora below it, and eventually the base would lose the ability to send out new growth if cut. The appearance of the hedge is important to Mr Marlowe-Thomas as he drives past it every time he leaves and returns to the farm.

Wildlife benefits when such a hedge is laid, mainly because the hedge is more likely to survive. It can be tempting to remove a thin, straggly hedge which looks untidy and does not provide a barrier to livestock. Hedgelaying also encourages thicker growth and so provides better nesting cover, and the light let in allows plants to grow on the hedge bank.

The hedge was laid between December and February by a farm worker who is often employed as casual labour. Stakes and binders had to be bought and the cost of the job was £33 per chain.

On FWAG advice Mr Marlowe-Thomas applied for and received a grant from the Ministry of Agriculture (MAFF).

Mr Marlowe-Thomas comments that, since being laid, the hedge has been full of birds and that plants are now beginning to grow on the previously bare hedgebank. He advises other farmers 'Do not underestimate the work involved in hedgelaying; it is a long and time-consuming job but it is worth it in the end. Other farmers asked why I did not just cut the hedge down with a machine, but it is a pleasure to drive along it now'.

The whole farm Howe Hill Farm, a few miles to the south-west of Oundle (TL02-86-), has been farmed by the Gent family since the end of the last century, and is now run by Messrs Bob and John Gent. The farm extends to about 590 acres, about half of which is owned by the family and half rented. Most of the farm is arable but there are about 250 acres of grass for beef and sheep, the sheep including a pedigree Suffolk flock. The grassland includes some land in the Nene valley subject to flooding. There is considerable variety in the soils, which include heavy clay, limestone brash, cornbrash, gravel and silt, often with considerable variation, even in the same field.

(DJW-P)

Over the last thirty years wildlife habitats have been managed, improved and added to, while the farm business has been run profitably and efficiently. Fields have been made larger by removal of hedges, but only where necessary, to give an average field size of 30 to 50 acres. The remaining hedges are carefully looked after as links between the other wildlife habitats on the farm. For economic and practical reasons they are trimmed mechanically, but they have been kept to a height of 5–7 feet and when possible some are left untrimmed for a year or two to encourage blossom and fruit. The farm was badly hit by Dutch elm disease, losing many mature trees. However, much of the hedgerow elm has put up shoots and there are now hedges and small belts of elm, kept healthy by regular trimming or coppicing because of their value as food plants for insects.

There was almost no woodland on the farm but trees, mostly native species, have been planted in areas which were difficult to cultivate, such as field corners, steep slopes, areas of very heavy soil etc. Planting a line of trees to straighten the irregular edge of one field has alleviated problems with cultivating the field on one side and created a 'new green lane' on the other. The latest planting combines trees with improving field boundaries, as the parish boundary, which once was marked with a hedge containing many elms, is replanted with native trees and shrubs, using the Northamptonshire County Council Amenity Tree Planting Scheme.

Existing ponds have been cleaned out and restored, and new ponds created so that there are now seven on the farm. One new pond was made on the site of a wet gateway in the corner of a field; the gateway was moved to a drier position about 25 yards away.

A small area, about four acres, has been sown with a mixture of legumes, with a view to attracting butterflies and providing summer grazing for the Suffolk rams. The farm has also experimented with sowing and planting small areas of wildflowers, in fields, on banks and in the largest spinney.

The initial tree-planting arose from an interest in shooting, but conservation is now carried on for its own sake. The work on the farm illustrates the possibilities for improving land for wildlife, by making use of the parts which are difficult or impossible to crop profitably; this was recognised when in 1984 the farm won the national Country Life Farming and Wildlife Award. The Gents have always worked closely with FWAG and their enthusiasm, their willingness to discuss problems or mistakes, and their success have encouraged many other farmers to follow their example.

There is considerable help available to farmers interested in wildlife conservation. Since 1973, Northamptonshire County Council and the Countryside Commission have run an Amenity Tree Scheme for farmers and landowners. The purpose of this is to help and encourage farmers who wish to create or maintain landscape features and wildlife habitat by planting native trees, for example in hedgerows, old parkland, field corners and small copses, by grant aid or the provision of trees. Areas larger than 0.25 hectares often qualify for planting grants from the Forestry Commission and may be managed to bring in a return from timber sales at some stage in the future. Looked at realistically however, the small, scattered groups of trees which are so important to the Northamptonshire patchwork of habitats and landscape features, are unlikely to bring any financial return to the landowner, but still need him to put resources of time, care and money into them if they are to survive.

Replacement relies heavily on tree-planting efforts – natural regeneration is in any case slow in hedges, and mechanical trimming makes it even less likely. Allowing for non-survival, 27,000 trees planted per year would keep pace with natural loss over the next decade. A further 17,000 trees planted per year would restore some of the decrease in the tree stock which had already occurred, particularly over the previous decade. This gives a minimum annual requirement of about 44,000 trees to be planted over the next 10 years.

The success of the Amenity Tree Scheme has been remarkable. In National Tree Week 1988 the milestone was reached – half a million trees planted through the scheme since it started. In 1987/88, 117 landowners used the scheme to plant a total of 70,659 trees which, even allowing for an unrealistically high failure rate of say 30%, more than meets the requirements suggested by the tree survey for replacement of natural losses of trees and rebuilding the tree stock.

Recognising that new trees are not the only things which contribute to the landscape and wildlife of the county which we all enjoy, and that managing features such as ponds and woodland can be expensive for the landowner, the County Council and Countryside Commission expanded the Amenity Tree Scheme in 1984/5 to become a Landscape Conservation Grant Scheme. This has allowed them to help financially with a wide range of conservation work on farms, including dredging old ponds which were silting up, making new ones, pollarding old willow trees to prolong their lives, fencing stock out of woodlands to give the ground flora a chance to grow, coppicing ancient woodland, and planting or restoring hedges. The combination of financial help from this or other sources (eg MAFF and the Forestry Commission) and the advice on conservation which is now available to farmers from the grant-giving organization and FWAG, is certainly having its effect. In 1987/88, 38 Landscape Conservation Grants were given, and the interest in conservation work on farms is now so great that more people are applying for grants than the annual budget can fund.

In many cases information is needed just as much as grant aid by farmers keen to improve their land for wildlife. Such advice is available from specialists such as the Northamptonshire Wildlife Trust, MAFF, Northamptonshire County Council and the Forestry Commission. In addition, in 1978 a Farming and Wildlife Advisory Group (FWAG) was formed in Northamptonshire to provide advice and information to such farmers, and also to bring together the various interests in farming, wildlife conservation, landscape conservation and countryside management. The FWAG is an independent group of individual farmers, representatives from organizations involved with agriculture, eg MAFF, the National Farmers' Union, the Country Landowners Association, those involved in wildlife or landscape conservation, eg the NWT, the Nature Conservancy Council, and those with an interest in countryside management, eg Northamptonshire County Council, the Forestry Commission and Anglian Water. The group aims to improve the understanding by farmers and conservationists of each others' problems and points of view; to show that these are not necessarily opposing camps but groups with mutual interests and complementary roles, and that the needs of modern farming can be reconciled with wildlife and landscape conservation. One way of doing this is by meeting several times a year to discuss topics whose interests overlap those of the different groups involved. Another is by providing an advisory service for farmers.

The advisory service, free to any farmer in the county who wants information on ways of fitting wildlife conservation and his farming business together, was originally provided as a voluntary service by FWAG members. However, the demand became too great to be satisfied in this way and in 1984 the Group decided to appoint a full-time adviser.

In June 1984 the writer was appointed as a Farm Conservation Adviser by Northamptonshire FWAG in association with the Farming and Wildlife Trust, the charitable trust to which all county FWAGs are affiliated. Northamptonshire was only the fifth county FWAG to raise enough funds from the local farming community to do this.

The main purpose of a Farm Conservation Adviser is to provide an independent and confidential source of free advice for farmers on the ways in which managing land with sympathy for wildlife and the landscape fits in with modern farming. Since 1984 over 200 farmers, who between them manage about 60,000 acres in Northamptonshire have been advised. The subjects of this advice vary; the commoner ones are about planting trees (29%) and the creation of management of ponds (27%), but farmers also ask about the management of hedges, woodland, old meadows, streams, and marshes. A high proportion of those seeking advice take the sensible view that we should look at the farm as a whole rather than at individual habitats in isolation. Many farmers, also use the Adviser as a contact with member organizations of Northamptonshire FWAG, who can give more technical help or, in some cases, grants for conservation work.

There are of course other ways of providing information: talking to farming groups in the county, running courses for the Agricultural Training Board and the Northamptonshire College of Agriculture, and leading farm walks. The shows at which FWAG has had displays include a wide range, from national events such as the Royal Show and the 1986 Farmers

Weekly Drainage Event, to local ones such as the East of England and Northampton Town Shows, to even more local ones like the ever-growing Blakesley Show.

We sometimes organize events to provide farmers with information on particular topics. With the Ministry of Agriculture and the Forestry Commission, we arranged a course on managing farm woodland which attracted 30 people. Over 150 people attended a meeting on restoring farm ponds which we held in association with ADAS in 1985, and another similar meeting was attended by about 50 farmers (the maximum which the site would accommodate).

Because Northamptonshire FWAG believes that, if a farmer develops an interest in wildlife when young this will benefit wildlife throughout his or her farming career, we run a competition for Young Farmers' Clubs in the county to plan and carry out practical conservation projects. This competition, which is sponsored by Barclays Bank plc and the winners of the Country Life Farming and Wildlife Award 1984, has been won for the last two years by Welford YFC, who planned and constructed an attractive pond.

Uncertainty about the future of farming is dangerous for wildlife. A farmer who thinks that restrictions may be placed on how much land he should cultivate can be tempted to bring even uneconomic areas into production, so that any future quota will be based on the largest possible baseline area on his farm. A farmer who sees prices and profits falling may only be able to compensate by increasing production, possibly at the expense of cultivating that little bit nearer the hedge, or by ploughing that little bit of 'waste' land. This land which at the moment has a reasonably high value for wildlife may paradoxically be put into danger by the problems of agricultural surpluses.

On the other hand, there are several hopeful indications of good prospects for wildlife on farms. Demand continues for advice on wildlife conservation. The interest of younger farmers in the theory and skills of wildlife conservation is shown by the demand for college courses on the subject, for Agricultural Training Board courses on subjects such as tree maintenance and hedgelaying, and by the interest of Young Farmers' Clubs in conservation projects and competitions.

At the same time new schemes related to the need to reduce agricultural overproduction, eg set-aside and the Farm Woodland Scheme, may provide new opportunities to create wildlife habitats on previously intensively cropped land. The possibilities offered by alternative farm enterprises which bring the public onto farms, from farm shops and pick-your-own fruit, through those involving the continuing interest in shooting and fishing, to such novel ideas as renting out private systems of tracks and rides for horses, all add to the incentive for farmers to make their land as attractive as possible for people and wildlife.

Red-legged partridges. (RP)

Southfield Farm marsh – the A1-M1 link road will obliterate this piece
of marsh. (PW)

Working for wildlife: ABOVE: chain-sawing, BELOW: five year coppice
at Thorpe Wood. (Both BG)

154

Conservation in the Future

(RP)

by Adrian Colston, Director, Northamptonshire Wildlife Trust

Northamptonshire has a rich and varied flora and fauna today but over the years a great deal has been lost. The great changes at the time of the Enclosure Acts had a tremendous impact on wildlife, and then again changes in agricultural practices since 1945 and more recently the pressures from development have further reduced the biological diversity of the county.

Today the wildlife of Northamptonshire represents a fraction of what once existed. The remaining sites are the products of chance and management practices not primarily concerned with protecting wildlife. Some sites are ancient and 'semi-natural' whilst others are new and created. Despite the losses over the years there have been some notable gains.

Since 1963, when the Northamptonshire Wildlife Trust (then called the Naturalists' Trust) was formed, concerted efforts have been made to protect, conserve and enhance the wildlife of the county. Much has been achieved but, as progress has been made, ideas have had to change.

Throughout this book a number of themes have occurred again and again: the old and the new; the natural and the created; the role of management, the threats and the opportunities.

The natural and old   For many years the conservation of wildlife has to a large extent been a site-based activity. Quite reasonably, naturalists have tended to go to places which are known to contain either rich assemblages of plants and animals or rarities. As a result, a number of important sites have been identified over the years and many have been notified as Sites of Special Scientific Interest.

Sites which have been left undisturbed or have been managed traditionally have formed the core. Ancient woodlands and pastures, meadows and hedges have been identified and cherished. Some of these are truly ancient and may be thousands of years old; others have shorter histories as sites, but are nevertheless hundreds of years old. These more recent ones, when created, were surrounded by natural habitats whence the plants and animals which colonised them came. Today, when sites are created, the surrounding areas are often devoid of wildlife, and therefore colonisation is either slow or non-existent.

Since the discovery of sites by the early naturalists, intensive surveys of the county, mainly during the 1970s and '80s, have been undertaken by the Trust, the County Council and the Nature Conservancy Council. These have included a habitat survey of the entire county,

155

ancient woodland, hedgerow, river valley and meadow surveys. In this way sites previously unrecorded have been discovered, some of which have subsequently been notified as SSSIs or acquired as nature reserves. Even today, new sites of high wildlife value are occasionally discovered in the more remote parts of the county.

Having extensive information on wildlife sites in the county has enabled the Trust to assist Local Authorities with planning applications, by providing informed and authoritative comments on wildlife importance. County and District Councils regularly consult the Trust on planning applications so that our views can be taken into account.

The Trust has based its reserve acquisition policy on sites which are good representatives of all the habitats found in the county. As a result the Trust now has under its management examples of ancient woodland, limestone grassland, old unimproved meadows and pastures.

Whilst concentrating on important sites has ensured that a large number of these now have some form of protection, it has meant that much of the rest of the countryside has been left unprotected and at risk from development and agriculture. Whilst nature conservationists (in Britain) have been successful to a large extent at protecting individual sites, they have been much less successful at ensuring that the fabric of the countryside is a hospitable place for wildlife despite their involvement with FWAG. Unfortunately the planning laws (or lack of them) have been of little use in protecting features and habitats of wildlife interest.

Many of our ancient sites of wildlife interest have long histories of sympathetic (traditional) management which has enabled a rich variety of plants and animals to survive and flourish. The conservation of these isolated sites is now vital if the character of Northamptonshire's wildlife is not to be diminished. Fortunately a number of these do receive protection under the Wildlife and Countryside Act 1981, some are managed by conservation bodies and some are owned and managed by sympathetic private landowners. However, we must not be complacent, as there are many interesting areas in the county receiving no form of protection or management, and therefore potentially under threat.

The new and created A number of the premier wildlife sites in the county are not ancient in origin or natural, but result from development or industry. They have often been the centre of much controversy. The extraction of minerals and the construction of reservoirs have resulted in opportunities for wildlife but there has often been a high environmental cost to pay.

Gravel pits The winning of sand and gravel is important and has radically altered the landscape; the Nene valley between Northampton and Oundle is a testament to this. Gravel extraction is to many people unpopular: machinery sites are unsightly, noisy and dirty and heavy vehicles aggravate traffic problems. Once gravel has been extracted large holes are left in the ground, which fit uncomfortably into the landscape. However, the gravel pits of the Nene valley are extremely important for wintering wildfowl, breeding birds and passage migrants. Without these new wetlands there would be a lot less wildlife in Northamptonshire.

These important gains have had an environmental cost. In some places where gravel pits now stand large areas of wet grassland and marsh once occurred. Unimproved wet meadows, pastures and marshland are now the rarest habitats in the county, and it is now difficult to find areas where snipe breed: well over 95% of the county's flood meadows have disappeared.

Where further gravel extraction threatens any of the remaining wet unimproved grasslands great efforts will be made to protect them, despite the possibility that the resulting gravel pit would be attractive to wildlife. There are now more gravel pits in the county than unimproved wet meadows.

Where gravel pits are inevitable the landscaping of resulting excavations is extremely important if the area is to be made attractive to wildlife. Over the years the gravel companies and the County Council have become more sympathetic to planning after-use for conservation, encouraged by the Trust and other conservation bodies. Good restoration schemes can be seen at the Thrapston gravel pit complex.

Central government expects huge amounts of gravel to be extracted from Northamptonshire for many years to come. No doubt further areas in the Nene valley will be considered, as will deposits in the Welland and Tove valleys. Paradoxically important sites would be threatened if new sites were created.

Quarrying Vast areas of the county have been quarried for ironstone to supply the old steel works in Corby but much of the worked land has now been restored to agriculture or forestry. There are a number of gullets (quarries) in Northamptonshire which over the years have developed into rich areas for wildlife. Some sites such as Twywell Gullet (SP94-77-) and some of the Cranford Quarries (SP92-97-) are extensive areas with rich flora and fauna. These limestone gullets have a rich mosaic of habitats from scree, cliffs and limestone grassland to scrub and pools. Many have an impressive number of unusual plants, with bee and common-spotted orchid often in great profusion.

It is somewhat ironic that there is now often as great an outcry, when quarry sites or gravel pits are planned to be infilled, for their wildlife value, as when the original extraction was proposed!

Reservoirs The primary role of reservoirs is water supply but they also provide extremely good habitats for wildlife, especially birds. Pitsford is the largest at over 1,000 acres and attracts the largest concentrations of birds, particularly wintering wildfowl. These birds are attracted by both its size and its tranquil atmosphere and the vast majority are to be found at the northern end of the reservoir in the Trust reserve. The rest is used by various recreational activities such as fishing and sailing. If Pitsford is to remain such an important refuge for birds there must be a balance between conservation and recreation and increased recreational pressures must not ruin the nature reserve area.

The urban conservation movement The majority of the population of Northamptonshire and the Soke of Peterborough live in large urban settlements and so do not have immediate access to countryside. There is an urban wildlife group in Peterborough and the Trust has an active group in Northampton. Both these groups are working to see wildlife catered for in the built up areas. This is being achieved by working with the planning authorities to deter development from important habitats in urban areas, by carrying out surveys of built-up areas, by managing and creating new wildlife sites and by involving the public in wildlife walks, talks and projects within town boundaries. Five years ago conservationists and naturalists spent the vast majority of their time in the countryside; now many people are demanding that wildlife should flourish in towns, where the majority of the population can also enjoy it.

Management The conservation of areas of wildlife importance only begins with their acquisition as nature reserves or notification as SSSIs. Once a site has been officially protected it still needs to be managed. It used to be thought that nature reserves should be left alone and nothing ever done to them; nothing could be further from the truth.

Grassland must either be cut for hay, grazed by animals or both. It is also essential that the grazing and the cutting is at the right time of the year. In a county which is now predominantly arable, it is becoming increasingly difficult to find farmers prepared to graze an important pasture, or to find someone willing to cut and bale hay. Without traditional management practices the biological interest of such sites will diminish.

157

Woodlands must be managed: they may need to be coppiced and standards felled. A lot of practical conservation work may appear to be destructive but, without detailed management plans and a source of labour to implement the work, the acquisition of such sites as nature reserves is futile in the long run: the importance of sympathetic management work cannot be over emphasised.

As time passes the Trust will continue to acquire more and more nature reserves along with other conservation bodies such as the Woodland Trust. One of our great challenges will be to ensure that sites of wildlife interest are correctly managed. Ways must be found to raise the ever-increasing sums of money needed, sources of cheap or free labour will have to be tapped, increased revenue will have to be raised from the sale of products from nature reserves without damaging the wildlife interest, and new skills will have to be learnt and passed on to future generations. Quite a tall order, but there are hopeful signs which suggest we will be able to do it.

There is a heightened awareness of the importance of reserve management, and organisations and individuals are now more willing to give towards management costs. In addition, Trusts are beginning to market products from their reserves and therefore derive better returns. Local communities are keen to become involved and look after areas of wildlife interest near where they live. With all the enthusiasm and concern for wildlife and the countryside evident in Northamptonshire we are optimistic.

Many local communities are already looking after small areas of land called Pocket Parks and a number of Trust reserves are managed by local groups with the guidance and assistance of the Trust.

Threats to wildlife Whilst many past changes have affected the county's wildlife there are many more to come. The most immediate is the escalating urban development in the county. New housing estates are being built, new factories are being erected and of course the infrastructure that goes with development also has to be built.

Much of this will not have a direct impact on wildlife but it will change the character of the county from a predominantly rural one to a far more developed one. In order to protect our wildlife it is important that developers are directed away from vulnerable wildlife sites towards areas with little wildlife value. Whilst this is beginning to happen in certain areas, far too many sites of both county and national importance are being destroyed. For example, the building of the A1–M1 link road across the county will directly affect at least four SSSIs: these are sites of national importance and we only have 60 or so in the county. In addition there will be ancillary developments in the wake of the road. Then there are threats posed to wildlife sites from gravel extraction.

The other main threats to our wildlife come from pollution. With an increasing population Northamptonshire faces pollution problems from a variety of sources. Rivers may have to cope with increased levels of sewage, there will be increased amounts of domestic and industrial refuse which will need to be disposed of, and increasing numbers of cars will inevitably cause more air pollution.

Perhaps in the longer term the effects of depletion of the ozone layer and global warming of the climate pose the greatest threat to wildlife (and people). Many researchers today predict a global warming of 3–4° centigrade which might cause a rise in sea level, due to the melting of the ice caps, of one metre within 30 years. This would have a profound effect on Britain: sites and species would be put at risk. The effects of global climatic change will become the most important environmental issue of the 1990s and all those concerned with Northamptonshire's wildlife will have an important role in trying to avert a major crisis.

Future opportunities Despite the problems there are also many opportunities open to conservation bodies anxious to improve the county for wildlife.

With increased development pressures come opportunities to work with developers. They are often prepared to create areas for wildlife and protect those already existing as long as the majority of their development can proceed. The Trust can therefore work with them for the benefit of wildlife without compromising its aims and objectives. Great Oakley Meadow would not now be a Trust reserve if we had not worked closely with the developers – it would be under bricks and mortar.

There is also some hope that, as agricultural land may in future be managed less intensively, this could provide environments less hostile to wildlife. Some hedges and woods will be replanted and roadside verges managed more sympathetically. It is a great challenge for all conservation bodies to try to persuade the farming community and big estates to reinstate some of what was removed in the last 40 years. Given the right incentives and advice the countryside outside special reserves and SSSIs could become as attractive for wildlife as it once was.

The fate of wildlife in the county depends on the attitudes and actions of people. The more people are involved in enjoying wildlife and countryside, the brighter the future. The Trust can play the leading role in this by encouraging people to visit nature reserves, both for enjoyment's sake and to get involved in the well-being of the area.

It is up to us all to be vigilant, to work with organisations like the Trust either as individuals, as businesses or collectively, in both the public and the private sector. Northamptonshire's wildlife deserves and demands our commitment.

ABOVE LEFT: Collyweston Quarries, a fine limestone grassland with clustered bellflower. (PW) ABOVE RIGHT: Twywell Gullet, limestone grassland on disused ironstone workings with knapweed broomrape. (PW) BELOW: Adder's-tongue fern: an indicator of unimproved neutral grassland. (JB) CENTRE LEFT: Bee orchid, found in both disturbed and undisturbed limestone grasslands. (AC) RIGHT: The green-winged orchid only occurs in a few unimproved grasslands. (RP) BELOW LEFT: Early marsh-orchid (AC) RIGHT: Common spotted orchid (RP) FAR RIGHT: Shining crane's-bill (RP)

Working for wildlife: LEFT: Bean poles from Short Wood. BELOW: Thinning at Thorpe Wood. RIGHT: Collyweston Quarries – Reserve sign. (All BG)

Fotheringhay Church from the Willow Brook. (DJW-P)

References

Bowen, H.J.M. (1980). A lichen flora of Berkshire, Buckinghamshire and Oxfordshire. *Lichenologist* 12: 199–237.

Brooke, M. de L. & Davies, N.B. (1987). Recent changes in host usage by cuckoos (Cuculus canorus) in Britain. *J. Animal Ecology* 56: 873–883.

Cannon, P.F., Hawksworth, D.L. & Sherwood-Pike, M.A. (1985). The British Ascomycotina: an annotated checklist. Commonwealth Mycological Institute.

Chester, T.W. & Hitch C.J.B. (1987). Field meeting in Northamptonshire. *Lichenologist* 19(1): 77-92.

Colston, A., Greenwood, B & Thomas, I. (1987). *Wildlife in Northamptonshire. A Guide to the Trust's Nature Reserves*. Northamptonshire Wildlife Trust.

Coppins, B.J. & Purvis, O.W. (1987). A review of *Psilolechia*. *Lichenologist* 19(1): 29-42.

Davies, F.B.M. (1981). *The Common Lichens of Bedfordshire*. Bedford Natural History Society.

Druce, G.C. (1930). *The Flora of Northamptonshire*. Buncle.

Frith, J.C. (1982). Short Wood SSSI. Reserve Management Plan. Northamptonshire Trust for Nature Conservation.

Fuller, R. (1982). *Bird Habitats in Britain*. T. & A.D. Poyser.

Gilbert, O.L. (1975). Lichens. In Peterken, G.F. & Welch R.C. (Eds) *Bedford Purlieus: its history, ecology & management*: 125–129. Monks Wood Experimental Station Symposium No. 7.

Green, R. (1988). Drummers in the Meadow. *Natural World* 22:22–24.

Hawksworth, D.L. (1975). *The changing lichen flora of Leicestershire*. Trans. Leicester lit. phil. soc. 68:32–56.

Hawksworth, D.L. & Seaward, M.R.D. (1977). *Lichenology in the British Isles 1568–1975: An Historical and Bibliographical Survey*. Richmond Publishing Co.

Hawksworth, D.L., James, P.W. & Coppins, B.J. (1980). Checklist of British lichen-forming, lichenicolous and allied fungi. *Lichenologist* 12(1):1–115.

Hawksworth, D.L. (1983). A key to the lichen-forming, parasitic, parasymbiotic and saprophytic fungi occurring on lichens in the British Isles. *Lichenologist* 15(1): 1–44.

Heath, J. (1974). A Century of Change in the Lepidoptera. In Hawksworth, D.L. (Ed.) *The Changing Flora and Fauna of Britain*. Systematics Association Special Volume 6. Academic Press: 275-292.

Hooper, M.D. (1977). Management Plan: Short Wood. Northamptonshire Naturalists' Trust.

Hoskins, W.G. (1955). *The Making of the English Landscape*. Hodder & Stoughton.

Kelly's Directory of Northamptonshire (1877). London.

Laundon, J.R. (1956). *The lichen ecology of Northamptonshire. In The First Fifty Years: A History of Kettering and District Naturalists' Society and Field Club*: 89–96. Kettering & District Naturalists' Society & Field Club.

Marchant, J. (1984). 1982-3 Common Birds Census. Index Report. *BTO News:* 134.

Marchant, J. & Whittington P. (1988). 1986-7 Common Birds Census. Index Report. *BTO News:* 157.

Morris, F.O. (1908). *A History of British Butterflies*, 10th edn. George Routledge & Sons Ltd.

Morton, J. (1712). *The Natural History of Northamptonshire*. Knaplock & Wilkinson.

Newton, I (1972). *Finches*. Collins.

O'Shaughnessy, K.J. (1983). *Northamptonshire farmland tree and hedgerow survey, 1982*. Northamptonshire County Council.

Owens, N.W. (1978). Common Birds Census at Short Wood. *Chronicle of Northamptonshire Naturalists' Trust:* 17–23.

Owens, N.W. (1980). *The Effects of the 1978–9 Winter on the Bird Population of Short Wood.* Northampton Bird Report.

Penistan, M.J. (1973). *Hedgerow Tree Survey in East England Conservancy, 1972.* Forestry Commission.

Perrins, C.M. & Birkhead, T.R. (1983). *Avian Ecology.* Blackie.

Peterken, G.F. (1976). Long-term changes in the Woodlands of Rockingham Forest and other areas. *J. Ecology* 64:123–146.

Peterken, G.F. (1981). *Woodland Conservation and Management.* Chapman & Hall.

Peterken, G.F. & Harding, P.T. (1974). Recent Changes in the Conservation Value of Woodlands in Rockingham Forest. *Forestry* 47:109–128.

Peterken, G.F. & Welch, R.C. (Eds) (1975). *Bedford Purlieus: its history, ecology and management.* Monks Wood Experimental Station Symposium No. 7.

Pollard, E., Hooper, M.D. & Moore, N.W. (1974). *Hedges.* Collins.

Purvis, O.W. (1987). *Psilolechia leprosa:* an overlooked species? British Lichen Society *Bulletin* 61:18.

Rackham O. (1976). *Trees and Woodland in the British Landscape.* Dent.

Rackham, O. (1980). *Ancient Woodland.* Arnold.

Rackham, O. (1986). *The History of the Countryside.* Dent.

Robinson, D.P. (1988). *Northamptonshire Inventory of Ancient Woodland.* Nature Conservancy Council.

Rose, F. (1976). Lichenological indicators of age and environmental continuity in woodlands. In Brown, D.H., Hawksworth, D.L. & Bailey, R.H. (Eds). *Lichenology, Progress and Problems:* 279–307. Academic Press.

Seaward, M.R.D. (1980). Lichen Flora of Lincolnshire. *Lincolnshire Natural History Brochure* No. 8. Lincolnshire Naturalists' Union.

Seaward, M.R.D. (1988). Lichen damage to ancient monuments: a case study. *Lichenologist* 20(3):291–294.

Sharrock, J.T.R. (1976). *The Atlas of Breeding Birds in Britain and Ireland.* BTO/IWC.

Shawyer, C.R. (1987). *The Barn Owl in the British Isles.* Hawk Trust.

Stagg, S.A. & Wynne, J.A. (1977). The Window Eaters. In Carry on Reading. *Red Series Book* 3:65–67. Schofield & Sims.

Stamp, L.D. (1943). The Land of Britain. *The Report of the Land Utilisation Survey of Britain*, parts 58 and 59: Northamptonshire and the Soke of Peterborough.

Wake, J. & Webster, D.C. (1971). *The Letters of David Eaton to the Third Earl of Cardigan 1725–1732.* Northampton Record Society.

Watson, W. (1933). A list of Northamptonshire lichens contained in the herbaria of Robert Rogers, now deposited in the Museum, Public Library Kettering. J. Northampton Natural History Society 27:24.

Watson, W. (1953). *Census Catalogue of British Lichens.* British Mycological Society.

Wilkinson, W.H. (1888). *Botanical excursion to Fawsley.* J. Northamptonshire Natural History Society 5:148–149.

Williamson, K. (1969). Habitat Preferences of the Wren on English Farmland. *Bird Study* 16:53–59.

Hunting hedgehog. (DJW-P)

Gazeteer of Nature Reserves in Northamptonshire and the Soke of Peterborough

SSSI stands for Site of Special Scientific Interest and this indicates that the area is of national importance for wildlife conservation.

NWT stands for Northants Wildlife Trust reserve.

Barnack Hills and Holes. Nature Conservancy Council reserve with part leased to NWT National Nature Reserve 9 miles north west of Peterborough. TF075046. 22 ha. rich limestone grassland over ancient stone quarry.

Barnwell Country Park. Northants County Council.
TL037874. 15 ha. area with gravel pits, reed beds and grassland and scrub. South of Oundle.

Bedford Purlieus. Part of site is an NWT reserve 2 miles west from Wansford.
TL033995. 21.5 ha. of ancient woodland. Very rich flora with over 400 species. Access from Kings Cliffe to Wansford road and then approx. 1 mile along forestry road.

Boddington Meadow. NWT reserve. 1.5 miles west of Byfield.
SP494532. 2.4 ha. Damp neutral, unimproved grassland. Species rich. Access: park at north west corner Byfield Reservoir – follow embankment of reservoir on west side, then over stile into meadow.

Brigstock Country Park. Northants County Council.
SP955854. Area of restored grassland, ponds and scrub. Rich flora and excellent for butterflies and dragonflies.

Bucknell Wood Pastures. NWT reserve.
SP645451. 25 ha. of neutral grassland with old hedges and many interesting species. Access from Abthorpe.

Byfield Pool. NWT reserve. 1 mile west of Byfield village.
SP500527. 4.5 ha. open water, reedbeds, willow carr. Good range of birds. Access – follow track along eastern side of reservoir for 0.5 miles.

Castor Hanglands. Nature Conservancy Council National Nature Reserve.
TF118023. 90 ha. of woodland, scrub, grassland and wetland. Access via public footpaths.

Collyweston Quarries. NWT reserve. SSSI. 7.5 ha. 3 miles south west of Stamford.
TF004038. Species rich limestone grassland on old stone quarry. Access – turn off A43 half way between Collyweston and Easton-on-the-Hill. Park in lay-by opposite bungalows.

Daventry Country Park. Daventry District Council.
SP575642. 70.8 ha. of reservoir with surrounding grassland and woodland.

Delf Spinney. NWT reserve. 1 mile north of Harlestone village.
SP698660. 4 ha. woodland, scrub, grassland, stream and pond. Access – from A428 follow public footpath 0.5 mile to railway.

Denford Churchyard. NWT reserve. In Denford village.
SP992767. A churchyard nature reserve on bank of River Nene. 0.5 ha. grassland, pond, scrub, springs and mossy walls. Access – off A605, through churchyard.

East Carlton Country Park. Corby District Council.
SP835895 40.5 ha. Parkland and grassland with magnificent trees.

Farthinghoe Reserve. NWT reserve.
SP518404. 3.5 ha. disused railway and landfill site. Vegetation types include hedgerows, scrub, damp meadow, pond and orchard.

Finedon Calcine Banks. NWT reserve.

SP903713. 2.4 ha. Small area at end of a disused railway. Scrub and grassland. Part of a larger area which makes up the Finedon Country Park.

Glapthorn Cow Pasture. NWT reserve. 3 miles north of Oundle.

TL003902. 28 ha. species rich secondary woodland and blackthorn scrub. Butterflies include black hairstreak. Nightingales present. Access — gate at south east corner of wood off Glapthorn to Upper Benefield Road.

Grafton Regis Meadow. NWT reserve.

SP765466. 2.2 ha. Unimproved neutral grassland with rich flora. Traditionally managed hay meadow. Access – via track from A508. Follow canal towpath then over stile in hedge.

Great Oakley Meadow. NWT and Corby District Council reserve.

SP863855. Neutral grassland reserve with many species of flowering plants. Access off the Headway, Great Oakley.

Harlestone Heath. NWT reserve. North-east of Harlestone Firs.

SP721646. 3.5 ha. acid grassland with heather. Large pond with newts and dragonflies. Access – via bridlepath through Harlestone Firs to strip near railway.

High Wood & Meadow. NWT reserve. SSSI. 5 miles south of Daventry.

SP589548. 20 ha. of oak/ash woodland (with many wild cherry) and acid grassland. Access – pull off Preston Capes – Upper Stowe road at north-west corner Mantles Heath. Follow Knightly Way south then turn right at first hedgeline.

Higham Ferrers Pit. NWT reserve.

SSSI. 10 ha. Gravel pit excellent for birds. Access from Higham Ferrers across bridge over A45.

Irchester Country Park. Northants County Council.

SP912658. 81 ha. Scrub, plantations and old ironstone workings.

Irthlingborough Newt Pools. NWT reserve.

SP940716. Access from Finedon on the A6, turn left just after Irthlingborough turn, one field from road.

Kings Wood LNR. NWT and Corby District Council reserve. Corby.

SP864874. 31 ha. of ancient oak and ash woodland. Acid grassland in glades. Ponds in wood. Access from Danesholme Road.

Kingsthorpe Nature Reserve. Northampton Borough Council.

SP743628 10 ha of water meadows, river, ponds and mill runs.

Lings Wood. NWT reserve. Northampton.

SP803638. Northamptonshire Wildlife Trust headquarters. 22.5 ha. mixed woodland with interesting grassland and ponds. Access from Lings Way, follow signs for Lings House.

Nene Park. Nene Park Trust. Peterborough.

TL145975. 200 ha. River meadows, gravel pits and woodland.

New Coppice. NWT reserve. 1 ha. East Carlton.

SP846894. Small piece of coppiced woodland with rich ground flora. Access off A427.

Newbottle Spinney. NWT reserve. 5 miles west of Brackley.

SP517365. 16 ha. Mixed mature secondary woodland. Elm, beech, ash, hazel on disused stone pit. Access from off Kings Sutton to Charlton Road.

Northfield Avenue Reserve. NWT reserve. Kettering.

SP861799. 1 ha. of grassland and scrub, gorse, birch and yellow stonecrop. Access – Cunliffe Drive off Northfield Avenue, behind tip.

Peakirk Wildfowl Refuge. Wildfowl Trust.

TF168069. 6.8 ha. wildfowl collection and duck decoy.

Pitsford Reservoir. NWT reserve. SSSI. 7 miles north of Northampton.

SP783707. 194 ha. open water, mudflats, grassland, plantation and marsh. Important nationally for wild fowl and passage migrants. Access – restricted – permit from B. Moore, 84 Norton Rd, Kingsthorpe, Northampton, NN2 7TN with SAE.

The Plens. NWT reserve. Desborough.
SP807837. 14 acres. Former ironstone quarry. Scrub with calcareous grassland. Access from road to Pipewell by railway bridge.

Ramsden Corner Plantation. NWT reserve. SSSI. 1.5 miles west of Upper Stowe.
SP625563. 3.5 ha. acid grassland, scrub and mixed woodland. Unusual and rare species in a small area. Access – from Upper Stowe to Farthingstone Road.

Rothwell Gullett. NWT reserve.
SP808818. 1.3 ha. Area of woodland, scrub and grassland in old mineral gulley. Access off A6 between Desborough and Rothwell.

Salcey Forest. NWT and BBONT reserve. SSSI. 6 miles south of Northampton.
SP812510. 13.5 ha. Excellent example of ancient woodland. Diverse ground flora. Access – along forestry track off Hackleton to Stoke Goldington Road. Other parts of the wood have Forestry Commission nature trails.

Short Wood. NWT reserve. SSSI. 2 miles north of Oundle.
TL015913. 25 ha. of ancient woodland and old secondary woodland. Renowned for display of bluebells in May. Access along footpath off Glapthorn to Southwick Road.

Southorpe Paddock. NWT reserve. SSSI. 2 miles north east of Wansford.
TF084022. 1.5 ha. of unimproved limestone grassland which is now scarce. Access –paddock off Southorpe to Sutton Road.

Stanford Reservoir. NWT reserve. 7 miles north east of Rugby.
SP604803. 5.5 ha. reservoir. Trust area is Blowers Lodge Bay. Important for large wildfowl numbers in winter. Access restricted – by permit from Lings House. Entrance from B5414 at SP593807.

Stoke Bruerne Brickpits. NWT reserve.
SP743497. 10 ha. Disused brickpits with reedbed, grasslands and ponds. Access from Shutlanger Road in Stoke Bruerne.

Stoke Wood. Woodland Trust.
SP801861. Ancient woodland adjacent to Stoke Wood End Quarter.

Stoke Wood End Quarter. NWT reserve. SSSI. 2 miles north of Desborough.
SP800861. 1 ha. ancient oak and ash woodland. Also coppiced hazel, field maple and many shrubs present. Access – follow track from B669 for 600 yards across arable land.

Sywell Country Park. Northants County Council.
SP830653. Country Park with reservoir, grassland and woodland.

Thorpe Wood. NWT reserve. Western outskirts of Peterborough.
TL160986. 9.6. ha. of ancient coppice with standards woodland with diverse flora. Access in to north section from car park at Holywell Way end of Thorpe Road, near A47/A1260 roundabout.

Titchmarsh. NWT reserve. 110 ha. Part SSSI. North of Thrapston.
TL007815. Consists of heronry, gravel pits and grassland. Excellent for breeding, wintering and passage birds. Access from Aldwincle on Lowick Lane at TL007815.

Walton Grounds. NWT reserve. 800 square metres.
SP509347. Site for green hellebore. Permission to visit must first be obtained from NWT.

Northants Wildlife Trust, Lings House, Billing Lings, Northampton, NN3 4BE. (0604 405285). Further details of NWT reserves can be found in the Trust's reserve handbook *The Wildlife of Northamptonshire* obtainable from Lings House, £3.40 including p&p.

Index

Figures in *italics* refer to illustrations

169

Subscribers

Presentation Copies

1 Northamptonshire Wildlife Trust
2 Royal Society for Nature Conservation
3 Nature Conservancy Council
4 Northamptonshire County Council
5 Extramural Department, Leicester University
6 Nene College, Northampton
7 Dr Miriam Rothschild

8 Adrian Colston
9 Dr Franklyn Perring
10 Rosemary Parslow
11 Clive and Carolyn Birch
12 David N. Robinson
13 Alan Dawn
14 Iaon Thomas
15 Jeffrey A. Best
16 Jonathon Spencer
17 Nick Owens
18 Susan Page
19 David Harper
20 Oliver Maxim
21 Ruth Moffatt
22 Gill Gent
23 Tom Chester
24 Phil Richardson
25 Robert Bullock
26 Cliff Christie
27 Peter Gent
28 Richard Eden
29 Rosemary Cockerill
30 D.W. Smith
31 L.C. Cook
32
33 Miss M.A. Blount
34 Dorothy Gurr
35 Mr Gilby
36 Mrs D.M. Aitken
37 Dr Stephen L. Jury
38 M.J.B. Butterfield
39 G.E. Rixon
40 Sean L.M. Karley
41 Jonathan & Susan Craig
42 Mark Green
43 Timothy J. Coles
44 Dr D.M. George
45 K.M. Colles
46 C.E. Parsons
47 D.N. Jones
48 Miss M.C. Harrison
49 R.G. Freebairn
50 K.M.B. Morrison
51 Miss R.S. Hooper WRAF
52 Leicestershire Libraries & Information
55 Service

56 Mrs E. Cadbury
57 C. Richards
58 Pamela Desmond
59 Dr M.P. Lewis
60 E.V. Owen
61 J.M. Griffin
62 M.C. Gosling
63 Ann Rowlett
64 Margaret Turnbull
65 Dr A.F.M. Little
66 S.A. & D.M. Pickard
67 P. & R. Buttenshaw
68 T.H. Preston
69 Michael J. Wareing
70 Evan Robinson
71 Major & Mrs R.F. Sykes
72 Mr & Mrs C.P. Brawn
73 David & Paula Cochrane
74 Kerstin Goulding
75 David Holmes
76 Mrs N.L. Christie
77 Mrs E. Jackson
78 Miss J.M. Pirie
79 Mrs Diana Briggs
80 Mrs L.A. Humfrey
81 P. Mullane
82 E.A. Brookfield
83 Ian M. Morris
84 David W. Holland
85 Miss Mary Spokes
86 Mrs C. McCormick
87 Linda Gale
88 R.J. Southgate
89 Mrs J.E. Coxon
90 Nicholas Millar
91 Miss M.J. Finn
92 Lt Col J.A.O. Napier (retd)
93 J. Ross
94 J.A. Stigner
95 Gary J. Austin
96 David T. Way
97 Mrs Beryl Lockhart
98 The University Centre, Northampton
99
100 Ann Kennard

101 Wendy Turner
102 Roy and Avril Burrell
103 Mrs Mary Hulbert
104 Miss Joan Coe
105 G. Moore Thompson
106 A.C. Roadnight
107 Mrs Jean Jackson-Stops
108 Chris Donnelly
109 R.D. Broughton
110 P.H. Blackman
111 Graham Rice
112 Frances Lavinia Chambers
113 Nita Davies
114 Jane Sheldon
115 Betty Blakeborough
116 Angela E. Bolton
117 Tim Boswell MP
118 Bernard Crowhurst
119 P.J. Kightley
120 Louise Andrew
121 Dr J.A. Bullock
122 Mrs L.D. Aucott
123 Miss J. Kench
124 H.K. Trayner
125 Dr Frank Clark
126 D.R. Clarke
127 M.D. Pool
128 Barbara Hodge
129 Harris S. Burry
130 David Raper
131 Keith Farrington
132 N.J. Zorzi
133 Owen & Alice Lougher
134 John Gale Clarke
135 Clifford J. Harris
136 Anna & Robert Wilson
137 Roy Copson
138 Joyce M. Evans
139 Trevor Hold
140 G.D. Bugby
141 Howard Morgan
142 Michael Duerden
143 Cynthia E. Wiggins
144 Muriel Jenkins
145 Kathleen Bunn
146 Mrs M. Partridge

147 K.E. Shackleton
148 Marjory Strongman
149 Henry Benjamin Tew
150 Brian Webster
151 Dr Paul Wix FIBiol
152 Mrs V.J. Lankester
153 S. Tilley
154 Michael Bower Manser
155 Ann Longhurst
156 Mr & Mrs P.F.A. Sharpling
157 Kathleen Thompson
158 Mrs D. Worrell
159 K.A. & Mrs M.E. Radford
160 Stephen J. Morris
161 M.J. Dickie
162 Peter Warden
163 J.W. & Mrs E.J. Ruecroft
164 Dr Robert Wrigglesworth
165
166 Caroline E. Rogers
167 D.K. Dennison
168 Nick Barnes
169 Gordon J. Penn
170 N.B. & A.C. White
171 Peterborough Central Library
172
173 B.S. Goodman
174 Gordon Rixon
175 RSPB (East Midlands Office)
176 Sheila Baggalay
177 David Reynolds
178 Paul Hillyard
179 Ian Thomas Foster
180 James Patrick
181 Peter & Margaret Adhemar
182 Ann & Peter Kennard
183 Judith A. Doughty
184 Harris S. Burry
185 Barbara Carpenter
186 A.O. Jones
187 Simon J. Leach
188 Everdon Field Centre

189 Ron Wilson
190 Miss P.M. Slarvie & Miss M. Vaughan
191 J.M. Griffin
192 Arthur A.K. Whitehouse
193 D. Ivison
194 George Twiselton
195 Josephine Booth
196 John D. Cole
197 Sue & Chris Green
198 George L. McDonnell
199 Mrs S.A. Wilch
200 I.S. & E.C. Colston
201 Mr & Mrs B.A. Pack
202 Mrs J. Davey
203 D.J. Stimpson
204 G.I. Crawford
205 S.P. Jackson
206 Dr I.S. Hodgson-Jones
207 Tessa Watts-Russell
208 Nick Craggs
209 Maureen Pritchard
210 Kevin Smyth
211 R.P. Cawthorne
212 J.M. Sharpe
213 Barry Joyce
214 Jack Knightley
215 Gwen Keech
216 J.E. Nash
217 Christopher Elliott-Binns
218 Rafe Warren
219 Geoffrey Andrew Smith
220 Ann Plackett
221 Nigel Muddiman
222 B.W. Broderick
223 Joan Stephenson
224 Jane Draper
225 Cambridgeshire
229 Library
230 Dr David Harper
233
234 John Michael Sharman
235 Maureen Bly
236 Michael Miley
237 Mrs Joan Ling
238 Dr C. Ringrose
239 M. Thompson Coon
240 Geoffrey Noble
241 Grace W. Penn
242 Alan Stewart
243 J.D.E. Wainwright
244 Jonathan Alan Calderbank
245 Axel Landmann
246 Isobel Peggy Tuffs
247 Heather A. Tait
248 P.C. Bromhall

249 Mr & Mrs R.A. Smith
250 John Fenton
251 Mrs Dorothy Harris
252 Doris Cage
253 Robin S. Arch
254 Tim Barfield
255 Edward T. Baxter
256 Kenneth Richard Harris
257 Graham Rice
258 P.D. Everden
259 T.N. Parker
260 Adrian Colston
261
262 Robin M. Vowles
263 D.J.A. Wrighton
264 Harry Pearson
265 David Emmerson
266 G.T. Gibson
267 Frank & Julia Moss
268 Geraldine Hunt
269 Tom Chester
270
271 J.P.G. Fletcher
272 P.J. Harder
273 Paul G. Jackson
274 Mark E. Bird
275 Lindsay Pentelow
276
277 Keith Reeve
278 Elmer Daniel Underwood
279 Mrs D. Burch
280 Miss Mollie Vaughan
281 P.D. Dickin
282 Mrs B. Graver
283 Miss A. Underwood
284 R.G.N. Bird
285 Brian Yates
286 Dr Rachel H. Carter
287 J.M. Litchfield
288 Dorothy J. Herlihy
289 Miss D.A. Phillips
290 D. Pickering
291 Clive Munns
292 M.C. Gosling
293 John Wotherspoon
294 Jeffrey A. Best
295 Malcolm Holliday
296 J. Ross
297 P.J. Bond
298 John & Eliza Bond
299 Peterborough City Council
300 A. Dawn
301 Judith Ann Craig
302 Miss Mary Jackson MBE
303 D.J. Knott
304 Geoffrey Winsor
305 Margaret Tait
306 K. Clarke
307 D.A. Phillips

308 Martin Ingram
309 K.A. & Mrs M.E. Radford
310 Elizabeth & Peter Crane
311 M.R. Wallis
312 Richard Charles Eckton
313 Margaret Gearing
314 Crispin Fisher
315 Malcolm Magee
316 Alan Roger Shepherd
317 Pippa Hyde
318 J.C. Jackson
319 P.M. Wade
320 William J. Jones
321 Dr John Buckley
322 M.O. Bryan
323 Pauline Wiles
324 Mrs Brenda Catchpole
325 Mrs Felicity Bickley
326 Mrs D. Whitehouse
327 Mrs Chris Rose
328 John W. Everett
329 Dr C.B. Wain
330 Derek Chapman
331 Higham Ferrers Nature Conservation Group
332 David Saint
333 Julie Wilson
334 Isabel Brown
335 Lawrence Bee
336 Ann Rowlett
337 Mrs Elspeth M. Cooke
338 Roy J. Collis
339 Elizabeth J. Marks
340 L.R. Fellowes
341 M.V.D. Champness
342
343 D.K. Cessford
344 Mrs Ann Window
345 Anne Senior
346 Raymond Howe
347 Elizabeth Ball
348 J.W.W. Metcalfe MBOU
349 Mrs Cristine Orr
350 Paul Davies
351 Tom Weed
352 Mrs S. Hinde
353 David Jeffrey
354 Lady Mary E. Jackson
355 Mrs Mary Cross
356 Janet Thompson
357 Sherry Brown
358 Gerald Henry Ginns
359 Mrs J.R. Marks

360 Cheryl Jeanne Hardwick
361 SPACE Ltd
372
373 Jill Charman
374 Jean Olive Newman
375 Miss Charmian Leah Worrall
376 R.T. McAndrew
377 Mr & Mrs R. Reed
378 Joan Plummer
379 Mrs Freda P. Willgress
380 J.M. & Z.F. Turner
381 Wallace B. Gulliver
382 Margaret Hammersley
383 Mr & Mrs I.F. Thomas
384 Mrs S. Jones
385 Dr D.F. Burton
386 R.F. Burrows
387 Mrs Kathleen Allen
388 Northamptonshire
461 Libraries
462 John Locke
463 John Simpson
464 Margaret A. Smith
465 Harold Binder
466 Mrs L.E. Percival
467 R.L. Gent
468 R.J. Holder
469 Thomas Henry Preston
470 P. Smith
471 Mr & Mrs M. Dix
472 Anthony B. O'Brien
473 Mary Hunt
474 Mr & Mrs Basil Naylor
475 Derek G. Gillam
476 Mrs D.J. James
477 Northamptonshire Countryside Ranger Service
478 John E. Skerritt
479 Tony Smith
480 Col T.R.L. Greenhalgh
481 Peter Kemp Spokes
482 Jack Purvis
483 Mrs J.R. Rusher
484 Susan Greasley
485 Audrey Marriott
486 Dr Eric Duffey
487 Mr & Mrs J.F. Brinsley
488 P.C.E. Clarke
489 Rev M.R.A. Wilson
490 Peter John Harris
491 Peter Scott
492 E.B. Wright
493 Kenneth George Freeman

Little grebe and bistort. (RP)

END PAPERS: Map of nature reserves in Northamptonshire and the Soke of Peterborough. (PN)

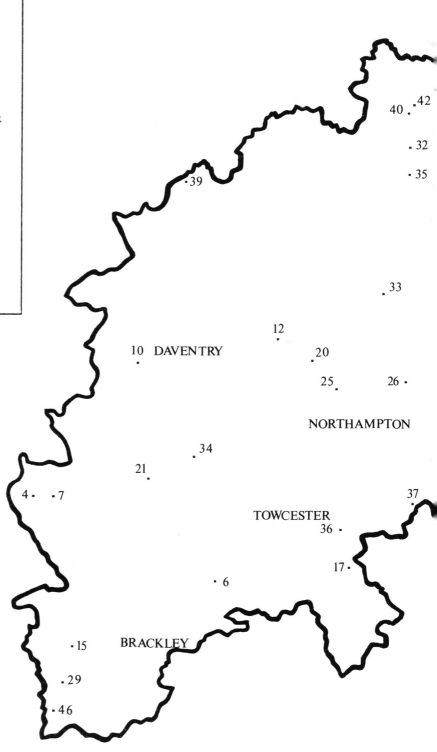

NATURE RESERVES

IN NORTHAMPTONSH

1	BARNWELL COUNTRY PARK
2	BRIGSTOCK COUNTRY PARK
3	BARNACK HILLS AND HOLES
4	BODDINGTON MEADOW
5	BEDFORD PURLIEUS
6	BUCKNELL WOOD PASTURES
7	BYFIELD POOL
8	CASTOR HANGLANDS NNR
9	COLLYWESTON QUARRIES
10	DAVENTRY COUNTRY PARK
11	DENFORD CHURCHYARD
12	DELF SPINNEY
13	EAST CARLTON COUNTRY PARK
14	FINEDON CALLY BANKS
15	FARTHINGHOE RESERVE
16	GLAPTHORN COW PASTURES
17	GRAFTON REGIS MEADOW
18	GREAT OAKLEY MEADOW
19	HIGHAM FERRERS GRAVEL PIT
20	HARLESTONE HEATH
21	HIGH WOOD AND MEADOW
22	IRCHESTER COUNTRY PARK
23	IRTHLINGBORO' NEWT POOLS
24	KINGS WOOD

40 . .42

. 32

. 35

.39

. 33

12 .

10 DAVENTRY
.

.20

25 .

26 .

NORTHAMPTON

. 34

21 .

4 .   . 7

37
.

TOWCESTER

36 .

17 .

. 6

. 15

BRACKLEY

. 29

. 46